The Linear B Decipherment
Controversy Re-examined

The Linear B Decipherment Controversy Re-examined

by

SAUL LEVIN, A.B., PH.D.
*Professor of Classics, Harpur College
of the State University of New York*

STATE UNIVERSITY OF NEW YORK

1964

Copyright © 1964 by State University of New York

Sole distributor: University Publishers Inc.
239 Park Avenue South, New York 3, N. Y.

Designed by NEIL GOLDWASSER
of Century Typographers, New York

Linear B Characters
Drawn by HEIDI WONG

LIBRARY OF CONGRESS CATALOG CARD NUMBER: 64-17579

Manufactured in the United States of America

To Ruth

PREFACE

One pleasure of publication is the opportunity to acknowledge before the world my deep indebtedness to many persons who have helped me in various ways and deserve the credit for whatever my readers may find good in this book. I can properly begin with Professor Emmett L. Bennett, Jr., of the University of Wisconsin, Institute for Research in the Humanities. Innumerable times I have drawn upon his singular familiarity with all Linear B material and studies; he has been, without fail, friendly and cooperative even while disagreeing with me fundamentally. Most recently I have borrowed, for one of the pull-outs attached to the flyleaf at the back of the book, his tables of the Linear B syllabary, which was adopted by the Third International Colloquium for Mycenaean Studies. Other scholars who have corresponded with me, sent me copies of their writings, and given me the benefit of their expert — and divergent — opinions are Miss Jane E. Henle of New York City; Professors A. J. Beattie of Edinburgh, Aram Frenkian of Bucharest, Ernst Grumach of Berlin, Konstantinos D. Ktistopoulos of Psychiko (Greece); and Mr. Henry D. Ephron of Missoula (Montana).

My former colleagues at Washington University discussed many major points with me orally, and through their reactions, challenges, and original ideas stirred me to work out a satisfactory answer to difficulties. In this essential regard I owe the most to Professors Hans Petersen (now at the University of Louisville) and William M. Sale III; several whole chapters would never have taken shape without them. Professors Phillip H. DeLacy (now at Northwestern University), James W. Marchand (now at Vanderbilt University), and Ernst A. Ebbinghaus gave steady and judicious backing to my research interests. Dean Lewis E. Hahn and the Graduate School of Arts and Sciences at Washington University granted funds generously to facilitate the preparation of this book. Professors Carl H. Kraeling and Ignace J. Gelb, of the Oriental Institute, University of Chicago, favored me with timely encouragement early in 1959, while I was deliberating about the dimensions of my inquiry. Finally, when I was appointed to the faculty of Harpur College in 1961, Professors Aldo S. Bernardo and Bernard F. Huppé very promptly put me in touch with Mr. Mort Grant, of the Research Foundation of State University of New York; so no time was lost on account of my moving.

The varied and always dependable assistance of Mrs. Elizabeth F. Hall, my secretary at Washington University, spanned nearly the whole time of my research and writing, and spared me many a tedious chore. As it was necessary to make up the deficiencies of local libraries, I often saddled their staffs with extraordinary problems, which they despatched most efficiently. At least four librarians — Miss Marjorie Karlson, Miss Victoria Bradford, and Mrs. Roma S. Gregory at Washington University, and Miss Janet E. Brown at Harpur College — have done much more for me than their duties required. Mr. and Mrs. Francis R. Bellamy, of University Publishers in New York, have applied their experience and sagacity to make this book clearer and more attractive, and have watched over the typographical accuracy of a difficult text.

My gratitude to my wife is naturally of an altogether different character, which can best be conveyed implicitly in the bare words of the dedication.

S. L.

BIBLIOGRAPHICAL ABBREVIATIONS

Greek authors are omitted from this list, as I spell out their names so that the titles of their works can be readily located in Liddell-Scott-Jones, *A Greek-English Lexicon* (Oxford [1925-1940]), pp. xvi-xli. But I usually cite *Il[iad]*, *Od[yssey]*, and Ventris's writings without the author's name.

My reader is presumed to have access to "Evidence" and *Documents.*

AJA = *American Journal of Archaeology* (new series, 1897–).

Beattie, *JHS*, LXXVI = A. J. Beattie, "Mr. Ventris' Decipherment of the Minoan Linear B Script," *Journal of Hellenic Studies*, LXXVI (1956), 1-17.

Beattie, *MIOF*, VI = "A Plain Guide to the Ventris Decipherment of the Mycenaean Linear B Script," *Mitteilungen des Instituts für Orientforschung*, Deutsche Akademie der Wissenschaften zu Berlin, VI (1958), 33-104.

Bennett, "MT" (1953) = Emmett L. Bennett Jr., "The Mycenae Tablets," *Proceedings of the American Philosophical Society*, XCVII (1953), 422-470.

Bennett, "MT" (1958) = "The Mycenae Tablets II," *Transactions of the American Philosophical Society*, new series, vol. XLVIII, part 1 (1958).

Bennett, *OOTP* = *The Olive Oil Tablets of Pylos*, supp. 2 to *Minos* (1958).

Bennett, *PT* (1951) = *The Pylos Tablets, a Preliminary Transcription* (Princeton University Press, 1951). The *PT* (1951) numbering of tablets, although followed by "Evidence" and *Documents,* is now fully superseded by *PT* (1955). .

Bennett, *PT* (1955) = *The Pylos Tablets: Texts of the Inscriptions found 1939-1954* (Princeton University Press, 1955).

Chadwick, *Decipherment* = John Chadwick, *The Decipherment of Linear B* (Cambridge University Press, 1958).

Chadwick, "Introductory Essay" = "A Historic Document: An introductory essay to Work Note 20" (1958, privately circulated).

Chadwick, "New Fragments" = "New Fragments of Linear B Tablets from Knossos," *Annual of the British School at Athens*, LII (1957), 147-151.

CIG = August Boeckh *et al.* (eds.), *Corpus inscriptionum Graecarum*, 4 vols. (Berlin: G. Reimer, 1828-77).

Deecke = Wilhelm Deecke, "Die griechisch-kyprischen Inschriften in epichorischer Schrift," in *SDGI*, I (1884), 1-80.

Documents = Michael Ventris and John Chadwick, *Documents in Mycenaean Greek* (Cambridge University Press, 1956).

EM = Michel Lejeune (ed.), *Études mycéniennes: Actes du colloque international sur les textes mycéniens* (Paris: Centre national de la recherche scientifique, 1956).

Evans, *PM* = Sir Arthur Evans, *The Palace of Minos*, 4 vols. (London: Macmillan & Co., 1921-1935).

"Evidence" = Ventris and Chadwick, "Evidence for Greek Dialect in the Mycenaean Archives," *Journal of Hellenic Studies*, LXXIII (1953), 84-103; also published separately.

Grumach, *Gnomon*, XXXII = Ernst Grumach, rev. of Chadwick, *Decipherment*, in *Gnomon*, XXXII (1960), 681-695.

Grumach, *OLZ*, LII = "Bemerkungen zu M. Ventris – J. Chadwick: Evidence," etc., *Orientalistische Literaturzeitung*, LII (1957), 293-342.

Guarducci = Margarita Guarducci (ed.), *Inscriptiones Creticae*, 4 vols. (Rome: Libreria dello stato, 1935-1950).

Hoffmann = Otto Hoffmann, *Die griechischen Dialekte in ihrem historischen Zusammenhange*, vol. I (Göttingen: Vanderhoeck und Ruprecht, 1891).

IG = *Inscriptiones Graecae* (Berlin: G. Reimer, 1873–).

*IG*² = *Inscriptiones Graecae*, ed. minor (Berlin: W. de Gruyter, 1913–).

IGA = Hermann Roehl (ed.), *Inscriptiones Graecae antiquissimae praeter Atticas in Attica repertas* (Berlin, 1882).

Kober, *AO*, XVIIᵃ = Alice E. Kober, " 'Total' in Minoan (Linear Class B)," *Archiv Orientální*, XVII, part 1 (1949), 386-398.

KT = *Bulletin of the Institute of Classical Studies of the University of London*, supp. 1, 2, 7:

KT [1955] = supp. 1, *The Linear 'B' Texts from Knossos*, transliterated and edited by R. Browning;

KT (1956) = supp. 2, *The Knossos Tablets*, a revised transliteration by Emmett L. Bennett Jr., John Chadwick, and Michael Ventris (ed.);

KT (1959) = supp. 7, *The Knossos Tablets*; 2d ed. by John Chadwick and Fred W. Householder.

Lang, *AJA*, LXII = Mabel Lang, "The Palace of Nestor Excavations of 1957: Part II," *AJA*, LXII (1958), 181-191.

"Languages" = Michael Ventris (ed.), "The Languages of the Minoan and Mycenaean Civilizations" (unpublished circular, dated New Year 1950).

Meister = Richard Meister, *Die griechischen Dialekte*, II (Göttingen: Vanderhoeck und Ruprecht, 1889).

Mitford, *Archaeology*, V = T. B. Mitford, "The Status of Cypriot Epigraphy – Cypriot Writing, Minoan to Byzantine," *Archaeology*, V (1952), 151-156.

"*MT*" (see Bennett)

OOTP (see Bennett)

Palmer, *Gnomon*, XXIX, = L. R. Palmer, rev. of *Documents*, in *Gnomon*, XXIX, (1957), 561-581.

Palmer, *OLZ*, LIII = "Mr. Ventris and his Critics," *Orientalistische Literaturzeitung*, LIII (1958), 101-117.

PT (see Bennett)

RE = Paulys *Real-Encyclopädie der classischen Altertumswissenschaft*, rev. by Georg Wissowa *et al.* (Stuttgart: J. B. Metzler, 1894–).

Schwyzer = Eduard Schwyzer, *Griechische Grammatik*, Handbuch der Altertumswissenschaft, zweite Abteilung, erster Teil; vol. I (Munich: Beck, 1939).

SDGI = Hermann Collitz (ed.), *Sammlung der griechischen Dialekt-Inschriften* (Göttingen: Vanderhoeck und Ruprecht, 1884-1915).

SM II = A. J. Evans, *Scripta Minoa*, vol. II, ed. by J. L. Myres (Oxford: Clarendon Press, 1952).

Vilborg = Ebbe Vilborg, *A Tentative Grammar of Mycenaean Greek*, Studia Graeca et Latina Gothoburgensia IX (Göteborg: Almqvist & Wiksell, 1960).

Work Note 1, 2, etc. = Ventris, "Work Notes on Minoan Language Research" (unpublished circulars, dated 28 January 1951 to 1 June 1952). On Work Note 20, see Chadwick, "Introductory Essay."

CONTENTS

The Linear B Decipherment
Controversy Re-examined

CHAPTER I

INTRODUCTION

MICHAEL VENTRIS's decipherment of the Mycenaean or Linear B script from Crete and the mainland of Greece has been widely praised as one of the major achievements of research in the historical sciences. But his work remains controversial and needs to be reassessed. It has yet to join the indisputably successful decipherments that have added so much knowledge about ancient languages and peoples in Egypt and western Asia. If Ventris's discovery is verified, it will deserve the renown of a decisive breakthrough, opening up the early Aegean civilization. The area was adjacent to the Near East and just as important or more so, because it became the setting for classical Greek culture. Even though the Linear B tablets are unimposing to the eye and record no great events or sublime thoughts, yet the reading of them carries with it the hope of penetrating into the origins of a singularly supple language and rich literature.

Those tablets tantalized the scholars ever since the first large find was made in Crete by Sir Arthur Evans, excavating at Knosos in 1900. Ventris, along with others, has ably narrated the vicissitudes of Linear B studies (see *Documents,* pp. 8 ff.); I need only draw attention to certain parts of the story which make the present controversy more understandable. Although Evans lived until 1941, he never got

3

around to publishing the bulk of the Linear B texts. Scholars and amateurs meanwhile did what they could with the meager selection that was available. Another great find was made in 1939 by Carl W. Blegen at Pylos on the mainland; and after a delay due to the Second World War, these tablets were expeditiously published in 1951 by Emmett L. Bennett. The next year the Knosos tablets finally came out through the efforts of J. L. Myres. In the interval between the two major publications[1] Ventris was busy with the research preliminary to his trial decipherment. He was not yet thirty and had already made his mark as an architect. He mailed out his Work Notes on the Linear B material to his correspondents; and in the momentous Work Note 20, dated 1 June 1952, he communicated his idea that a number of important Linear B words could be transcribed into Greek. His subsequent publications — of which John Chadwick, a professional Greek scholar, was the coauthor — were essentially the working out of what he announced in that last Work Note.

The mysterious script had thus defied solution for fifty years since Evans's first excavations, but Ventris produced his key to it only a year after an ample number of Linear B texts became accessible through Bennett's edition. Ventris rapidly gained the approval of innumerable scholars. Opposition arose more slowly, but it has lasted;[2] and ten years since the decipherment was disclosed, its validity is still at issue.

As I begin a lengthy appraisal of it, I wish to avoid the bitterness that mars some of the literature of the controversy. I recognized that both sides have made some good points, and I have enjoyed friendly conversation and correspondence with individuals of diametrically opposite views. Although I shall express disagreement now with one and now with another, I respect the sincerity of all. If they

4

have erred in certain of their arguments, that is only human; and I venture to state my own position in the human hope of surmounting the errors previously made, and of finding readers who can correct me if I go wrong, and who may gain from adopting my conclusions where correct.

At the beginning of this or any other intellectual controversy, the parties doubtless intended not to forget their good manners; nevertheless quite a few cruel words have been written. These are best ignored, as irrelevant distractions from the real issue. It would be futile to investigate who was the first to hurt someone's feelings. Several men have retorted in anger to criticisms not leveled at them but at others whom they agreed with. I wish that my work may conduce only to the enlightenment, not the distress, of any person interested in the Linear B texts. I myself have been singled out for unkind mention in print by an author who was (so far as I can make out) acquainted with only a brief summary of the paper I read to the American Philological Association and the Archaeological Institute of America in 1958. While I consider his conduct unfair and his reasoning faulty, I prefer not to press my case against him and not to publish his name, as my present study can do without a discussion of his remarks.[3]

Writers on both sides of the controversy have on occasion cited only part of the evidence relevant to the point they wished to prove, when the rest would have weakened their case. I do not chide them for dishonesty, because a convinced partisan may sometimes take for granted the familiarity of the audience with the entire body of evidence and therefore confine himself to emphasizing what is favorable to his side. But I feel free of that temptation and not entitled to that excuse, since I profess an intermediate position on the decipherment as a whole. On each particular I mean to set forth all the data that appear to have any bearing; or if they are too lengthy to cite in full, I will at least indicate where they can be looked up. I see no harm in the formula "etc." to dispense with repetition of identical data; but otherwise I will not leave any data unmentioned, unless by inadvertence. I have tried not to overlook any Linear B texts published up to the time of writing, but a considerable part of the scholarly literature is inaccessible to me. I especially regret that my ignorance of eastern European languages (except Greek) shuts me off from many long and undoubtedly valuable articles. On the other hand, a great many works are known to me which I shall not cite individually or take issue with, because the authors began by taking the whole decipherment for proven; it would be useless for me to criticize the specific arguments that they have built upon that foundation.

The need for further evaluation of the decipherment. Having thus appealed to the reader's good will, I must now insist that the ensuing critique of Ventris's work is not superfluous, but warranted by the circumstance that competent judges stand opposed in accepting or rejecting virtually the whole decipherment. Competent judges are of course not infallible, but it will not do to challenge their qualifications. Although Ventris himself was an amateur, his research has been scrutinized by many whose right to a professional opinion of it is unassailable — whose advice, indeed, had been sought by him at various early stages — and these scholars do not come out in agreement. Some have made it plain that their judgement on this question is no longer tentative: they have made up their minds and are not enlightened but irked and disgusted by views contrary to theirs. It is fair to remind them not to give way to *odium philologicum,* but to reply to stubbornness with patience and to keep a mind open to instruction from any quarter. The controversy will not be dispelled by breaking off communication. Until the experts arrive at a consensus, they cannot be stopped from expressing their disagreement in the pages of the best journals; and other people interested in the subject can be expected to have sense and perceive that it is unsettled. No one should be misled by attempts to belittle the competence of either side; such tactics amount to bullying the less expert readers so that they will be afraid to listen respectfully to counterarguments. Each of the experts has, of course, his individual attainments, but it is wrong to entertain thoughts like these about an opponent: "He knows less than I do about a certain field that bears upon the decipherment; therefore I can dismiss his opinion of it." Rather one should reflect, "I know less than he does about another relevant field; so I owe it to myself, to him, and to the altar of truth to follow his arguments through with the utmost care and learn whatever I can from them. Besides, I can remember times when I have had to change my mind." In a scholarly controversy, even if it turns out eventually that one party has been not just basically wrong but quite wrongheaded, still that party is bound to have made at least a few worthwhile remarks; so the other party and the learned public will be better off for having paid attention.

Some supporters of the decipherment have naively drawn comfort from the fact that they are greatly in the majority. This illusory advantage comes from misapplying to the Republic of Letters the analogy of legislatures and courts of law. In the practical world an issue often cannot be argued on and on with no time limit until ultimately the question ceases to be controversial. Instead, those in authority may be convinced that the issue is urgent enough to require a decision, premature though it may be — when the alternative of letting the contest continue is liable to bring more harm. But in academic questions it is not so. No one can and no one should limit debate or call for a vote.[4] An editor, to be sure, has a right to decide when he has given a certain controversy all the space he can afford; but the other right, to decide which side has won, does not belong to him. The controversy will continue in other publications and deserves to go on so long as the parties bring in more facts and fresh arguments. One can sympathize with those who wish the controversy would die down, so that they could simply acquiesce in the outcome of it; but such a wish is not to be gratified until the disputants are exhausted.

The present controversy over the Linear B tablets is inconvenient to many scholars; for example, to an economic historian writing about changes in the pattern of land tenure. Suppose this hypothetical person does not reckon himself an expert in any of the fields that bear directly upon the correctness of the Ventris decipherment; nevertheless it matters to him whether to use the results of it in his own studies or to leave them aside as speculative and unconfirmed. Either way that he may decide involves a considerable risk. If he is bold by temperament, he will be inclined to treat what is debatable as if it were established; if he is conservative, he will avoid whatever is not established securely. Assuming that the Mycenaean period is really indispensable to his subject, one can only advise him that the world can wait as long as necessary for a definitive work to be written, even if he thinks he cannot wait any longer to write it! He would be ill-advised to turn, in his inexpertness, to the authority of Professor A, or of Professors A, B, C, and D together, if they happen to agree. To say "What's good enough for them is good enough for me" does not befit a scholar, when he knows there are other experts who disagree. Nor can he rightly weigh which persons are the more reputable authorities. The only valid criterion is, which *reasons* will stand up under examination; there may be some such on both sides. Whoever is conscious of not being equipped to apply this test, should consider the issue to be in suspense until a consensus is reached by all those acknowledged to be experts. Meanwhile anyone who professes a degree of expertness can contribute to an eventual settlement by publishing the arguments that lead him to such and such a conclusion.

While a mature consensus of experts is an excellent goal, its usefulness to a scholar in a tangential field ought not to be exaggerated. It enables him, in safety, to treat the bare facts as authentic, and the interpretation of them — on the most simple, straightforward level — as certain also. But a consensus in interpretation beyond that level is, in effect, no more than a currently accepted theory, useful indeed to the degree that it helps us to see coherent relations between facts, but not otherwise having any claim upon us to accept it as true. For instance, if a professor of philosophy knows just enough Greek, at best, to follow the text of Plato when accompanied by a translation, he is entitled to feel confident of the plain sense of any passage that is rendered substantially the same by all reputable translators; but their agreement upon any higher matter of dialectical or literary structure is in some danger of signifying less about Plato than about themselves and their own way of thinking. I am far from decrying the need for theories; only in the light of a theory can we gauge the import of each fact — which facts to pass by fleetingly and which ones to dwell upon. However, if we have to handle other men's theories based on facts that lie mainly outside our knowledge, we are not on the safest ground. Few of us manage or even desire to tailor our research so that it falls entirely within the field of our particular expertness. Yet the more we have to rely on the conclusions reached by others, the more we become like a general dependent upon allies not under his command. It amounts to saying, "If generalization A is right (which I have on good authority but cannot vouch for personally), and generalization B likewise, and so on, then my inferences are right too." Great and ambitious syntheses usually rest on such a framework, more or less hidden. Few of them are good enough to satisfy the specialists whose authority in the several fields has been drawn upon; for when we try to handle what we have not mastered, we invite serious mistakes.

The dilemma, of either using only what one can vouch for or using what one cannot vouch for, has to be compromised by each author to the best of his ability. I, for instance, have studied far too little of the archaeological evidence for dating the Knosos tablets earlier than the Pylos tablets. The chronological interval could make an important difference in the study of the Linear B language. The view that the Knosos tablets were written about 1400 B.C., and the Pylos tablets two centuries later, passed with virtually no challenge until recently; yet it would have been imprudent for me to rest any major point of my research upon it. Now it has been sharply questioned by L. R. Palmer,[5] and we can look forward to a clarification of the age of the tablets.

The need for verification of individual details. A related principle of scholarship — often overlooked in studies of Linear B — is that in the solution of a problem every detail is tentative and provisional until individually proved. It is admissible to say, "This step is not impossible, involves no immediate contradiction, so let's proceed with it." But an error of method enters later if one supposes explicitly or implicitly, "In retrospect it does not appear that anything has obliged us to reconsider this step; so we may now take it for certain." Even if we are satisfied with our experimental solution of the problem as a whole, we should be prepared to justify each part against any reasonable doubt. Any part that cannot be shown to be more than merely probable or possible must not be reckoned as established. When critics challenge us to explain what undeniable evidence such and such a point rests on, they do a better service than when they acquiesce in everything that they cannot prove to be absolutely wrong. The discoverer of something new ought in all cases to assume the burden of proof. Any competent critic is entitled to set up requirements for demonstrating the reality of the discovery; and the discoverer who refuses to do it on the critic's terms is not entitled to plead, "I am right anyhow; for other critics do not insist on such stringent conditions." [6] Any part that is no longer in the experimental stage must hold up positively under cross-examination.

This can indeed be demonstrated in any ancient language of which scholars have real knowledge. No challenge, however captious, can undermine what is solid. If anyone asks how we know that ἵππος in the great majority of Greek passages stood for the kind of animal that we now call a *horse* in English, the proof are overwhelming. Each of us may have initially accepted the equivalence ἵππος 'horse' on the authority of a teacher or a printed vocabulary list; but we are not limited to such authority, which we have found by experience to be not in every instance infallible. That experience is our extensive reading, which confirms this meaning of ἵππος time after time, likewise confirming countless other pieces of knowledge about Greek, although it also shows — on occasion — that the traditional doctrine on such and such a detail is wrong.[7] Any point that turns out, when scrutinized, to rest on nothing more than a conjecture or convention previously unchallenged ought to be labeled *unverified*.

Criticizing a dead author. In passing, I had better bring into the open and reply to a sentiment which is too unscholarly to appear in learned publications but has often been expressed orally and may be shared instinctively by some readers: that any adverse criticism of Ventris's work is indecent because he died prematurely and cannot defend it. His death in an auto accident (an increasingly frequent evil of our age) is truly lamentable; but the motto *De mortuis nil nisi bonum* cannot fairly be extended beyond its proper sphere. Persons (even living persons!) should be respected, but what they have produced should be impartially examined. It would be mistaken piety to exempt Ventris's writings from the full range of critical reactions. On the other hand, there is no reason why a severe castigation of his methods and results should become an attack upon his memory. In any case he left behind many able supporters. While they have, in one sense, every right to speak for him, in another sense we cannot be sure. When he was killed on September 6, 1956, just one thoroughly critical review of the decipherment had been published, that of Nikolaos Platon;[8] it was possible for Ventris in *Documents* (p. 24) to dismiss Platon's objections as "criticism from a 'Minoan' partisan." Other criticisms since then have been rejected by Chadwick and the supporters of the decipherment. Ventris might have done the same had he lived, or — for all we know — he might have seen some merit in the counterarguments and made more or less considerable changes, looking toward an accommodation with the opposing views. Since his death, any scholar who writes under his own name is no literary executor of Ventris but an individual expressing what he himself understands. I point this out for the sake of fair-mindedness to all who engage in this controversial subject. They are entitled to take extreme positions, according to their own judgement — regardless of what Ventris might say if he now had to face the same problems they do. Scholarship cannot help but go its way, after a pause for mourning, and try its best to hammer out a true statement, based on the facts.

12

While on the subject of due regard for the reputation of individuals, I want to apologize for my practice, throughout this book, of attributing to Ventris everything contained in the works that he published in conjunction with Chadwick. Of course I have no desire to detract from Chadwick's very great contribution to those works, for which both of them assumed responsibility. Chadwick himself, more than anyone else, has generously and unequivocally insisted that the fundamental discovery was Ventris's (see *Decipherment*, pp. 1, 68-70). While praising Ventris's modesty, he cannot successfully hide his own, and it redounds to his credit. I beg my readers to understand that when I write "Ventris" in reference to anything that appeared under both names, the one word stands for "Ventris with Chadwick's collaboration."

The desideratum in a decipherment. The whole issue, compressed into one sentence, is: By applying the Ventris decipherment to the Linear B tablets, do we make them into *comprehensible Greek texts?* Obtaining Greek *words* would not be enough, not even if every single word were recognizable as Greek (which of course has never been claimed by Ventris or anybody else). Apparently Greek words, if they do not fit together into a text, could be produced by great ingenuity while the language of the tablets would remain something quite different. A playful sort of ingenuity has concocted the following illusory sequence of Latin words:

> O Sibylle, si ergo
> fortibus es in ero;
> o nobile Themis trux,
> siue at sinam causam dux.

It is actually an English jingle, which my readers may enjoy figuring out, in case the trick has never been pulled on them before.

While we demand that the decipherment must yield Greek texts, not just Greek words, we cannot insist that the language be *identical* with the Greek we know. It need only be enough like a known language to be understood. If no Romance language besides French were known, a sentence such as

Lasciate ogni speranza, voi ch' entrate

could be understood as a dialectal equivalent of

Laissez —— espérance, vous qui entrez.

On principle, discrepancies between the newly discovered language and its known relative are to be expected, but each particular discrepancy must be noted with reserve until it is shown to fall into a coherent pattern, as the *-ate* : *-ez* discrepancy of the first word recurs in the last one. To move now from this easy, made-up example of reading Italian as French to a real experience in the history of linguistic scholarship, the Old Persian cuneiform inscription at Behiŝtun was successfully deciphered in the nineteenth century when a transcription was worked out that made it tolerably comprehensible as Avestan, which had never ceased to be used and understood by the Parsis as their scriptural and liturgical language and had lately begun to be studied by European scholars too. The solution was clinched when the discrepancies between Avestan and the language of the inscription were shown to be not chaotic but regular.

A decipherment is essentially a transcription that pierces the secret and opens up the text to anyone with a reading knowledge of the language. If the transcription is not legible throughout, whatever remains obscure is a limitation upon the value of the decipherer's work, at least to this extent: he has not made the meaning of the entire text accessible. Whether it is his fault is another matter. A message in a modern language, intercepted while being sent by radio, may be garbled in places before the decipherer receives it from the intercepting technicians; obviously he is not to blame for producing gibberish in the garbled places. A somewhat parallel case comes up in ancient texts which before decipherment were presumed (or might have been presumed) to be in a language not identical but only similar to a known one. To this cause the supporters of Ventris have attributed the admitted fact that a large part of the Linear B material, when transcribed, does not square with anything Greek. They apply their erudition and acumen to the reconstruction of a prehistoric type of Greek in which much that is unintelligible on the basis of classical Greek can be plausibly if not certainly interpreted. On the other hand, their opponents argue that the unintelligible passages are so extensive as to signify the failure of the decipherment as a whole, and that whatever may look like Greek is illusory. No one on either side, to my knowledge, has made more than the slightest concessions, which leave the issue unchanged. One who admits that Ventris's transcription may contain a tiny percentage of error agrees virtually with one who accepts the transcription in full. And a critic who allows that there may be — by coincidence — a bit of real Greek in it might just as well deny even that.

Notes to Chapter I

1. Listed in my bibliography (above, pp. ix, xii) as Bennett, *PT* (1951), and *SM* II, respectively.

2. A bibliography in Grumach, *Gnomon*, XXXII, 691.

3. My readers are not obliged to take my word for this. Whoever wishes to form his own opinion can obtain an exact reference by writing to me. So much I owe to any interested scholar who makes a private inquiry; nor would I have a right to limit such a person's use of published material. But I feel another duty not to make more of the incident than absolutely necessary. It would not be candid of me as a scholar to take no notice whatever of something written to my discredit and called to my attention by a person other than the author; on the other hand, it would be petty to vindicate myself by showing how unjustified the critic's words were. I had this study planned before he wrote anything about me.

4. Cases arise in practical life that require expert opinion, and it is found that the experts disagree; for instance, on the benefits and the possible dangers of fluoridation. Then the public authority may have its reasons for not waiting until the experts reach a consensus. The Ventris decipherment is not an urgent issue in the same sense. Nobody's teeth are at stake. The only impact it is likely to have on people's lives would be in the direction that it may give to scholarly leisure and to the subsidies paid out by research foundations.

5. "The Truth about Knossos," *The Observer* (London), July 3, 1960, p. 1.

6. Even in the kind of experiment that results in the making of a new machine, the author may commit some errors that he never perceives or corrects until they are later pointed out by a critic. The success of the product demonstrates that the process must have been right in the main, but not that it was free from all flaws. The product may operate more or less well in spite of built-in defects.

Such literally spectacular proofs, addressed to the senses and not merely the intellect, are seldom possible in the solution of problems set in the past.

7. All readers of scholia will remember meeting, here and there, an incorrect explanation of some difficult word or construction.

8. In Κρητικά Χρονικά, VIII (1954), 143-63; excerpts translated by Henri Grégoire, "Le déchiffrement des inscriptions en LINEAR B de Crète et de Pylos," *Académie royale de Belgique, Bulletin de la Classe*

des lettres et des sciences morales et politiques, 5th series, vol. XL (1954), 683-89. Massimo Pallottino voiced serious reservations, particularly in view of the highly systematic but illusory decipherments of Etruscan; "Sulla decifrazione dei testi cretesi-micenei in lineare B," *Atti della Pontificia Accademia Romana di Archeologia,* ser. III, *Rendiconti,* XXVIII (1954-55), 19-29, actually published in 1956.

Chadwick, *Decipherment,* p. 90, tells of a correspondence that he and Ventris had with Beattie, beginning in 1952; but in this passage there was no occasion to say whether Beattie wrote out in his letters the detailed objections that he later used in his *JHS* article.

CHAPTER II

VENTRIS'S METHOD: THE GRID AND THE CYPRIOTIC SYLLABARY

IN ANY OTHER decipherment presenting such a mixture of what can and what cannot be taken for an intelligible ancient language, one might expect another reaction in between adherence and refutation — to wit, a suspicion that the decipherment is right only in part, that the method was valid up to a point but not without serious faults. This is my view of Ventris's work, but I have not heard of anyone else who cares to maintain it actively. Ventris's use of a cryptographic grid has led people to presume that the solution must be practically all right or all wrong.

It was indeed a novelty to bring a grid into the process of deciphering ancient documents; at any rate this was the first time it was used with any show of success. The classical scholars who wished to form an opinion of Ventris's work did not have previous experience with this sort of decipherment to guide them in the present case. So it was not easy for them to estimate how much the preliminary use of the grid by Ventris ought to affect their criteria for determining the value of his results. Some may not even have heard of the word *grid* before, except in its homely meaning — a utensil for baking waffles. Ventris emphatically asserted that the grid (a cryptographic term for a rectangular work sheet of columns and rows) made a crucial difference. But the theory claiming superior reliability for a decipherment based on a grid was set forth by him very briefly; and I must discuss it much more lengthily, because I see that in spite of his intention he has mystified rather than enlightened the learned public on this key point. No authority on the art of cryptanalysis has come forward with a critique — whether favorable or not — of Ventris's procedure. I gained a moderate acquaintance with cryptanalysis during the Second World War, but I wish we could hear from real experts. Nearly all writers who discuss the Linear B decipherment are Hellenists and not cryptanalysts. Ventris himself was an amateur in both fields. Emmett L. Bennett, who — more than anyone else — carries the two in balance, has not yet published an account of his unfinished attempt to decipher the tablets before he saw Ventris's solution and, with some hesitation, accepted it. Such an account, accompanied by a comparison with Ventris's method, would be no mere curiosity but a clarification of an obscure and essential subject. Without a professional cryptanalyst to guide them, some scholars proficient in Greek or in general linguistics, but not visibly so in cryptanalysis, argue nonetheless about Ventris's grid and taunt their opponents for not understanding its implications. I shall try to show that the proper function of the grid could only be, at best, to *suggest* tentative phonetic values for the Linear B characters, and that then each value needs to be *individually proved* by occurring in contexts that do not admit of a reasonable difference of opinion.

The possibility of using a grid occurred to Ventris doubtless because of a previous inference, made by Vladimir Georgiev, Konstantinos Ktistopoulos, and himself,[1] that the Linear B script (as well as the Linear A) is a syllabary constructed on principles similar to those of the Cypriotic syllabary of classical times, in which each character stands for a consonant followed by a vowel or for a vowel alone. The grid was produced by lining up in a certain column all the Linear B characters that were deemed to have a vowel in common with each other, and in a certain row all the characters that were deemed to have a consonant in common. That Ventris did this to the Linear B characters does not at once prove the process had any decisive importance in the decipherment. He stated in his publications (especially "Evidence," p. 88) that the grid had played a fundamental role; but it appears to me from studying his previous, unpublished circulars that the grid was ancillary rather than fundamental.[2]

The basic procedure of Ventris's grid. The question may be put this way: Was the phonetic value of the Linear B characters deduced from their position on the grid, or did their placement on the grid merely record the phonetic value already assigned to them? To the extent that the former is true, the grid served as a device to obtain phonetic values for the characters, not one at a time (as other methods would do) but in groups. This great methodological advantage of the grid depended upon first arranging the characters in rows and columns without assigning phonetic values. Then the assignment of a consonant-plus-vowel value to a single character would spread that consonant to the other characters in the same row and that vowel to the others in the same column. But if any character is placed on the grid after a value has been assigned to another in the same row or column, the newly placed character has been individually judged to possess the consonant characteristic of that row or the vowel characteristic of that column. The nature of a syllabic grid would allow it to serve two functions, each partially: to obtain consonantal or vocalic values for the characters previously aligned, and to register the values obtained by other means for the previously unaligned characters. In the latter function the grid is a mere table helping the cryptanalyst to keep track of his progress.

Actually the Work Notes present the grid in three states:

First state	28 January 1951	Work Note 1
Second state	28 September 1951	Work Note 15
Third state	20 February 1952	Work Note 17

All of these are less complete than the grid published in "Evidence" and *Documents*.

Phonetic values assigned by Ventris in his early research. In "Evidence" (p. 88) Ventris went to the extreme of claiming that "the consonant and vowel equations tabulated below had all been deduced from internal evidence before any phonetic values were allotted. They are based partly on inflectional evidence, partly on accidental or deliberate spelling variations." The words "all" and "any" are manifestly irreconcilable with what Ventris had actually done in Work Note 1 (28 January 1951) — so irreconcilable that his later statement in "Evidence" must be an idealization (not a willful falsification) of his procedure. But readers took these published words at face value, and thus their judgement of Ventris's work was gravely, even fatally, misguided. It is of capital importance to set the facts straight.

Work Note 1 contained the first very incomplete attempt at a grid. The inflexions and other variations that are cited in the Note are too few to permit the grouping of more than a minority of the Linear B characters. Nevertheless, eight of the ten rows of the grid are assigned a tentative consonantal value:

1 *t*- ?

2 *r*- ??

3 *ś*- ??

4 *n*- ??
   s- ??

5

6 *l*- ?

7 *ḫ*- ??

8 θ- ??

9 *m*- ?
   k- ?

10

The headings of the four vowels are

Vowel 1	Vowel 2	Other vowels ?	Doubtful
-NIL (*-o* ?)	*-i* ?	*-a, -e, -u* ?	

Even before this first Work Note with its preliminary grid, Ventris had expressed in the "Languages" circular (p. xiv) the opinion that "9-odd" characters common to Linear A and Linear B are readily identifiable in the Cypriotic syllabary.

Shape and numerical transcription in Linear A and B	Phonetic value in Cypriotic[3]
⊦ 01 (AB)[4]	ta
† 02 (AC)	lo
‡ 03 (AD)	pa
⊤ 05 (AG)	to
∧ 37 (AJ)	ti
⊼ 39 (AL)	si
⫶ 76 (EB)	zo
⊔ 60 (IJ)	li
⊤ 06 (IS)	na

Besides these nine, he ventured in the same circular to give a phonetic transcription of twenty-five other characters in Appendix 1, "Experimental phonetic values," and Appendix 2, "Sign-groups identified as vocabulary words" (pp. xxi-xxx).[5] Of the identifications that Ventris thus made before constructing any grid, eleven reappear in the grid shown in the "Evidence" article, either unchanged or with a minor modification:

> 01 is now *da* (*ta* in "Languages")
> 02 " " *ro* (*lo* in "Languages")
> 03 remains *pa*
> 05 " *to*
> 37 " *ti*
> 06 " *na*
> 09 is now *se* (*şe* in "Languages")[6]
> 31 " " *sa* (*şa* in "Languages")
> 57 remains *ja*
> 08 " *a*
> 12 is now *so* (*ş" in "Languages")[7]

23

Ventris's later policy of minimizing his dependence on the Cypriotic syllabary. We might be tempted to conclude that Ventris attached these values to the eleven characters all along, from before he made any grid to the time when he drew up the grid for the "Evidence" article. It would follow that whatever other characters he placed in the same row or the same column with any of the eleven had thus a consonant or vowel determined before or upon entering the grid, not afterwards. However, in Work Note 15 (3-27 Sept 1951) and on the grid in its second state (28 Sept 51) he gave no phonetic values, except for labeling the row with *o8* and *61* "pure vowels ?" (i.e., not preceded by a consonant) and the row with *57* and *59* "a semi-vowel ?" (i.e., *j-* preceding the vowel).[8] He also declared:

> I have completely ignored the Cypriot syllabary in trying to put Figure 10 [the new, or second, stage of the grid] together. Though I believe it to be descended from a form of the Minoan Linear scripts, its signs have evidently undergone such a radical transformation that it is only in the case of the very simplest and commonest, such as ⊦ *ta*, ⧻ *pa*, ✝ *lo* etc, that there is any realism in trying to interpolate their values into Minoan sign-groups. However, if we compare the Cypriot syllabic table *as a whole* with a Minoan "GRID" such as that of Figure 10, there is a rather better hope of noticing any simultaneous identities, and of analysing the way in which the Cypriot signs have undergone modification. I have not embarked on this.

The policy announced in this latter Work Note, much more than his early procedure, accords with the remarkable claim that he made for the grid in "Evidence." He seems in this Work Note to be almost but not quite renouncing the majority of his early identifications of certain Linear A and B characters with certain Cypriotic ones. Yet a closer look makes it hard for me to believe that in setting up the grid he really renounced them. I cannot give absolute proof, because he did not carry the columns and rows of the grid in its second state "to the point of suggesting actual phonetic values for any vowels and consonants, though the prospect is always tempting." At any rate, of the nine Linear characters that he had identified with Cypriotic characters in the "Languages" circular, he now placed seven in positions where they were to receive, in the third state of the grid (20 Feb 1952, with Work Note 17), phonetic values still agreeing with those of their Cypriotic counterparts:[9]

01   *ta* ?[10]
02   *lo* ?
03   *za* ? or *pa* ?
05   *to* ?[10]
37   *ti* ?[10]
60   *li* ?
06   *na* ?

He discarded the other two of his original identifications, *39 = si, 76 = zo*, which are not among the "very simplest and commonest"; *39* became *zi* ? or *pi* ? and *76* became *ra* ? or *la* ?

There is no need to suspect a dishonest intention in those statements of his, professing not to have used the Cypriotic syllabary in constructing the second state of the grid, and not to have assigned any phonetic values until he had deduced from internal evidence which character had some vowel or some consonant in common with which other characters. His sincerity hinges on a distinction between the subjective and the objective, or between Ventris as a amateur prone to hunches and whims and Ventris as a disciplined researcher intent on demonstrating his case to learned colleagues and professors. He had the highest regard for the American scholars; he wrote, in Work Note 15 accompanying the grid, "Only our colleagues in the United States seem to me to have so far shown the realistic approach." He was therefore determined to present his research in a fashion acceptable to them. Alice Kober, before her death in 1950, had curtly refused to answer his questionnaire, calling it "a step in the wrong direction"; Emmett L. Bennett, in his brief answer, had given a rule of method to which Ventris at that time was not yet ready to adhere: "For the phonetic portions of the inscriptions the first steps should not be the substitution of values, but rather the investigation of the frequencies and combinations of the characters; the principles of formation within the sign-groups; the relationships of nearly identical sign-groups, which may yield evidence of inflection or of word-formation; the classification of the functions of the sign-groups, which might separate names of various sorts from the connective or predicative portions of the languages" ("Languages," pp. 7-8, 37). The second state of the grid and the Work Notes leading up to it were a new start, more in conformity with the rigorous standards of Kober and Bennett.

Ventris uneasily made their objective approach predominate over his subjective one. From his own experience and that of others, the Cypriotic syllabary was clearly an insufficient basis for deciphering Linear B; no successful decipherment could come out of an attempt to assign a Cypriotic phonetic value to as many Linear B characters as were shaped somewhat like Cypriotic characters. He could not shake off an unprofessional (though not unintelligent) hunch that at least a few Cypriotic characters were descended from Linear A and B characters and had retained nearly the same phonetic value. But by the time that he came to plot out the grid in its second state, he perceived the fallacy of deciding by mere intuition which cases of similar shape were significant, and which ones coincidental. He saw no proof of any phonetic values in Linear B and therefore limited himself to stating the relations between characters. Some of these relations were in accord with his original inferences from the characters shaped similarly in the Linear A and B and the Cypriotic syllabaries; but he was not prepared to argue that the graphic similarity in these several cases contributes any cogent reason for placing the characters on certain spaces of the grid. He therefore subdued the temptation to assign phonetic values expressly, though he had such values in mind for some of the characters and hence for their entire columns and rows. He indulged his fondness for the Cypriotic values only where he had internal Linear B evidence that seemed sufficient to establish the relations of those characters to the other characters.

Ventris's unwillingness to read 11-02 as po-lo. One character ⌐ *11* received very curious and yet typical treatment from Ventris. It had been noted by Sir Arthur Evans as similar to the Cypriotic *po,* because it occurs in the group ⌐† to the left of a foal's head twice on the Linear B tablet Ca895; the syllables would be *po-lo* in Cypriotic, equivalent to πώλω 'foals,' a dual form suiting the number written ideographically ‖ to the right of the foal's head (*PM,* IV[b], 799). Evans implied that the resemblance to a Greek word was coincidental; but Ventris in "Languages" (p. xxiii) recorded that it was accepted by Vladimir Georgiev and Bedřich Hrozný, not by himself. At that point he strangely refused to admit that the Linear B character *11* had anything to do with the Cypriotic. Later, in the second state of the grid, he in effect came around to the view of Georgiev and

27

Hrozný: he placed 11 in the same row as 03 and in the same
column as 05 and 02. These were labeled z- ? p- ? and -o ?
(-e ?) in the third state; but then the character 11, while
remaining in that row, was moved to a new column labeled
"vowel uncertain."

Ventris's early reluctance to identify 11 with the Cypriotic
character seems explicable only by his avowed hunch that
the Linear B language was Etruscan or related to Etruscan.
Had he accepted po as the value of 11 at the same time as lo
for 02, he could hardly have avoided reading po-lo as the
Greek word for 'foals.' By the time he reached Work Note 15,
his adherence to Kober's method required him to set aside as
premature any attempt to guess at the affinities of the Linear
B language; so he no longer had a reason to shun the conse-
quences of allowing a connexion between the Linear B
character 11 and the Cypriotic. On the other hand, he had
some internal evidence of variation between 11 and 03 (the
Cypriotic pa):

```
10-11-60-67-53-57
10-03-60-67-53-57 (Work Note 9, p. 78, item F 2)
08-27-11-20-61
08-27-03-75[   (Work Note 14, p. 100, item P 21)
```

This encouraged him to place 11 in the same row as 03. I
have not found in the Work Notes any such ground for
placing 11 in the same column as 02 and 05 (the Cypriotic
to). Ventris himself seems to have realized later, in the third
state of the grid, that the vocalic connexion expressed in the
second state was not warranted by the Kober-Bennett method; hence he was obliged in the third state to remove 11
from that column and call its vowel "uncertain."

The grid published in "Evidence" has 11 back in the -o
column; but like all the other changes recorded at that late

stage, it was not due to an internal analysis made of the occurrences of the character while the assignment of phonetic
values was held in abeyance. On the contrary, Ventris must
have decided upon *po* for the sake of obtaining Greek words
on the horse tablet and elsewhere in the Linear B texts.

Ventris's incomplete commitment to the grid. If it can be
properly claimed that the correctness of the grid must be
judged as a whole, the claim must be limited to those characters which were placed there no later than Work Note 17
(the third state).[11] The vowel designations of the columns
and the consonant designations of the rows were all at that
time shown to be tentative by means of question marks. It
was proper for Ventris to revalue a whole row or column
later, as he did in changing the ninth consonant from *f-* ? to
m-. But his claim that the grid stands as a whole is weakened
by his moving of individual characters to another position
on the grid between the third state and the "Evidence" article; e.g., *28* got shifted from the *vi* ? or *ri* ? space to the *i*
space, *61* from the *i* ? to the *o* space, *55* actually from the θ*e* ?
or *re* ? space to the *nu* space.[12] The moving around of several
characters implies that he did not then feel wholly committed
to those relations between them which he had discovered
in his internal cryptographic research. He was still less
committed in regard to certain other characters that he distinguished on the grid by reducing their size. ("Small signs
indicate uncertain position.") Hence it is no wonder that he
moved ♀ *20* from the *ʰ/χa* ? or θ*a* ? space in the third state
of the grid to *z?o* in "Evidence" (*zo* without a question mark
in *Documents*, p. 23). In the third state some cases of uncertainty were vividly and candidly expressed by placing
one character in two different spaces; e.g., *57* is shown full-
sized in the *ja* ? square, reduced in the *śa* ? square, and *46*
full-sized as *śi* ?, reduced as *śe* ? Surely the position of even

the full-sized character in these cases indicates just a preference, not a commitment.

Uncertainties about the efficacy of the grid method. For a considerable residue of the characters, the placement in a certain square of the third stage of the grid was not only unequivocal at the time but also turned out to be final, as they stayed put in the subsequent publication. For these characters only it is a tenable though not a necessary deduction from Ventris's procedure to say that their relation to one another was adequately established by internal evidence — with a corollary that if we accept Ventris's phonetic value for one of them, we must accept the same vowel for the other characters in the column and the same consonant for the other characters in the row. I have some doubts about the reliability of the grid, even within the limits I have set in this paragraph and the preceding one. First, does the "American" method of Kober and Bennett, which Ventris embraced, get at enough material that reveals sure — not merely tentative — connexions resting upon the phonological structure of vowels and consonants in the language? Secondly, did Ventris owe such success as he achieved in the decipherment to a rigorously faithful application of the "American" method, or rather to an eclectic flexibilty? I see plenty of room for reasonable difference of opinion on both questions.

On both theoretical and pragmatic grounds it is debatable whether the Kober-Bennett method, even if carried to the extreme of observing every detail about the occurrences of every character, could so dependably handle all the preliminaries to decipherment and so penetrate the structure of an unknown or, at any rate, unidentified language that the grid would serve as an immediate test for any phonetic values which the cryptanalyst (or anyone else) might wish to try out. Kober and Bennett were systematic and cautious;

their hopes too were modest. Kober's published observations — and I dare say Bennett's unpublished ones — on the Linear B script and language were nearly irreproachable. Nevertheless, linguistic theory is not so far advanced that anyone could do more than guess what sort of peculiarities to allow for in this script and language, which Kober and Bennett did not identify and which could not be identified with any reasonable confidence. On the other hand, one could intelligently surmise that at least a small percentage of the relations discovered between the characters and used in gridding them would turn out not to have the expected phonological significance — if ever one progressed to the point of a successful decipherment. The utmost authority that I would grant to any grid constructed under such adverse conditions is the privilege of *suggesting* phonetic values to be applied experimentally to the texts, where each character's value, if true, ought to find unmistakable confirmation.

Besides my theoretical reservations, it is a fact that Kober and Bennett did not arrive at a decipherment, nor did they complete the major preliminaries — sifting the internal evidence and arranging the characters upon a grid. Kober died too soon; Bennett was occupied with editing and with interpreting the nonverbal contents of the Linear B tablets no less than with cryptanalyzing the verbal part of them. It is useless to speculate on how much more they might have accomplished had things gone otherwise for them.

The change of method in Work Note 20. The success of Ventris's decipherment has generally been ascribed, first by himself in "Evidence" and subsequently by others, to his use of the grid constructed in conformity with the analytical method of Kober and Bennett; credit has also been given to his extraordinary speed. I believe, however, that something else contributed at least as much to Ventris's achievement: while making use of their method, he never put all his eggs into that one basket. He perceived, in the third state of the grid (Work Note 17), that the method, far as he had gone with it, still left many uncertainties—some characters doubtfully placed on the grid, others not placed at all. He had worked chiefly with the material in *The Pylos Tablets, a Preliminary Transcription* by Bennett (Princeton, 1951). I cannot judge whether a more complete and reliable grid might have been extracted, had Ventris or anyone else worked longer on the same material. But at that time an abundance of additional material became available, as he announced at the beginning of the Note (p. 162):

> The publication by the Clarendon Press, Oxford, of Sir John Myres' SCRIPTA MINOA Vol 2 introduces the third, and I hope final, stage in the decipherment of the Aegean inscriptions. Before going on to study the structure of the Knossos sign-groups, it may be helpful to draw up a revised form of the *syllabic grid,* incorporating all the phonetic evidence we have so far managed to extract from the Pylos material (Figure 11). This may have to be considerably modified in the light of the Knossos evidence, but something on these lines is bound to remain our most valuable instrument of analysis.

Ventris's subsequent writings indicate that he did not analyze the Knosos texts like the Pylos, but instead resumed his long-suspended efforts to transcribe words from the Linear B script into a pronounceable consonant-and-vowel syllabary. The next two Notes (18 and 19) did not deal with Knosos material; in Work Note 19 (20 March 1952) he charted out the declensions which he inferred from the Pylos texts, and at the end he wrote: "The next step will be to test out this paradigm against the forms occurring in the

Knossos tablets published in Scripta Minoa Vol 2, which I have not yet seen." Then Work Note 20 (1 June 1952) began as follows:

> *Are the Knossos and Pylos tablets written in Greek?*
> With the publication of the Knossos tablets in Scripta Minoa volume II, and with the promise of Dr Bennett's revised Index, we are in a position to begin a detailed analysis of the whole Linear B material under its various aspects. One of the first studies of this is Ktistopoulos' "Recherches sur les mots minoens", which I have just received. Until this work has been done, it will be as well not to start with any preconceived notions about phonetic values or about the language relationships.
> The Note which follows is in the nature of a frivolous digression, and is not intended to prejudice that analysis.

Ventris here implies that Work Note 20 is not based to any great extent on this recent research of Ktistopoulos; my examination of the two papers enables me to confirm that Ventris indeed did not incorporate Ktistopoulos's findings into his own grid. Doubtless there was too little time between his receipt of Ktistopoulos's paper and his writing of Work Note 20. Moreover, in the ten weeks between Notes 19 and 20 Ventris, far from analyzing the newly available Knosos material in the same manner that he had analyzed the Pylos material, apparently profited little from *Scripta Minoa* II; at any rate, in Work Note 20 the words cited from Knosos tablets were nearly all available for years in Kober's articles. The "frivolous digression," which he chose to write up in Work Note 20 before returning to the laborious method of the previous Work Notes, brought good enough results so that he never had to take up that method again.

As I understand his procedure, he worked on the grid no more than necessary. He resorted to it in 1951 because he had not obtained a decipherment by means of his previous method, which had rested mainly upon the Cypriotic syllabary. In 1952, when the bulk of the Knosos tablets became available, he was far from jumping at the opportunity to extract from them more relations between characters and thereby to perfect the grid. Instead he made what use he could of the grid as it was, on the chance that he now had enough for a decipherment by applying to certain characters on the grid the more trustworthy of the Cypriotic values that had impressed him much earlier. I commend him for being flexible; I do not censure him for impatience or lack of rigor. But I deplore the fact that in his publications "Evidence" and *Documents* he minimized — to the point of denying — his dependence on the Cypriotic syllabary and exaggerated the role of the grid.

Use of the Cypriotic syllabary in Work Note 20. Since Work Note 20 contains the essentials of the decipherment, we can show from it how, along with the grid of Work Note 17, he used key phonetic values that had been inferred by him before he ever began to make the grid. Three of these inferences were explicitly announced in Work Note 20 (p. 173):

1 That ⊢ᛏ [*08*] - ,[13] because of its great initial frequency, represents *a*-, as Ktistopoulos has also suggested ["Recherches sur les mots minoens," p. 3; likewise in earlier writings].

2 That the series ᛘ ᛤ ᛦ ╤ [*30, 52, 24, 06*] contain the consonant *n*-, because of Cypriot ╤ = *na*, because -*n*- is a verbal ending in Etruscan (and on Lemnos ?), and because of the adjectival use of -*n*- in Etruscan, especially after the forms of the genitive singular.

3 That *Vowel 1*, including 𐀹 𐀛 𐀴 𐀯 𐀖 𐀑 𐀪 [40, 30, 37, 41, 73, 67, 53] etc., represents *-i*, because of Cypriot 𐠳 = *ti*, and because this vowel seems very common before - 𐀊 (*-ja* ?) [57] but never occurs before 𐀃 (*-i* ?) [61].

Two of the three identifications were taken from the Cypriotic syllabary, just as Ventris had given the Cypriotic phonetic value to these two Linear B characters in the "Languages" circular. The third identification *08* = *a* is not from Cypriotic, but Ventris had given this one also in "Languages."

The variable policy of sometimes adhering to the grid and sometimes departing from it. To judge from the chronology of Ventris's research, the grid method was not, after all, a new start so much as a supplement to the Cypriotic-syllabary method. The research leading up to the grid, if not the grid itself, uncovered characters that would share with *06* either the consonant *n-* or the vowel *-a,* others that would share with *37* either the consonant *t-* or the vowel *-i,* and so with still other rows and columns. The grid also enabled him to discard several misleading Cypriotic values for Linear B characters, such as *zo* for *76,* which seemed inconsistent with the distributional relations of *76* to other characters. We must not imagine that he went according to the grid when it pleased his fancy but otherwise overrode it in favor of the Cypriotic syllabary. Rather he tried to fasten upon those Linear B characters whose phonetic value was most persuasively suggested by the two converging criteria – the pattern of their occurrences in the Linear B texts and the similarity in shape to certain Cypriotic characters. On account of distributional evidence he renounced at least one Cypriotic value from "Languages" which would have been handy in Work Note 20 (p. 176) for the decipherment of a Greek word. This is *si* for *39*, which would make a fine dative plural ending -σι in *08-30-57-39* *ἀνίασι 'with reins,' occurring in the Knosos chariot tablets. But the second and the third state of the grid placed *39* in the same row as *03*, and Ventris tacitly judged the consonant of that row to be *p-* because *03* looks like the Cypriotic *pa*. He therefore identified the four-character word with the Greek instrumental form *ἀνίᾱφι.[14] The grid would not allow him to keep both Cypriotic values, *si* for *39* and *pa* for *03*; he chose the latter. The value *si* was assigned to *41* at an earlier point in Work Note 20, when he was experimenting with the ethnic *a-mi-ni-si-jo*, *a-mi-ni-si-ja* 'Amnisian' (masculine and feminine, respectively). *41* 𝓗 resembles the Cypriotic *si* character anyhow, almost as much as *39* 𝗔 does. From the second state of the grid on, *41* was in the same row as *12* and *31*, which he had much earlier called *ṣᵘ* and *ṣa*, respectively.[15] Thus he reconciled the grid as much as he could with the Cypriotic values of the characters.

Respect for his grid did not deter him from suddenly revaluing two characters in the first word of the *08-60-26-57 08-30-57-39*, in order to get *a-ra-ru-ja ' ā-ni-ʲa-phi* (p. 176).[16] According to the third state of the grid *60* is *li* ? and *26* is *la* ?. Now the consonantal change from *l-* to *r-* is no great matter; he had labeled the *l-* ? probably for the sake of identifying *02* with the Cypriotic *lo*, but in Work Note 20 (p. 174) he proposed to neutralize the *l ~ r* opposition. Still that would not have done much for *08-60-26-57*; *a-ri-ra-ja* is not reminiscent of any Greek word. So he quickly juggled the characters in that row of the grid to come out with *a-ra-ru-ja* instead of *a-ri-ra-ja*. That gave him a translation 'fitted out with reins'; otherwise he would have been at a loss for a 'with' construction to account for the instrumental ending -φι. The revaluation of *60* 𝖑 was all the easier because it bears some graphic resemblance to the Cypriotic *ra* and *la,* as well as *li* (see Grumach, *Gnomon,* XXXII, 688). Even so, Ventris remained ill at ease because one of the chariot tablets (Sd0408+0411), for no perceptible reason, has *08-60-26-42-57* (not *08-60-26-57*) *08-30-57-39,* and *a-ra-ru-wo-ja* is not a Greek formation. Another difficulty, which he did not consider — nor have I seen it pointed out by any critic — is that ἀραρυῖα and related forms in Homeric Greek do not normally have the vague meaning 'fitted out, equipped' but rather 'fitted in place, fastened, held tight.'[17] It does not make neat sense to describe a chariot as 'fastened with reins.'

The ancillary rather than decisive role of the grid. My comprehensive judgement of the grid is that it was, in effect, never more than an aid toward decipherment and was liable to be overruled at whatever moment it seemed to be blocking some other advance toward decipherment which occurred to Ventris apart from the grid. Such procedure was not unsound cryptanalysis; but the corollary is that the interrelations shown on the grid were in reality just tentative, not established. They could be verified only by successfully assigning phonetic values that transcribe the Linear B tablets into intelligible, satisfactory texts. Ventris did not treat each character on the grid in its third state as immobilized within a certain square; but the only ones he moved were those which gave no tolerable Greek words in Work Note 20 or thereafter. Otherwise, the sum of his results pleased him well enough to leave characters where they were on the grid.

Ventris's criteria for valuing individual characters correctly. Characters not yet on the grid were to receive a phonetic value in one of three ways: "For a sign to be allotted a fixed syllabic value it must occur in a vocabulary word (not merely in a personal name!) whose Greek identification is absolutely certain from the context; or be found in a larger number of words whose identification is at least probable; or else be shown to alternate regularly with a sign whose value is already known" (*Documents,* p. 26). I am uncertain whether or not these three criteria were meant to test the proposed phonetic value of all characters, including those which had been placed on the grid in the Work Notes. Nowhere does Ventris or Chadwick go over the list of Linear B characters systematically and try to prove by one of the three criteria that each one has such and such a value. A statement to that effect would have greatly facilitated the task of any sincere critic. Whatever they may have intended, I maintain that only the first criterion is adequate and that no character should be exempted from meeting it. The second and third are too liable to subjective guessing and may clash with each other; e.g., in *08-60-26-57* the characters *60* and *26* had previously been placed in two columns on the basis of their alternations, but were given quite different vowels in order to get a Greek word ἀραρυῖα, which is not, after all, very probable. This case suggests something more than that the alternation method (or distribution method) falls short of infallibility; not only this time but in other cases too, its results are liable to be illusory unless proved by the finding of unmistakably Greek words. For in the Linear B language, which at best is like the known Greek language only in part, there can be no prior assurance that a given alternation will correspond to a known Greek alternation.

Ventris would doubtless have justified every one of his phonetic values by the first criterion — occurrence "in a vocabulary word . . . whose Greek identification is absolutely certain from the context" — if such proof were available. But for a great majority of the characters it is not available; if it were, there would be no controversy. When he was writing the Work Notes, it was scarcely available for any characters at all. Had he been able to make use of the tripod-and-jug tablet Ta641 (Pylos) and the missing piece of the horse-head tablet Ca895 (Knosos), he — or any other competent person without his unusual qualities — could have proceeded to direct and conclusive proof of the value of several characters. As it was, he followed an indirect and less cogent method, not by choice but by necessity.

The need for verifying each item in Ventris's table of values[18] has not been faced squarely. The easy but wrong way out is to say either that enough of the decipherment is valid to establish all the rest, or that enough is unacceptable to invalidate the whole thing. All or nothing leads to a futile confusion of what is sound with what is unsound. Ventris may seem to have invited this wrong kind of wholesale acceptance or rejection in "Evidence" (p. 90): "With no bilingual or other external aids to decipherment available, the reality of a proposed transliteration can only be tested by applying it to the material as a whole. If consistent series of vocabulary and grammatical forms result, which are in agreement with the probable context of the tablets, then we may be justified in believing that even those features which remain intractable will eventually be accounted for."[19] I maintain that "consistent series of vocabulary and grammatical forms" are inadequate unless they fit together to form meaningful and comprehensible texts. Besides, the reliance on "probable context" set up a particularly unwise criterion and lured Ventris into a vicious circle. Presumably he meant that the nonverbal context of a tablet — i.e., the ideographic part — would be a check upon his decipherment of the verbal part. But, as he said later, "Except where they are clearly pictorial (like MEN, WOMEN, CHARIOTS and TRIPODS) the meanings of the ideograms and other abbreviations are impossible to guess unless there are generous clues in the context" (*Documents*, p. 27). Here *context* must mean the

Linear B words as transcribed into Ventris's phonetic values. In the majority of the tablets the ideographic part of the text is not identifiable and will neither prove nor disprove a proposed interpretation of the verbal part.

The announced limitations upon the decipherment. I must in fairness say that right after calling for an application of his phonetic values to the Linear B material as a whole, Ventris went on to indicate that he was not demanding all or nothing; for the ensuing points are moderate and sensible ("Evidence," p. 90):

> From experience gained in the unsuccessful testing of many previous lines of attack on the Mycenaean script, we are confident that the results so far yielded by this transliteration are too numerous to be attributed to pure coincidence; that some considerable part of our chain of deduction will have to be re-followed by even a rival decipherment; and that it would be very difficult for any system of values to yield a comparable mirage of Greek forms, however uncertain in its outlines, if the language was in fact of a totally different affinity.
>
> But to those approaching the research from the viewpoint of classical scholarship, for whom the transliteration may seem vitiated by the eccentricities of the Greek and by the relatively small proportion of the tablets interpreted, we would offer the following in extenuation:
>
> 1. If the language is Greek, we are seeing it at a stage 1000 years older than Plato (a difference in date as great as between Beowulf and Shakespeare), and separated from the classical idiom by a Dark Age. It is set in a different environment, and surrounded, possibly closely intermingled, with barbarian languages spoken

by peoples of equal or superior culture. Some elements of the vocabulary may be either 'Aegean', or distorted by non-Greek scribes, or part of an older stratum of Greek unfamiliar to classical philology. There is no doubt that all the Mycenaean archives are in the *same* idiom, whether Greek or barbarian, but there is still the possibility that this idiom contains some fixed proportion of elements too unfamiliar to be comprehensible, more embarrassing in some contexts than in others.

2. The palace archives are written in a highly abbreviated style, in which literary syntax has no place. Their text contains few regular 'sentences' and consists largely of personal names, many of which are probably those of non-Greeks, and of place-names, presumably 'Aegean' in formation. Even the names of Greeks, like many of those in later epic and myth, may be pre-Hellenic in form.

3. The transliteration is the preliminary result of only the first three months of a very laborious investigation. Many of the proposed values may have to be reconsidered, and the rules of orthography may not yet be fully understood: many of their most baffling features are probably due to Linear *B* being a script imperfectly adapted to Greek from the conventions of a quite different language.

4. We believe that prolonged study, and the aid of the new unpublished tablets from Pylos, will eventually enable the whole Mycenaean material to be interpreted in detail. But at this initial stage, when any translation must be extremely tentative, we have preferred to concentrate on a limited number of tablets which typify the most significant contexts and formulae. They together contain all the passages most crucial as linguistic evidence, and the light which they throw on the me-

chanics of the Mycenaean adjective, noun and verb will be useful, we hope, even to those who doubt whether they are specifically Greek.

Unfortunately these points have been heeded too little in the research and discussion since the publication of "Evidence." In the three years between "Evidence" and *Documents* the only characters revalued were the following rare ones:

	"Evidence," p. 86	*Documents*, p. 23
48	nu_2 ?	*nwa*
58	qo_2 ?	*su*
79	$z?o_2$	*zu* ?

Four others were reconsidered to the extent of allowing an alternative value, bisyllabic in three cases:

25	a_2	a_2 (*ha*)
66	ta_2	ta_2 (*ti-ja*)
68	ro_2	ro_2 (*ri-jo*)
76	ra_2	ra_2 (*ri-ja*).[20]

It would be well if we could justly say that continued experience has confirmed the value of every other character from the grid in "Evidence." But the fact is that while some scholars are convinced, others are suspicious. The whole question — What constitutes proof of a decipherment? — has been treated often but inadequately.

Notes to Chapter II

1. "Languages," pp. 28, 38, xii-xiii.

2. The circulars are "The Languages of the Minoan and Mycenaean Civilizations" and "Work Notes on Minoan Language Research."

3. For a table of the Cypriotic characters, see *Documents*, p. 64.

4. The numerical transcription, to cut down on the labor of copying the characters in facsimile, was not yet in use, being introduced by Bennett in *PT* (1955), p. 201. Ventris employed a less desirable transcription into digraphs consisting of a vowel followed by a consonant, both in capital letters. These capital digraphs were meant as a code suitable for typing —AB for ⊦ , AC for ✝ , etc. — not at all as a phonetic transcription.

5. No Appendix 1 came with my photostats, but Bennett very kindly looked up on his own copy the information I needed.

6. The value *ṣe* for ⊫ *o9* (EP) should count as an identification based on the Cypriotic *se*. He apparently did not feel happy enough about the identification to mention it along with the other nine in the body of the "Languages" circular (p. xiv). However, he did express it in Appendix 1. Several other such identifications in the Appendix he eventually abandoned.

7. *73* (ER) is a special case; for its vowel was identified as *-i* in "Languages," but the consonant *m-* was not assigned to it until the "Evidence" article.

8. Ventris has somewhat regrettably used the letter *j* for the semivowel related to *i*. It stands of course for the same sound as in *young* (German *jung*).

9. In Work Note 17 (p. 162), explaining the third state of the grid, he commented: "The tentative phonetic values shown in the first column are not to be taken too seriously. They pay scarcely any regard to supposed similarities with the Cypriot syllabary, but represent the values which seem the most useful in giving an 'Etruscoid' character to Pylos names, words and inflexions."

10. *05* and *37* are in the row next below *01*, both rows being labeled *t-* ? The value *d-* for the row containing *01* was first mentioned in Work Note 20 (1 June 1952, p. 176). This involved a departure from one principle of the Cypriotic syllabary, which consistently fails to distinguish between voiced, unvoiced, and unvoiced aspirate plosives. Linear B according to the Ventris decipherment behaves the same way in regard to labial and velar plosives, but dis-

tinguishes the voiced dental plosive *d-* from the unvoiced; see below, pp. 73-4, 153-4.

11. With the further restriction that characters in the "vowel uncertain" column are part of the grid only in respect to their consonant, and characters in the "other consonants" row are part of it only in respect to their vowel.

12. The last character was moved by Chadwick, according to his statement in "Introductory Essay," p. 5. The moving of characters on the grid in order to obtain Greek words was begun by Ventris unobtrusively in Work Note 20. See Beattie, *MIOF*, VI, 45, written before he studied the Work Notes.

13. Ventris's hyphen here was probably meant to suggest the position of *o8* as the first character of a word.

14. See Chadwick, "Introductory Essay," p. 7.

15. *o9* was not gridded as *se* until the "Evidence" article, but he had transcribed it *ṣe* as early as the "Languages" circular — mainly, it seems, but not avowedly, because of its resemblance to the Cypriotic *se* (see above, note 6).

16. Ventris's typewriter character ' at the beginning of the second word is meant to be the "rough breathing."

17. E.g., κνημῖδας . . . ἀργυρέοισιν ἐπισφυρίοις ἀραρυίας 'leggings fastened with silver ankle-pieces' (*Il.* 3.330-331, etc.), κουλεὸν . . . χρυσέοισιν ἀορτήρεσσιν ἀρηρός 'a scabbard fastened with golden straps' (11.30-31). Only one passage, ζώνῃ ἑκατὸν θυσάνοις ἀραρυίη 'in a girdle fitted with a hundred tassels' (14.181), may indicate as loose a fit as reins in a chariot.

18. "Evidence," p. 86; repeated with a few modifications in *Documents*, p. 23.

19. Quoted in *Documents*, p. 23, with an added expression of mingled caution and assurance: "Similar reservations must be made today, for the much larger number of texts discussed in the present book. It may be difficult to assess the point at which ultimate scientific proof can be conceded, but a relative degree of certainty must be granted to the theory when we try to estimate the odds against its results having been obtained by chance, and when we consider the success with which it has been used by independent researchers to interpret new texts, unknown when it was first formulated."

20. See Beattie, *MIOF*, VI, 34.

CHAPTER III

THE NEED FOR OBJECTIVE DEMONSTRATION RATHER THAN SUBJECTIVE CONVICTION

A BODY OF TEXTS in an obscure script that cannot be read poses a problem, which is solved when we arrive at an understanding of the texts. We understand them only insofar as we can give a sufficient reason for each detail and the evidence leaves no reasonable alternative. If the writing system is wholly or partly phonetic, the solution must show how such and such sequences of sound, represented in writing, express such and such a meaning. The phonetic side of the solution may temporarily outrun the semantic side; but unless the latter catches up, the solution is unsatisfactory. For the language remains unknown to one who can pronounce it, approximately or even exactly, while being unsure what an utterance or a text in it means. Now uncertainty or downright ignorance of a word or phrase here and there is a normal limitation upon anyone's knowledge of even his native tongue. But a decipherment, a professed solution to a particular kind of linguistic problem, cannot afford to shrug off any part of any text as semantically obscure or uncertain — unless it is physically damaged and therefore phonetically doubtful. We repeat the sounds in vain if we can only speculate about their meaning. To maintain that the phonetic side of the decipherment is right, even where it leaves us beset with semantic enigmas, we need to be very certain indeed of the individual phonetic values. Such certainty can legitimately come only from a demonstration that precludes all circular argument, all begging of the question, all assumptions later elevated arbitrarily to the level of proved facts. Morever, it is necessary to distinguish between subjective and objective certainty – without, however, immediately condemning the former as unworthy of learned men.

The conditions necessary for an objective demonstration. Objective certainty, where it is obtainable, is independent of all accidents, such as when a given piece of evidence came to light, and how effectively or impressively an individual author has presented the evidence. For objective certainty we need only the data themselves: any sure conclusions that are inherent in them will be remarked by all persons of ordinary intelligence, provided they have the patience to work through the data. Or if it takes one unusual mind to extract the conclusions in the first place, others will not have trouble following the demonstration. In case some room is left for difference of opinion, it can be clearly defined and narrowed down.

Unfortunately, no such objective demonstration of any part of Ventris's decipherment was possible before the tripod-and-jug tablet (Ta641) came to light. Without it, everything that he wrote in "Evidence" was open to reasonable doubt; not one text deciphered by him was more than a conjecture. Even the impressive occurrence of 𐀡 𐀫 next to the foals' heads (see above, p. 27) did not quite prove that the Cypriotic values *po-lo* could be safely applied to Linear B. πώλω is a Greek word of Indo-European origin, and some good scholars doubted that Greek, or any other Indo-European language, could have reached Crete so early. They also wondered why the word for 'foals' should be redundantly written beside the drawing. However, Ta641 contains the proof of redundant writing.

Consider what it takes to demonstrate objectively the correctness of a decipherment. To stand up as a whole, it must — apart from an occasional obscurity — produce completely and unmistakably comprehensible texts according to the detailed pattern of a certain language. The Linear B texts transcribed by Ventris are far from that state. To demonstrate a decipherment in part, the meaning of the text at that point has to be known independently of the decipherment, and the characters at that point have to be shown to occur just as they would according to the rules of one language. Our independent knowledge of the meaning may come from an accompanying text in another language that is accessible to us: e.g., on the Rosetta Stone and the Obelisk of Philae, by reference to the royal names in the accompanying Greek texts Champollion knew where to look for the Egyptian renderings of 'Ptolemy' and 'Cleopatra,' and the "cartouches" enclosing the hieroglyphs delimited the names convincingly.[1] Or, even though the text is not bilingual, it may have an equivalent resource, an ideographic accompaniment favoring us with some particulars that are redundantly expressed in words. This is what we have in Ta641; but Ventris, before that tablet came to his notice, had practically no clues to the precise or even the approximate meaning of anything written in Linear B characters. He could only see that the tablets were inventories or records of various kinds. For the sound of a few characters he had the meager guidance of the Cypriotic syllabary. A less determined man would have resigned himself to an impasse, but Ventris did not. He did what he could with the unpromising material at hand; for "to wait for a *bilingual* to help us to solve our problem is to cry for the moon" (Work Note 15, p. 145). Naturally he had no ground for expecting a tablet like Ta641 to turn up. So he directed his energy to methods that could not, in themselves, lead to an objectively valid decipherment — unless by some luck the language of the Linear B tablets were virtually identical with a known language and would therefore betray itself solely by its phonetic and morphological pattern and its vocabulary.

Procedure for demonstrating objectively the phonetic value of Linear B characters. In rare cases where the meaning of part of a Linear B text can be proved, not merely conjectured, from the accompanying ideograms, we are further able to prove that the meaning is expressed in Greek. This will be explored in detail in the next two chapters; for the present I confine myself to a summary statement of principles. The inference that a certain Linear B word of known meaning is Greek rests upon a series of observations. First, the number of characters in it must be appropriate to the Greek word of that meaning, if written out syllabically. Moreover, each character under consideration must recur with the same phonetic value, either in Cypriotic Greek inscriptions or in the right syllabic position of another Linear B word (more precisely, another Linear B morpheme) that can also be transcribed into Greek with its meaning assured by the context. In case some but not all of the characters of a Linear B word meet the test, then a weaker character, with no provable recurrence, may be sustained by stronger ones on both sides, and may be transcribed with the syllabic value which the Greek word requires to fill the gap between the transcribed values of the other characters. In such a case of supplementation we have not strictly proved that the character in question has the phonetic value we assign to it; for if that one character were obliterated by damage to the tablet, we would have just as good an argument for assigning the same value to the lost character that had occupied the space.

The argument, either way, is that we can make out enough of the word to identify it with a Greek word of a certain meaning; so any part that we cannot identify must nevertheless fall into line. Our transcription, anyhow, should not be taken for more than a rough normalization of the Linear B words to the phonology of Greek. For we can show, here and there, that the Linear B language has a closer affinity to Greek than to any other known language; and to that extent our transcription can indicate to which Greek sound each Linear B character corresponds.

Since the relevance of the Cypriotic syllabary has been in principle denied by Ventris, I ought to explain my use of it. Apart from my reasons for maintaining that Ventris was only halfhearted in his renunciation (see above, pp. 24-7), it is quite justified to cite the Cypriotic value of a character as a clue to the Linear B value. It turns out to be efficacious only to a limited extent, but that should not condemn it altogether. To be sure, the wholesale transcription of Linear B tablets, according to the values of similarly shaped Cypriotic characters, would give gibberish for the most part. But nearly the same result arises from transcriptions made upon any other principle, including Ventris's combination of principles. The Cypriotic syllabary is proved, *by his work,* to have a genuine, though limited, utility for solving the Linear B decipherment problem. Even before it was so proved, he had good reason to expect something helpful from it. It was next to impossible that the similarities in shape between many Linear B and Cypriotic characters could be all devoid of phonetic significance. The two writing systems flourished in countries that were partly inhabited by the same nationality, but the Cypriotic documents are many centuries later. It was natural to infer that the Cypriotic script continued some parts of the older system. But the identification of those parts would be unsafe if made casually, as Ventris did at first in the "Languages" circular (see above, p. 23).[2] The presence of *11-02* (which would be *po-lo* in Cypriotic) by the foals' heads deserved to be taken seriously, because such perfect identity was unlikely to be due to coincidence. Yet every attempt by professional or amateur scholars to build something more upon this isolated case, by applying Cypriotic values to Linear B characters, was speculative and inconclusive until Ta641 came to light. It at once supplied what had been lacking — a clue to the precise meaning of a Linear B text, regardless of the language. Then several phonetic values could be brought in from Cypriotic to test for a relation to a known language. We ought to follow essentially the same order in the analysis of other tablets too: after we have from the context a clue to the meaning, we can draw upon the Cypriotic syllabary, as far as it will serve, to fill in the sounds.

Subjective conviction beyond objective demonstration. The characters whose phonetic values we can and will demonstrate objectively in the next chapter, mainly by reference to Ta641, were given the same (or nearly the same) values by Ventris in "Evidence," without any recourse to that all-important tablet. Any intelligent reader of "Evidence" might feel that it was all hypothetical, unproved; again and again it could be objected that the experiment was not bringing decisive results. No Linear B tablet cited there could be read as Greek except by making violent assumptions about prehistoric Greek that were not supported by any known facts. This was most obvious in the tablets that are not mere lists but contain sequences of words which presumably are linked to one another syntactically ("Evidence," pp. 92-93, 98-101). Yet the publication of the one additional tablet made a tremendous impact.[3] The application of Ventris's transcription from "Evidence" to the new tablet brought out several unmistakable Greek words, whose correctness was guaranteed by the ideograms. The values of the characters in those words were already given but not proved in the "Evidence" article. It was proper to consider them hypothetical until proved, and no longer hypothetical after they were proved. But something bigger than this entered with the realization that no part of the hypothetical decipherment was disproved. Through a tendency of the human mind, which deserves the name of credulity, people concluded that the whole decipherment must be right, even though it left parts of this very tablet utterly obscure.

Those who slipped into the paralogism included some excellent Hellenists, at a disadvantage perhaps because cryptanalysis was a mystery to them. A regrettably misleading statement in "Evidence" (p. 88) contributed to their error:

> But it should be made clear that the consonant and vowel equations tabulated below had all been deduced from internal evidence before any phonetic values were allotted. They were based partly on inflectional evidence, partly on accidental or deliberate spelling variations.

> If correctly determined, these equations enable the most frequent signs of the syllabary to be arranged in a two-dimensional pattern, or 'grid', which we must expect to be adhered to by *any* suggested system of phonetic values. The problem of decipherment is in this way reduced to the correct distribution of five vowels and twelve consonants to the columns of the grid; and since a proposed reading of only two or three words may, by a 'chain-reaction', predetermine rigid values for almost the entire syllabary, a very severe discipline is imposed on the earliest stages of a decipherment. If the initial moves are wrong, it should be quite

impossible to force any part of the texts into showing the slightest conformity with the vocabulary or grammar of a known language; even though that might be quite easy if one were free to juggle with the values of eighty-eight mutually unconnected signs.

Here was an assurance that Ventris had obtained all the values by one clear-cut method, which contained a (so to speak) built-in guarantee against any danger of an illusory decipherment. The last sentence of the quotation, if subjected to a normal logical conversion, declares that if any part of the texts show the slightest conformity with the vocabulary or grammar of a known language, the initial moves must not have been wrong. But that last sentence was a mere assertion. Neither the experience nor the theory of cryptanalysts obliges us to go nearly so far in our reliance upon any grid, least of all on a grid as incomplete and unsettled as Ventris's had been during the whole time that he used it. Besides, the first sentence of the quotation is by no means fully borne out by my examination of the "Languages" circular and the Work Notes (see above, pp. 21-37). Some values were set before he started on the grid and were never revoked. Some others were added only after he had finished using the grid. In order to find out whether he gave a certain character its permanent niche before, during, or after his work on the grid, we have to trace it through those unpublished writings of his. In "Evidence" he idealized his former procedure, which had in fact combined various approaches.[4]

Of those characters whose values are authenticated by means of Ta641, the majority did not depend on the grid at all. Several were given values by Ventris from the Cypriotic syllabary; others were given values in Work Note 20 and later, contrary to their positions on the grid. How much or how little Ventris relied on the grid for each character, I will point out in the next chapter; such knowledge was of course not available to the readers, who could judge only from the "Evidence" article and the text of Ta641. While they were somewhat rash in their innocence, they still had something to go on. We who now have the means of checking up on Ventris can show that before writing "Evidence" he shifted many characters on the grid and changed his mind about the value of quite a few. Nevertheless, in "Evidence" he came out with a set of values that were later either verified by Ta641 or at any rate not contradicted. This was a signal accomplishment, far surpassing anyone else's attempt to decipher Linear B. It fostered an inference that Ventris must indeed have used a reliable method, as he claimed, and that his procedure had been substantially infallible — exempt from any but incidental errors.

The trouble with making or accepting such an inference was that people did it without a detailed understanding of what went into Ventris's work. They were dazzled by the result, which was truly vivid if not extensive. As men they can be freely excused, but as scholars they ought to have been more circumspect. He intended no fraud; but they jumped to a premature conclusion.

The motives for relying on a token demonstration. In modern problems of military cryptanalysis, dealing of course with a fully known language, you can tell you are on the right track as soon as a small amount of unmistakable "plain" text emerges from the cipher. But you are not absolutely guaranteed that nothing can go wrong. If you fail to transcribe the rest of the secret text into something intelligible — and intelligible without torturing the language — you must have some wrong assumption mixed in with the right ones. Ventris's supporters want to eat their cake and have it. They are not content to cite the small amount of unmistakable

Greek as proof that the decipherment is partly right. "Because of the arbitrary nature of language comparatively few words will suffice to 'prove' a decipherment, which must satisfy an intricate pattern of phonemic cross-relationships" (Palmer, *OLZ*, LIII, 117). Insisting thus upon the whole decipherment, they attribute the unintelligibility of many "deciphered" texts to our partial ignorance of the prehistoric language. But this blanket excuse is too handy; it would doom us to the confusion of positing differences between the Linear B language and Greek where the difficulty may be due merely to an error or hasty guess of Ventris. Palmer's argument from "comparatively few words" has a converse: A small amount of gibberish, irreconcilable with the pattern of a certain language, will just as well prove the decipherment cannot be right for that language. Ventris's transcription gives us on the one hand some acceptable Greek in Ta641, but on the other hand words that begin with *jo-* in several tablets and the word *o-pi-i-ja-pi* — violations of Greek phonology (see below, pp. 83 and 99, note 31). What entitles us to treat only the favorable evidence as significant? Scholarly caution should, if anything, lean in the opposite direction, laying the burden of proof upon the discoverer and not receiving one partly successful test as though it were so decisive as to remove any further need for equally stringent verification. We must decline to put the verified and the unverified parts on the same footing.

I accept the verified Greek words in Ta641 as proof of the correctness of some of the decipherment; Palmer and others have taken them for a token of its total correctness. No doubt it is not by choice that they rest their case upon so little; if the decipherment as a whole were directly demonstrable by producing ample amounts of plain Greek text, nobody would bother to attach so much importance to a token. However, they are convinced and at the same time (so it seems to me) lacking in the means to demonstrate in full what they believe. They dispense with such proof by recurring to a generality about language. They do not perceive a weighty responsibility upon them: to deduce from incontrovertible foundations of linguistic theory a corollary that a token demonstration is enough to prove an entire decipherment of any script whatever, in any language whatever.

They lay capital stress on instances of this decipherment being successfully applied to tablets not yet known to Ventris when he produced it. Each instance then counts as a prediction fulfilled.[5] When the decipherment yields nothing recognizable in Greek or any other language, that is passed over as no reflection on its correctness; some interpretation or other, farfetched but perhaps not quite impossible, will be excogitated. The adherents of Ventris are sincere scholars and would be shocked to hear that their attitude is not one of disinterested respect for scientific prediction, but rather reverence for prophecy. When we are in total darkness, we are humanly grateful to anyone who can cast a little light. Before Ventris the scholarly world was as completely baffled by the Linear B texts as mankind in general has been baffled by the future. Whoever can offer some helpful insight will be appreciated as much as he deserves, or even more; "au royaume des aveugles les borgnes sont rois." And people require of a prophet not a full demonstration of what he tells them, but only a token of his superior insight; when the token passes the test of experience, it suffices for a conviction that his whole message is true. Palmer saves his conviction in the face of admitted difficulties by enunciating a novel principle, " 'Decipherment' must be clearly distinguished from 'interpretation' " (*OLZ*, LIII, 117, cf. 108) — i.e., the validity of a decipherment is not in proportion to how much sense it enables us to obtain from the texts. Who before ever had to resort to such an apology for a decipherment?

The fundamental irrelevance of prediction. I do not maintain that Ventris was devoid of extraordinary insight; but I see no need to approach his decipherment as a prophecy of which the diverse ingredients lay hidden in the depths of his mind. The Work Notes, while unpublished, are accessible. Although they are not easy to read through, they do allow us to see what data he paid attention to, and his characteristic way of handling them. In a field where the best-qualified scholars had been utterly perplexed or halting or fumbling, an amateur needed some of the brashness of a prophet, and Ventris had it. But his manner was amiable and more likely to sharpen our analytical powers than to deaden them. His bright and clever mind deserved something better from the world than the uncritical veneration he got during his life and after his death.

On the other hand, the most unpleasant side of Beattie's attacks upon him can be understood as a reaction to this. Sensing that Ventris was, in substance though not in name, esteemed a prophet, Beattie set out to show by "circumstantial" evidence that Ventris's successes were virtually *uaticinia ex euentu* (see below, pp. 63, 164). Had Beattie proved it directly and to the hilt, still it would hardly touch the essential question, whether the Ventris decipherment makes the Linear B texts plainly intelligible. If it does, then as a corollary a text discovered subsequently ought to yield a meaning in harmony with the accompanying ideograms. Palmer's criterion, though intended to clarify the main issue, has side-tracked it: "the ultimate test is the application of the solution to texts which did not enter into the original calculations: this has been provided by the Pylos no 641 (1952), as yet unpublished, which fully confirms the following values: *TI, RI, PO, DE, O, WO, WE, DI, PA, E, QE, TO, RO, JO, A,*

NO."[6] Even if such a test succeeded in full (unlike the application of Ventris's transcription to Ta641), it would be just a short cut for the purpose of convincing people who cannot or will not go over the arguments behind each detail of the transcription, as scholars should. Any point that needs the new material to prove it, must before have been merely a surmise. The new evidence, if available before, would have proved the point before. It ought to be just incidental whether the decipherer had a particular specimen before his eyes to work with or learned of its existence later. What matters is whether all the evidence, taken together, will establish his decipherment point by point.

In science, a future event accurately predicted may seem to clinch a theory announced previously; but to one who understands the theory, that event is just one more case in which the same laws or processes operate. The theory in the present controversy is Ventris's transcription of an ancient writing system, and instead of a future event there can only be a tablet that comes to light subsequently. In one respect, therefore, we depart from the rigor of a scientific test: we must depend on the good faith of men not to have cards up their sleeves but to lay everything on the table. If someone were to base his theory partly on evidence whose existence he kept secret, and if he later exploited the publication of that evidence (or of equivalent evidence), the independent corroborative value of the newly presented evidence would, of course, be illusory; but its intrinsic value in support of the theory would be the same, no matter when the author paid attention to it. This, I hold, is the proper answer, both to Palmer's criterion that prediction efficaciously proves the decipherment, and to Beattie's charge that Ventris, when he made the "prediction," had (or may have had) sole access to tablets from which he already knew what no colleague learned until later.

The discipline of philology has in the past been obliged to cope often with unreliable testimony, and has learned to draw conclusions principally from the data themselves. The main trouble with witnesses in matters of philological concern is levity: whether they err through mere inaccuracy or through bias or dishonesty, they fall short of the requirements of scholarship to present the truth pure and whole, and to prevent any foreseeable misunderstanding. Witnesses become important in cases where the original data are no longer extant; but even then the reputation that entitles some witnesses to be trusted more, some less, is established by reference to other original data. For instance, we have only remote copies of the Greek and Latin classics, but we know pretty well how much we can rely on the spelling of each manuscript: for many words the spelling of inscriptions will provide a norm for judging how good or bad the orthographical standards of the manuscripts are; and then, where the inscriptions give us no specific guidance, we prefer the testimony of manuscripts whose spelling is generally good. The philological preference is first to establish to the maximum extent a solid base of knowledge that can be proved regardless of the competence of any individual witness; and finally, if need be, to take up that which cannot stand without an individual's authority.[7]

Ventris's superior knowledge of the Linear B texts. In short, we want everything to stand to reason. Or, to take a commercial metaphor, we prefer cash. In a short-term loan we may have no trouble remembering what we have allowed on credit; but if the transcription becomes complicated, we are liable not to keep it all in mind, forgetting where we really stand. This has happened to the scholars who incautiously embraced Ventris's decipherment. They had reason to admire him, but they went to unreasonable lengths. He showed that he could get much more out of the Linear B tablets than they could, proficient though they were in Greek. To surpass them he must have been brilliant indeed, and they ungrudgingly acknowledged the greatness of his discovery. Why he had accomplished more than anyone else, was a mystery and remains so; but I can at least suggest a cause that would obviate the necessity of attributing to him a genius so superhuman as to dispel all rational reservations on our part. He mulled over the texts as few others did, and saw them with his "architect's eye," as Chadwick says (*Decipherment*, p. 4). His approach was the most versatile, and time and again possible interpretations of words or phrases would enter his mind, to be entertained and — though not adopted then and there — not forgotten either. The most remarkable of his hunches, that *14-38-02* is *do^welo(s)* 'servant' (Work Note 11, p. 40), I shall discuss where it is pertinent to the value of the character *14* (see below, pp. 152-3). If the secret of the Linear B labyrinth was at some points penetrable, he was the man to penetrate it, thanks to his scouting and his probing. His intimacy with the unknown object of his love gave him alone some insight into its probable nature. Yet, while we freely grant this, we should not exempt his insight from the requirement of being backed up, in each case, by reasons that we can understand. In judging emendations of classical texts, even though we grant that a few editors have excelled because they were extraordinarily familiar with the language, sympathetic to the literature, painstaking and flawless in their exercises in Greek or Latin composition, nevertheless each emendation must stand on its individual merits, expressible in reasons, not on the general merits of the scholar who proposed it. So it is with Ventris's work: the best compliment we can pay the author is to weigh the work on its merits. Any other praise would verge on adulation.

Notes to Chapter III

1. *Lettre à M. Dacier . . . relative à l'alphabet des hiéroglyphes phonétiques* (Paris, 1822), pp. 6-9, concluding with the words, "The phonetic value of these twelve signs, already very probable, will become incontestable if by applying these values to other cartouches or little circumscribed figures (*tableaux*), containing proper names and drawn from Egyptian hieroglyphic monuments, we get without strain a regular reading, producing proper names of rulers, foreign to the Egyptian language." The Linear B material is less propitious, and the application of Ventris's phonetic values never yields such good results without strain.

2. An imaginary analogy from a more familiar writing system may clarify the problem of working back from the value of the characters in Cypriotic to the value in Linear B. Suppose we had only the minuscule letters of our alphabet and came upon ancient Latin inscriptions in capital letters. Some of the shapes are identical, others nearly so, but still others are drastically different. Besides we might be misled by the illusory likeness of capital I to minuscule l. (In modern printing we are accustomed to a preposterous distinction located in the top serif, I l.) The assignment of a phonetic value to a capital letter from its similarity to a minuscule would be justified only if we found it in a word whose meaning we could make out.

3. Ventris, "King Nestor's Four-handled Cups," *Archaeology*, VII (1954), 15-21; Carl W. Blegen, "An Inscribed Tablet from Pylos," Ἀρχαιολογικὴ Ἐφημερίς (1953-54, actually publ. 1955), pp. 59-62. Later in *Documents*, pp. 336-37 and pl. III.

4. Chadwick joined in the work at a late stage (July, 1952) and cannot be regarded as accountable for the inaccurate statement about Ventris's earlier method.

5. Ventris did not make actual predictions that the Linear B word for 'tripod' would be *37-53-11*, 'tripods' *37-53-11-45*, etc. But it was proper to infer from his decipherment that if words of such meaning should ever turn up, they would be written so — unless the Linear B vocabulary happened to differ from Greek in this regard.

6. Review of "Evidence" in *Gnomon*, XXVI (1954), 65. Palmer does not claim here, as in his later and more polemical writings, that Ta641 validates the decipherment as a whole. He adds, however: "One may have *confidence,* therefore, that the cryptographic solution is in the main correct" [my italics]. I will show in the next chapter

that Ta641 does not at all confirm the values *wo, di,* and *pa,* and that it gives something short of full confirmation to several others.

7. Philology, unlike natural science, occasionally has to cope with fabricated antiquities, presented as primary data. We do not begin by granting offhand that everything is authentic. We set up a norm founded on what has been least exposed to any danger of falsification, and that norm helps us to judge whatever has come to us thinly attested. The authenticity of all Linear B tablets seems safe from even the slightest suspicion of forgery.

CHAPTER IV

OBJECTIVE DEMONSTRATION, PRIMARILY BY MEANS OF THE TRIPOD-AND-JUG TABLET (Ta641)

A CONSIDERABLE minority of the Linear B tablets have recognizable drawings; and a majority — at least of the well-preserved tablets — have numbers written in an easy ideographic system. But rarely does this non-verbal information enable us to prove that Ventris has transcribed any of the words correctly. It was simple economy on the part of the scribes not, on the whole, to convey the same information both verbally and ideographically, but to use one means of graphic symbolization to supplement the other. However, it is our luck that now and then they did express their meaning redundantly, so that the words convey something that is also in the ideograms. The most important tablet of this sort is Ta641 (see above, p. 60, note 3), which I present in the numerical transcription and in Ventris's decipherment (see pull-out attached to the front flyleaf). It proves what we could only surmise from a few other tablets: that Linear B scribes were not wholly averse to redundancy.

Ta641 in relation to Ventris's previous work. This tablet did more than anything to convince scholars that Ventris's decipherment is correct. In my view it proves that the decipherment is *partly* correct. One great reason for its effect upon scholarly opinion is that it came out after Ventris finished his decipherment, and that it was then transcribed on the basis of his grid without necessitating the revaluation of any Linear B character. That he could not have known or used this tablet while working out his decipherment was taken in all quarters as an unquestionable fact, until Beattie astonishingly challenged it in 1958 (*MIOF*, VI, 84-90). Beattie tried to demonstrate that Ventris knew the characters on the tablet when he wrote Work Note 20; but Beattie could not find any direct proof. At most he showed it might not have been quite impossible chronologically; however, any shadow of suspicion was utterly dispelled by Carl W. Blegen's exact history of the tablets from excavation to reading.[1] In my present inquiry, as I have said (see above, p. 56), it would make no essential difference even if Ventris did know the tablet as early as Beattie said. It would be very distasteful to me if I thought that the validity of Ventris's research could be safely judged only at the price of doing or countenancing detective work in order to determine his whereabouts on certain days of June 1952 and to spy into his private correspondence during those days.[2] If his widow or his friends wish to make public any facts, that is their business; but they do not owe the world an accounting of what Ventris did. Scholars can properly steer away from unnecessary inquiries about the *man* toward the truly professional question of what is worthwhile in his *work*.[3]

Even supposing that Ventris in the first place based the decipherment largely on Ta641, we could still confirm, from the scattered evidence of other tablets and from the Cypriotic syllabary, all the phonetic values on this tablet that emerge from a comparison of the verbal with the nonverbal text. The indispensable rule of verification is that we must avoid circular reasoning. For example, in *08-52-75* (the last word in Ta641) standing next to a jug with no handles, if we posit *08 = a* in order to get a transcription *a-no-we* that can be understood as a Greek word for 'earless,' then we must not turn around and claim the transcription *a-no-we* for proof that the Linear B character *o8*, corresponding to the Greek vowel α, occurs in a negative prefix and has the phonetic value *a*. But we should point to Uc160 (Knosos), where *o8-39-11-27-75* stands next to an amphora followed by the ideographic numeral 3; the transcription *a-pi-po-re-we* comes close enough to the Homeric Greek form ἀμφιφορῆες 'amphoras' (*Od*. 13.105) to confirm — among other things — the value *o8 = a*. Either the juxtaposition of *o8-39-11-27-05* and the amphora drawing confirms the *a* value of *o8* posited in the tripod-and-jug tablet, or else the juxtaposition of *o8-52-75* and the jug without handles will serve to confirm the *a* value posited in the amphora tablet. One way or the other the value *o8 = a* is confirmed.

All unprejudiced observers ought to recognize that Ta641 contains the material for a beginning, at least, of a decipherment of the Linear B script — even if Ventris had never appeared on the scene. It is regrettable that Ventris's critics, being suspicious of his decipherment in general and unwilling to grant that Ta641 fully upholds it, have been impelled to minimize the conclusions that can reasonably be drawn from the juxtaposition of verbal and ideographic data on this tablet. They have thereby deprived themselves of the knowledge about the Linear B script which they could gain from the tablet, and they have also detracted from the cogency of the good arguments they have against Ventris and others for making unwarranted inferences. Now, benefiting from what my predecessors have written, I will try to escape the errors of both sides.

37-53-11 = ti-ri-po. Almost at first glance the tablet shows us which characters express the meaning 'three-' as the initial element of a compound word. On the top line *37-53-* stands at the beginning of the first, second, and third items, which also contain drawings of tripods.[4] 37-53- also stands in the word next to the drawings of three-handled jugs; these belong to the third item on the middle line and the first item on the bottom line. Supposing the language to be altogether unknown, we would still have no choice but to associate the meaning 'three-' with the characters 37-53-, all the more because these characters are replaced in the word next to the four-handled jugs:

$$78\text{-}05\text{-}02\text{-}75 \quad \text{FOUR-HANDLED JUG} \quad 1$$
$$37\text{-}53\text{-}61\text{-}75\text{-}38 \quad \text{THREE-HANDLED JUG} \quad 2$$
$$78\text{-}05\text{-}02\text{-}75 \quad \text{FOUR-HANDLED JUG} \quad 1$$
$$37\text{-}53\text{-}36\text{-}75 \quad \text{THREE-HANDLED JUG} \quad 1$$

To get the phonetic value of the two characters, it is of course not enough to reason that the Greek prefix τρι-, if spelled according to the rules of the Cypriotic syllabary, would need two characters *ti-ri-*. That would be close to begging the question, What language is in the Linear B texts? The most we may assert so far is that a sequence of two characters with the meaning 'three-' is *not incompatible* with Greek. But we take a big step by noting that 37 is shaped much like the Cypriotic character which is phonetically *ti*. Ventris had noted the similarity as early as 1950; subsequently the grid in its first, second, and third states indicated that he continued to associate this value with 37, and in Work Note 20 he gave this same identification as one of the keys to the exercise in decipherment (see above, p. 35). Whatever way he arrived at his other phonetic values, this one was unquestionably deduced not from the position of the character on the grid, but from the Cypriotic syllabary. In his publications and at one point (see above, p. 24) even in his unpublished circular he was not candid on the matter of his dependence upon Cypriotic values. He was convinced, apparently by Bennett, that it was a weakness in his method; for, as he said in *Documents* (p. 20): "It was tempting to compare Cypriot values (see fig. 12 [*Documents*, p. 64]), but clearly unrealistic: ǂ [*03*] might be taken at its Cypriot value of *pa*, but then it was impossible to read Ƨ [*75*] in quite another line of the grid as *pe* by the same analogy." Such thinking is another case of the all-or-nothing fallacy: since we cannot successfully decipher any Linear B tablet merely by transcribing the characters as though they were Cypriotic, it is inferred that we have no criterion for separating those Linear B characters to which the Cypriotic value applies from those to which it does not. My proposal is that we should try out the ones that occur in Linear B words whose meaning is given to us by the context.[5] Any phonetic value is purely tentative until verified — whether Ventris got it from the Cypriotic syllabary or from his grid.

Until we discover the language of Ta641, the meaning 'three-' for the characters 37-53- does not confirm the phonetic value *ti* for 37. 53 is not shaped anything like the Cypriotic *ri* character (nor like the Cypriotic *li*). But what follows 37-53- helps us. 37-53-11 in the single tripod entry and 37-53-11-45 in the entry with the tripod and the number 2 establish the value *po* for 11 and thereby favor *ti* for 37 and (less emphatically) *ri* for 53. They establish *po* beyond any likelihood of illusion or coincidence because 11-02 stands next to the foals' heads in Ca895 (see above, p. 27), which would make the Greek word πώλω if read with the Cypriotic values, and because 11 is in the right syllable of 08-39-11-27-75 next to the amphora drawing, so that it corresponds to φο in the Homeric word ἀμφιφορῆες. That the same character should correspond both to πο and to φο is in accord with the rule of the Cypriotic script not to distinguish between nonaspirate and aspirate (or between unvoiced and voiced). That the same character should serve where

Greek has πο and πω is still less surprising; not only does the Cypriotic syllabary make no such distinction, but neither does the Greek alphabet except in the standard Ionic variety familiar to us, which eventually superseded all the local varieties. As the identification $11 = po$ is on so many grounds irreproachable and this consonant-plus-vowel series makes up a substantial part of the Greek word for 'foot,' we are invited in addition to relate the characters 37-53- to the Greek morpheme that means 'three-.' Now that we have the support of $11 = po$, we need not hesitate to identify 37 in the same word as *ti*, since this results from the convergence of two independent pieces of evidence — the similarity to the Cypriotic character, and the phonetic interpretation of 37-53-11 as cognate to the classical Greek word τρίπος or τρίπους 'tripod, kettle on three legs' (*Il.* 22.164; Euripides, *Supp.* 1197; etc.).

$53 = ri$ is not on so firm a footing, because it rests solely on the need to fill the gap between *ti*- and -*po*. We might add, in favor of both equations $37 = ti$ and $53 = ri$, that Ventris had assigned the values before the discovery of the tripod-and-jug tablet. However, we need to understand his reasons in each case, if we are to make an intelligent appraisal. 53 was in the -*i* ? column from the first state of the grid on; in the second and third states it was in the row to which the label *r*- ? *l*- ? was added in the third state, along with the character 76 (later called *ra₂*) and in reduced size 04 and 20 (later called *te* and *zo* respectively). One might industriously go through the Work Notes hunting for the alternations that persuaded him to put the four characters into the same row. But on his own showing he did not find evidence for putting 53 into the next row *l*- ?, which was filled up with

	$60=li$?	$02=lo$?	$27=le$?	$26=la$?	$33=l$ + uncertain vowel
later[6]	*ra*	*ro*	*re*	*ru*	*ra₃*

67

The reshuffling of the characters of this row, to make 08-60-26-57 read *a-ra-ru-ja* instead of *a-ri-ra-ja* or *a-li-la-ja* in Work Note 20 (as we saw above, p. 36), left the *-i* space of the row vacant; so Ventris in the "Evidence" article was able to move 53 into it, while he disposed of 04 and 20 elsewhere. Such proceedings argue that he had no strong evidence about the consonantal affiliations of 53. But provided we are willing to assume that 'three-' is a monosyllabic morpheme in Linear B, the value *ri* fits better than anything else — whether the language is Greek or not. Given a syllable consisting phonetically of two consonants followed by a vowel *CCV-*, the syllabary will show it as *CV-CV-*. Since the first character has been identified as *ti-*, we get *ti-Ci-* for the syllabary notation of what would be phonetically *tCi-*. In the languages of the world the consonant most likely to fit between *t* and *i* is *r*. Furthermore, if the language is Indo-European, it is likely to have *tri-* for the 'three-' morpheme, as in Latin, Sanskrit, etc., no less than Greek. In favor of taking the word for Greek is the identification of *11* as *po,* which gives a Greek vocalization of the Indo-European morpheme for '-foot.'

78-05-02- = *te-to-ro-* (*qe-to-ro-*). While the characters that express the 'three-' morpheme are 37-53-, the characters that express 'four-' are not just 78-05-. The next character is not the same in the words for 'three-handled' and 'four-handled.' In 'four-handled' the next character is 02, which was read *lo* next to the foals' heads in Ca895. 05 is shaped much like the Cypriotic *to.* 'Four-' in Greek is τετρα-, but in a few words the vowel α disappears through elision or absorption when the other member of the compound begins with a different vowel: τέθριππος 'four-horsed' (Euripides, *Hipp.* 1212, etc.), τετρώβολον 'four-obol piece' (Aristophanes, *Pax* 254). Since 05 and 02 appear to share the vowel *-o*, we can interpret them as the syllable -*tro-*, provided we find confirmation (as we shall presently) of Ventris's analysis which makes the '-handled' part of the word begin with an -*o* sound. Reading -*05-02-* as -*tro-*, we have an indication that the Linear B script does not distinguish *r-* from *l-*. This is contrary to the rule of the Cypriotic syllabary. We are not in a position — certainly not at this point — to infer whether the language had or had not a phoneme contrast between the two consonants. Greek does; but in the ancient Indo-Iranian languages *l* is rare or lacking: where Greek has λ, the Indo-Iranian cognates normally have *r*.[7]

78 occupies the initial where the Greek 'four-' has τε-. It also occurs in Au102 (Mycenae)[8] at the end of the second word in each two-word entry, followed by the MAN ideogram and the numeral ‖ [TWO, not ELEVEN].[9] The one-word entries, followed by the same ideogram and the numerical ∣ lack this character.[10] The natural interpretation of 78 in this tablet is as an enclitic conjunction signifying 'and,' like the Greek τε. The two words that it joins would be the men's names or some other identification of them. Many of the words, however, as transcribed by Ventris, do not look Greek by any stretch of the imagination. An1281.3,5 (Pylos)[11] shows precisely the same correlation: -78 comes at the end of the second word in those lines which have ‖ [= 2] after MAN, while -78 is lacking in the MAN ∣ entries. Here too the names themselves seem non-Greek.

Ventris's phonetic value *qe* was introduced not in the Work Notes but in "Evidence" (p. 102), to indicate a sound much like the Latin -*que*.[12] In the third state of the grid this character appears in the -*e* ? column and the *m*- ? row, along with 32 (identified as *qo* in "Evidence") and 58 (*qo₂* in "Evidence" but changed to *su* in *Documents!*). The character *04*, on which Ventris in "Evidence" settled the value *te*, does not occur in any word corroborated by the ideographic context.

Ventris found its distributional relations quite indecisive. In the second state of the grid he had placed it (reduced in size as an indication of uncertainty) in the same row as *53, 76,* and *20,* none of which has ever been thought to have the consonant *t-.* In the third state of the grid all four characters remained in the same row, now labeled *r-* ? *l-* ?; but another *04,* also of reduced size, made its appearance in the *te* ? square. Whatever considerations in the interim may have led Ventris to put *04* into the *t-* ? row, while not removing it from the *r-* ? *l-* ? row, no reason is given in the Work Notes. We lack a firm basis for attributing to *78* a labiovelar consonant rather than *t-; 04* has no clear title to the *te* space, such that we would have to find another row to house this other character *78.*

A transcription *te* for *78* is appropriate to the early stage of decipherment when our phonetic values are just a rough *normalization,* indicating not what the sounds were in the Linear B language but what sounds they are related to in Greek. We cannot yet depend on these Linear B characters to correspond equally well to the same Greek sounds in other words, although it is reasonable to hope that some of the characters will continue to behave tractably in relation to Greek sounds.

At a later stage, if our progress continues, we may be able to achieve a *phonological transcription* which will show how the Linear B sounds are related to each other; e.g., we may then know whether the difference between *27* and *02,* now transcribed *re* and *ro,* is indeed front vowel as opposed to back vowel, while they share an equal degree of aperture. A further stage, which our material may never allow us to reach, would be an accurate *phonetic transcription* giving the true pronunciation of the sounds; e.g., in classical Attic we know not merely that ε and ο are of the same degree of aperture, but even that they are the closed vowels [e, o] of the International Phonetic Alphabet, rather than the open ones [ε, ɔ].

45 = de (*not improbable*). Whatever may now be conjectured or later proved about *78*, which corresponds to the Greek τε in τετρ(α)- 'four-' and the enclitic 'and,' a different Linear B character is found at the end of *37-53-11-45*. Given a transcription *ti-ri-po-* for the first three characters, the ideographic context calls for the Greek dual τρίποδε, or possibly the plural τρίποδες.[13] Ventris as late as the third state of the grid was very doubtful of the place of *45;* he set it, reduced in size, at the bottom of the *-e* ? column, in the "other consonants" row, and again at the extreme right of the *ʰ/χ-* ? θ- ? row, in the "vowel uncertain" column. In Work Note 20 he gave *45* the value *de*, on account of its occurrence at the end of words where it reminded him of the Greek suffix -δε: (1) attached to what he took to be place names, although the context gave him no clues;[14] (2) in the word *05-12-45*, whose context sometimes calls for a word expressing the idea of a total, somewhat reminiscent of τοσόνδε, τοσόσδε 'so much' (neuter or masculine singular), τοσοίδε 'so many' (masculine plural). The only altogether sure instance, not compromised by any damage to the tablet, is in Jn415 (Pylos), where the line of summation

05-12-45 *77-70* |Ξ| ⊿Τ⊿   ² ‖ ² ‖

comes below six items ² ‖‖ and one item ² ‖ . The drawing of a balance almost certainly stands for TALENT, and ⋛ for DOUBLE MINA; for both here and on other tablets (slightly damaged) the balance ideogram is not used if the total of ⋛ remains under 30, and it takes 30 of ⋛ among the addends for each ǀ marked to the right of the balance.[15] En609 (Pylos) has at the beginning of its second line *05-12-45* and at the end MAN — ‖ [i.e., 14 men]. This may be a total, though not unmistakably so, because the sixteen lines below it contain, at most, 13 occurrences of an unclear ideogram 𐀷 conjecturally taken for WHEAT.

We have already identified $05 = to$ on the basis of the 'four-' morpheme and the shape of the Cypriotic *to* character. This would encourage us to transcribe *to-so-de* for 05-12-45, provided that the word alternates with another of similar meaning but lacking the last syllable, as Greek has τόσον, τόσος, τόσοι besides τοσόνδε, τοσόσδε, τοσοίδε.[16] Here again we have but one sure instance, in As1520 (Knosos): 05-12 next to MAN — [i.e., 10 men], below ten items each ending with a separate vertical | stroke.[17] To recognize 05-12 alternating

with 05-12-45 as the Linear B cognate of τόσο $\left\{\begin{matrix} v \\ ς \\ ι \end{matrix}\right\}$ alternating

with τοσό $\left\{\begin{matrix} v \\ σ \\ ι \end{matrix}\right\}$ δε, is possible though not inescapable. The

Greek words, unlike the Linear B ones, are not used in contexts where they would mean 'all told, in all, total';[18] this Linear B meaning, however, is not so far removed from the known Greek meaning 'so much, so many' as to prohibit a comparison with Greek. However, it is weakened by the lack of confirmation for the second character $12 = so$ (see below, p. 75). Along with 37-53-11-45 referring to the two tripods (τρίποδε or τρίποδες in Greek), 05-12-45 converges toward establishing the value *de* for 45. A pure coincidence here would be surprising.

The equation $45 = de$, although not quite assured, is of unusual interest. For one thing, the Greek suffix -δε has no plausible etymology, Indo-European or otherwise; if we have correctly identified it in 05-12-45, we have found in Linear B a feature characteristic of Greek *and no other known language*. [19] Besides that, the equation confronts us with something contrary to the Cypriotic rule. The Cypriotic script does not distinguish between voiced and unvoiced; Greek δε and τε (as well as θε) are indicated by one Cypriotic character ⋎ . But the Linear B correspondents of τε and δε differ from each other. In the two verified occurrences of 78, the cognates outside of Greek, such as the Latin enclitic suffix -*que*, suggest that the consonantal sound in Linear B may not have been a pure dental consonant like the Greek τ. But it remains just a suggestion, until we find a reliable case of another Linear B character — either *04* or something else —occurring where Greek calls for τε and the rest of the Indo-European languages also have a dental, not a labiovelar. Ventris's *04* = *te* is unverified (see above, pp. 69-70); we have yet to prove whether *45* could correspond to the Greek τε, θε (with dental, not labiovelar cognates). If it cannot, while some other character is proved to correspond to κε, χε, γε alike or to πε, φε, βε, that will demonstrate an asymmetry in Linear B as transcribed by Ventris. We might correlate it with the failure of Linear B to distinguish *lo* from *ro* (see above, p. 69). In case the Linear B language had just one sound — on the order of [r] — where Greek has the λ ~ ρ opposition, then what is δ in Greek could be articulated in Linear B more like the related lateral consonant [l] than like the plosive [d]. Such reasoning belongs, however, to a later stage of the decipherment, for which we are far from being ready.

12 = *so*, *31* = *sa* (*both doubtful*). The alternation between *05-12* and *05-12-45* will fit the pattern of Greek, provided we allow the omission of a Greek sound in the second syllable, right after the vowel *o*. The probability of a Greek interpretation has been enhanced because the *to* value for *05* and the *de* value for *45* appear also in *78-05-02-75* 'four-handled' and *37-53-11-45* '(two) tripods' — whereas these facts do not fit the pattern of any known language apart from Greek. The value *so* for *12* is inferred in order to read *05-12* and *05-12-45* as Greek words. Earlier we judged that *53* = *ri* in order to get a Greek word for *37-53-11* 'three-footed (kettle).' and similarly in 'three-handled.' The equation *53* = *ri* is stronger than *12* = *so* in two ways: *tri-* 'three-' is shared by other Indo-European languages; moreover, the context shows that *37-53-* means exactly the same as τρι-. *05-12* and *05-12-45*, in the few instances where we can prove their meaning from the context, are semantically related to

$$\text{τόσο}\begin{Bmatrix} ν \\ ς \\ ι \end{Bmatrix}, \ \text{τοσό}\begin{Bmatrix} ν \\ σ \\ ι \end{Bmatrix}\text{δε but not the same. In practically all}$$

other instances the two Linear B words occur in the vicinity of a number written ideographically; while this does not prove any precise meeting, it is compatible at any rate with a meaning expressive of quantity, on the order of the Greek words signifying 'so much, so many.'[20]

12 = *so* has a different sort of advantage: it exhibits a likely though not conclusive alternation of gender. That was what led Ventris to put the characters *12* and *31* into the same row, from the second state of the grid on; in the third state the columns are labeled *-o* ? and *-a* ? respectively, matching the Greek "second" (masculine) and "first" (feminine) declensions. Much earlier, in "Languages" (pp. xxii-xxiii), he had transcribed *05-12* as *tŭṣ"* and *05-31* as *tŭṣa*, "probably not a feminine inflexion," although he had seen Kober's arguments for taking *05-31* to be the feminine of *05-12*. In L598 (Knosos) the edge has *05-31* followed by the ideographic ⊞ ☰ [i.e., 40 of something]; this is fine as the total of the three items 1, 37, and 2 on the face of the tablet. The loss of part of the tablet does not compromise the arithmetic, so far as one can judge. But on a similar tablet (pieced together complete from the fragments L596, 589, 587) the number given on the edge, following *05-31* and the same ideographic symbol, is 149 – which is altogether wrong if intended as in L598 to stand for the total of the items on the face;[21] of those five items the largest is 372! Also, in what remains of L584, the number (which again follows *05-31* and the same ideogram) is 5, while the two items on the face are 4 and 5 respectively. So we can hardly depend on *05-31* to stand for 'total' as *05-12* and *05-12-45* do; that it seems to in L598, may be a coincidence. As for the gender of *05-31*, the ideogram leaves us in the dark. But the word occurs also beside the WOMAN ideogram on the sixth line of Ap639 (Knosos). In this long but incompletely preserved text we cannot prove whether the number 𐄓𐄋 [i.e., 45] is a true total. But the whole layout is in the main reminiscent of As1516 (see p. 102, note 17); so 𐀵𐀭 *05-31* before WOMAN may well stand for the feminine counterpart of 𐀵𐀰 X (*05-12* plus the check mark) before MAN.[22] *05-31*, like *05-12*, is not known to occur outside of quantitative contexts – which is a point favoring Ventris's transcription of them as *to-sa* and *to-so* respectively.[23]

I hesitate upon the identification of the two characters *31* and *12* more than any other that I have scrutinized up to this point. The evidence that *05-31* corresponds to τόσα(ι) – neuter plural or feminine plural – and *05-12* to τόσο- is by no means overwhelming. That they occur in contexts expressing quantity, becomes less impressive when we reflect that most of the Linear B corpus is like this. The meaning 'total,' where it applies to *05-31*, *05-12* (sometimes followed by x), and *05-12-45*, is no argument for *identifying* these Linear B words with Greek words that only mean 'so much, so many.' Supposing Ventris's identifications here to be correct, we can understand how the words might have simply lost their use in formulae of totaling, when the practice of elementary arithmetic declined in the collapse of Mycenaean civilization. When arithmetic again emerges in texts from the classical period (naturally at places other than the old cities of Knosos and Pylos), it is no wonder that a different term, κεφάλαιον, has arisen. This reasoning could help to support the values *sa* and *so* in these words, if the values were otherwise verified. But the verification needs something stronger than a loose similarity in sense, such as the one between the Greek words for 'so much, so many' (but not 'total') and the Linear B words for 'total' in a few passages and for some other quantitative meaning, perhaps, in the remaining passages.[24]

-61-75- = -o-we-, 08-52- = a-no-. Returning now to the tripod-and-jug tablet, we take up the part of 37-53-61-75-38 that refers to the handle. It consists of two characters whose values, *o* and *we* respectively, are confirmed elsewhere. The second line of Ca895 begins with 61-52, well to the left of the three drawings of equine heads.[25] The transcription *o-no* agrees with ὄνος, ὄνοι 'ass(es),' except that no Linear B character stands for the last letter of the Greek words (see below, pp. 230-2). The Greek word for 'ass' belongs to the "Mediterranean" rather than the Indo-European vocabulary. The identification 'ass' rather than 'horse' is suggested by the lack of a mane, such as is sketched in the two drawings of adult horses on the line above.[26] Moreover, two parallel lines ⦀ — coming out of the top rear of all the heads in the second line — must represent asses' ears, lacking in the three horse heads. It is fair to add that nobody seems to have recognized asses distinct from horses in the drawings till after Chadwick in 1955 found the fragment with the words 28-32 and 61-52 and part of one drawing of an ass's head.[27] With the advantage of hindsight we can now safely argue that the drawings themselves, even without the words, adequately distinguished the two equine species, and that the words

28-32, 61-52, and *11-02* — even if undeciphered — ought to signify in the Linear B language 'horse(s),' 'ass(es),' and 'foal(s)' respectively.

The meaning of the words is guaranteed by the drawings; but the words, so understood, do not futilely repeat in mere redundance what ought to be obvious without them.[28] The first line shows an ideogram of a MARE with the numeral 5, then of a STALLION with the numeral 4, then the word *11-02* and an ideogram with neither the $\int$ stroke for FEMALE nor the = strokes for MALE.[29] In the second line, *11-02* and the ideogram of an immature ASS with the numeral 2 come between the JENNY ASS and JACKASS ideograms, each with its numeral. The lack of a sex mark might in itself allow the *inference* that an ideogram stands for immature animals; but it surely does not make it altogether superfluous to write *11-02* and thereby *express* the meaning 'foal' outright. Neither is a word 28-32, at the left in the first line, superfluous to express what class of animals is comprised under the three headings that are inventoried ideographically in that line; nor, again, is the word 61-52 superfluous to express the other class of animals in the second line.

The value *61 = o* did not come from the grid but from Ventris's subsequent attempt to read Greek in the Linear B texts. On distributional grounds he had placed 61 in the -*i* ? column and the "pure vowels ?" row of the grid in its second and third states, because the other characters in that column do not occur before it, frequent though it is. That would indeed be a good reason for inferring a value *i*; at that time he did not have Ta641 with the sequence -53-61- in the word that means 'three-handled,' and he pardonably overlooked 08-39-61-05 in An857.r6 (Pylos).[30] Greek, like many other languages, rarely has a sequence *Cii* (*i* as the nucleus of two successive syllables, with no consonant separating the identical vowel sounds). But in

Work Note 20 (pp. 173, 175), although he still regarded 61
as *i* ?, he wondered briefly what to do about it in order to
make it serve for a Greek genitive ending. In "Evidence" he
revalued it *o* to fit the masculine "first declension" genitive of
the type ἱκέτᾱο 'suppliant' (*Il.* 21.75).[31] The experiment succeeded marvelously; for 61 turned out to occur just where *o*
is needed to yield a Greek word for 'ass(es)' and a Greek
morpheme that means '-eared, -handled.'

The fourth character in 37-53-61-75-38 and 78-05-02-75,
describing the jugs, occurs also in 08-39-11-27-75 next to an
amphora and the numeral ⫼ (Uc160; see above, p. 65). 75
corresponds to the ε in ἀμφιφορῆες, or rather to the (ϝ)ε; the
singular ἀμφιφορεύς (*Il.* 23.92) evinces a stem in -ευ- ∼ -ηϝ-.
Ventris's transcription *we* need not yet commit us to any
phonological judgement in regard to the *w*; it stands merely
for whatever sound in the Linear B language may precede
the vowel in this syllable and thus be cognate with the Greek
ϝ. That 75 was really pronounced /we/ is suggested by the
similarity of its shape ⟨ to the Cypriotic Ζ , Ζ .[32] The
relation between the rounded Linear B character and the
angular one in Cypriotic adds somewhat to the probability
that Ventris's value *we* is phonologically correct and not just
a normalization of Linear B to Greek for the practical purpose of carrying on the decipherment. However, the phonological question will need more evidence before it is settled.

The morpheme -*o-we*- '-eared' corresponds to -ῶες in
ἀμφῶες 'two-eared, two-handled' (Theocritus 1.28), where it
described a kind of cup. The derivation of -ῶες from οὖς 'ear'
(*Il.* 11.109; Sophocles, *El.* 27; etc.), ὦς (Theocritus 11.32),
or some such form is incontestable; but the details are
obscure. Beattie (*JHS*, LXXVI, 13) would forbid an intervocalic -*w*- in any form of the Greek word for 'ear.' But the
stem of the Greek word for 'ear' exhibits incoherent variation
within dialects as well as between them; its cognates in other

Indo-European languages do not present a clear picture either. We must therefore be prepared for surprises in the 'ear' morpheme when used in compounds. There is no telling whether or not the -ῶϵϲ of Theocritus ever had a *[w] sound between the two vowels.[33] If the Linear B character 75 contained such a consonant, it would be no barrier to the identification of -61-75- with -ῶϵϲ (apart from the final -ϲ).[34] -owe- is a possible structure for 'ear' (or '-eared') in Greek or a closely related language; but the known fluctuations in Greek prevent us from arguing that the Linear B characters which stand for '-eared' *must* be read -owe-. The -o- and the -e- parts are established; the -w- is liable to correction.

Ventris placed 75 on the grid without knowledge of either the jugs of Ta641 or the amphora of Uc160. He noted in Work Note 14 (pp. 97-122 *passim*) the many words in which 75 as a final character alternates with 10 and 42, and with the two characters 40-36 or 40-57. The row that 75 belonged to was therefore relatively easy to fix in the second state of the grid; but it was almost alone in its column, with only four spaces occupied out of seventeen. The Work Notes in between that and the third state give the reasons that led Ventris to merge this nearly empty column with a nearly full one, which was now marked -e ? His reasons tended in favor of the -ϵύϲ declension of Greek, with the nominative plural in -ῆ(ϝ)ϵϲ; but he was troubled by the difficulties in the way of such an identification (Work Note 16, p. 150). He most indecisively labeled the row s- ? v- ? θ- ? c- ? Two characters in the row were identified as wo and wa in Work Note 20 (see below, p. 110); and shortly after mailing it to his correspondents, he became certain of the -ϵύϲ declension, which seemed to assure the value we for 75 as the nominative plural (cf. *Documents*, p. 22). He had gone too far to be upset by having to make we serve also for the "dative" singular.

79

The transcription *a-no-we* 'earless,' for *08-52-75* beside the jug without a handle, fits in perfectly with the first character *08* in *a-pi-po-re-we* 'amphoras' and the second character *52* in *o-no* 'ass(es).'[35] The value *a* for *08* had been assumed by Ventris as early as the "Languages" circular (Appendix 2, items 24, 46), before he began working on the grid. He, like Ktistopoulos, doubtless based it on the fact that this is the most frequent character at the beginning of words. Later he found little in the pattern of alternations to confirm the original surmise (e.g., Work Note 9, p. 81), but still less to contradict it, so it went into the *-a* ? column and the "pure vowel ?" row of the grid.

The equation *52* = *no* exemplifies how Ventris made good use of the grid method in conjunction with the Cypriotic syllabary and pure hunches. He had transcribed it θ^u or $\theta\dot{u}$ in "Languages" (Appendix 2, items 32, 57, 61, 68, 75, 77). His vowel ^{u} or $\dot{u}$ in this appendix is the same as he attributes to *05* (= Cypriotic *to*) and *02* (= Cypriotic *lo*).[36] I have no idea what made him hit upon θ^u; at any rate he never revised his original surmise in regard to the back vowel. In Work Note 14 ("Pylos sign-groups showing inflexion," 28 Aug 1951), antedating the second state of the grid, he studied the alternation of *52* and *06* (particularly on p. 114, item P 103). Contrary to his general practice in the Work Notes of that period, he gave tentative phonetic values, *no* and *na* respectively. He had got *06* = *na* from Cypriotic (see above, p. 23); and in view of the alternation he made the consonantal part of *52* agree, while not needing to change the vocalic part as he had previously conceived it.[37] For he called attention, further on in the same long Work Note (p. 127, item K 12), to a phenomenon of the Knosos tablets:

53-36-52
53-36-30-36
53-36-30-57

This was parallel to

> 26-67-05
> 26-67-37-36
> 26-67-37-57 (same page, item K 9; cf. K 2, K 10).

Since he had $05 = to$ and $37 = ti$ from the Cypriotic sylla-bary, the pattern called for $52 = no$ and $30 = ni$. He did not at once announce the value ni for 30, but he placed it on the grid where it was destined to receive that value. Besides these relations, which facilitated the arrangement of the characters in one row, he perceived another between 52 and 46; but he classified it as "an alternation which is apparently extraneous to their most probable consonant and vowel equa-tions."[38] He therefore placed 46 in a different row, with ar-rows to show the relation to 52, judged by him to be insignifi-cant. So his identification of 52 as no has been splendidly ratified by the words $o\text{-}no$ and $a\text{-}no\text{-}we$, which were unknown to him in 1951. He already had a substantial lead over any other person working toward the decipherment of Linear B.

$36 = jo$ or o_2 *(problematical)*. The *-owe* morpheme '-eared' that comes out in *ti-ri-o-we-e, te-to-ro-we* (or *qe-to-ro-we*), *a-no-we* is complicated by the alternation in the third character of

> 37-53-61-75-38 *ti-ri-o-we-e*
> 37-53-36-75   *ti-ri-?-we*

Ventris had committed himself to $36 = jo$ in Work Note 20, before Blegen wrote to him about Ta641. In the third state of the grid he had called it *śo* ? and had not placed it in the same row as 57 (*ja* ?), in spite of their recurrent alternation at the end of words, following 37 (*ti*) and other *-i* characters. Only when he ventured to transcribe Greek words in Work Note 20 did he change it to *jo*, in order to transcribe

08-73-30-12   *a-mi-ni-so*   (i.e., ᾿Αμνισό(ϛ), the city)

08-73-30-41-36 *a-mi-ni-si-jo* (i.e., ᾿Αμνίσιο(ϛ), etc., the masculine ethnic)

08-73-30-41-57 *a-mi-ni-si-ja* (i.e., ᾿Αμνισία, the feminine ethnic).

His previous reluctance to recognize the pattern — that if *57* is *ja*, *36* ought to be *jo* — may be traceable to an oddity in the Cypriotic syllabary. When a Greek word has the sequence ια, the latter vowel is represented not always by the Cypriotic sign for the plain vowel *a* but often by the sign for *ja* instead; e.g.,

ta-ni-e-re-wi-ja-ne ta-se a-ta-na-se
(= Attic τὴν ἱέρειαν τῆς ᾿Αθηνᾶς) 'the priestess of Athena'

to-ni-ja-te-ra-ne
(= Attic τὸν ἰᾱτῆρα) 'the physician'[39]
ta-se-pa-pi-ja-se (= Attic τῆς Παφίας) 'the Paphian (goddess)'
but *ta-se-pa-pi-a-se* (Deecke, pp. 13, 16, nos. 1, 15, etc.).

When the Greek sequence is ιο, the latter is regularly represented by the plain *o* character; e.g., *e-ta-li-o-ne* (= ᾿Ηδάλιον),[40] *o-se-la-mi-ni-o-se, sa-la-mi-ni-o-se* (= Attic ὁ Σαλαμίνιος; Meister, p. 182, nos. 147[a],[b], etc.). The existence of a rare Cypriotic sign for *jo*, 𐙢 in Paphos and 𐠲 elsewhere, is a matter not yet beyond debate. Until Work Note 20, Ventris could not see a Linear B alternation *ja ~ jo* that was lacking or poorly represented in Cypriotic. This strikes me as whimsical rather than logical, particularly because the

Cypriotic *j*- characters bear little graphic resemblance to anything in Linear B.

Nevertheless the value *jo*, which Ventris after long hesitation applied to *36*, does work nicely in *ti-ri-jo-we* 'three-eared, three-handled.' The transition between the vowels *i* and *o* likely to be an off-glide homorganic with the *i*. Otherwise it would be hard to imagine what the difference between *36* and *61* (plain *o*) consists in. But a grave difficulty arises: whereas no Greek word ever begins with *j*-,[41] *36* comes at the beginning of seven Linear B words at least. Of them, five occur at the beginning of a tablet:

> *36-08-73-30-12-45* (Og0467, Knosos)
> *36-08-09-12-41* (Cn608, Pylos)
> *36-14-12-41* (Jn829, Pylos)
> *36-28-46-41* (Cn3, Pylos)
> *36* as a separate initial word (Ge602, Mycenae).[42]

The sixth, *36-04-27-03-05* (Fp14+27+28, Knosos), is almost initial in a way: what precedes it on the first line is a word in big characters followed by an interval of blank space; above the blank space another word is placed near the top edge of the tablet. The seventh, *36-38-44-05-32* (Gv863.1, Knosos), comes second after a word in big characters on the same line. In Og0467, *36*- looks like a prefix; for *08-73-30-12-45* occurs several times without it (Fp14, Fp48, F953). But the other *36*- words have no counterparts without the *36*-; it is just guessing to call *36*- a prefix in them. Out of the six words (leaving aside the one-character word from Mycenae), the three from Pylos all end in -*41*, and the three from Knosos are all followed by another word that ends in -*41*. Ventris transcribes this character *si*;[43] it certainly resembles the shape of the *si* in Cypriotic (see below, p. 115). Whether or not the occurrence of -*41* in the

environment of the initial 36- is accidental, we are at a loss
for anything in Greek to relate, either phonetically or semantically, to an initial *jo-* in Linear B. The phonetic difficulty
is not lessened by speculation (as in *Documents,* p. 79) that
what is transcribed *jo* may have been pronounced [ho]
rather than [jo]. If it brings us nearer to the phonology of
Greek in regard to the beginning of the Linear B words, it
does the opposite in the far more numerous cases where 36
follows another character; for we would then have to posit
sequences like *iho, eho, oho* — altogether foreign to Greek,
including the inscriptions written in non-Ionic varieties of
the Greek alphabet, in which H was available as a consonant.
On the semantic side, Ventris's interpretation of *jo-* as a
relative adverb 'how' (*Documents,* pp. 205, 207, 228) or a
demonstrative adverb 'thus' (pp. 357, 409) is desperate. His
translation of the Linear B words in which 36- occurs is not
even superficially attractive in the context of the neighboring
words.

We have in 36 a Linear B character whose relation to
Greek is so far intractable, except that its occurrence in
37-53-36-75 on the tripod-and-jug tablet argues that its
vocalic element is *o*. Until something further can be demonstrated about whatever other element may precede the *o,*
I recommend that 36 had better be given a noncommittal
transcription o_2.

39 = *pi,* 27 = *re.* We have used the amphora tablet Uc160,
with the word 08-39-11-27-75, to corroborate Ventris's values
a, po, and *we* found in Ta641. The elements ἀμφι- and -φορ-
are Indo-European, but the -εύς declension is not. The case
for 08 = *a* and 11 = *po* is overwhelming; the equation 75 =
we is not quite so solid (see above, p. 79). The value of
the other two characters 39 and 27 is verified only by their
position in this word. Ventris had gridded both of them

before the publication of *SM* II, as shown by the second state of the grid ("28 Sept 51"). Evans in *PM* IV^b (published in 1935) had not made any reference to Uc160; so we can reasonably presume that Ventris did not have this word from Knosos in mind as he was constructing the grid. He strangely wavered about the vowel of *39* when he came to the third state; although leaving it where he had placed it before (in the -*i* ? column), he added a little *39* in the -*e* ? column (see above, p. 29). His reason for that is as obscure as the reason for moving another character of the same row, *11*, out of the -*o* ? column to the "vowel uncertain" column (see above, p. 28).

At any rate, we find no clear-cut proof of the value *pi* for *39* and *re* for *27*, apart from the word *08-39-11-27-75*. For additional proof of the former, Chadwick (*Decipherment*, p. 93) cites two words — *39-25-60*, transcribed *pi-a₂-ra*, and *39-46-33*, transcribed *pi-je-ra₃* — which he and Ventris in *Documents* (pp. 324-25) identified with φιάλη, φιέλη. In Greek these are variant forms of the same word;[44] but the Linear B tablets prove no such thing about *39-25-60* and *39-46-33*. The former appears next to a drawing of a two-handled basin with a flat bottom (Tn996), the latter near a drawing of a two-handled bowl on a stand (Ta709, both from Pylos; Beattie, *MIOF*, VI, 50). We are in no position to affirm that *39-25-60* and *39-46-33* are interchangeable variants of the same word, applied to both vessels in spite of the difference between them. Nor can we determine whether one or both or neither of the vessels was of a type called φιάλη (φιέλη) in Greek. From Homer on (*Il.* 23.270, etc.), the kind of vessel designated by this word shifted a great deal;[45] and the literary references often tell too little to afford a precise identification of the object.[46] Lasting uniformity in the nomenclature of such artifacts is scarcely to be expected. All this makes it harder, not easier, to apply Greek to the reading of the Linear B texts concerning pottery. In order to identify 39-25-60 safely with φιάλη (-ᾱ) or 39-46-33 with φιέλη (-ᾱ), we would first have to show that not just conceivably but quite definitely the meaning of φιάλη, φιέλη embraces vessels of the sort depicted on the Linear B tablets.

38 = e (not improbable). In 37-53-61-75-38, followed by the three-handled jug and the numeral ‖ (TWO, not ELEVEN, of course), the character 38 is plainly a number suffix; for it is lacking in the words that come in the other jug items before the drawing and the numeral Ɩ . The morphological function of 38, to indicate a number other than the singular, does not in itself establish the phonetic value of the character. But we can narrow down the possibilities by considering that ἀμφῶες, the Theocritean *hápax legómenon* for 'eared on both sides, two-handled,' has all the appearance of a "third declension" adjective. The dual suffix of this declension would be -ε, regardless of gender; the masculine or feminine plural would be -ες, the neuter plural -α. The Linear B script, which has in our prior experience exhibited zero where Greek has a final -ς, is not going to distinguish the dual -ε from the masculine-feminine plural -ες. So it might seem that we have five chances out of six that the suffix in the Linear B language corresponds to -ε or -ες, rather than -α. But this is a wholly inconclusive speculation, particularly when we are unable to identify the noun 07-03-38 at the beginning of this item, or its singular form 07-03 at the beginning of the other items, or the gender.[47] We do not know whether to suppose the Linear B language used the dual with the consistency of Sanskrit, Old Slavic, and the Attic inscriptions (until 408 B.C.) or in competition with the plural, as Homeric and literary Attic do.[48] Compound adjectives in the dual are scarce in any dialect or style of Greek. So the correlation of the suffix -38 with the numeral ‖ does

not rule out the possibility of a neuter plural.[49] On this basis
the Greek counterpart to 38 is not necessarily ε; it could be α.

But a quite independent argument in favor of ε comes from
the Jn tablets (Pylos). In the first line of most of these we
find the formula 77-44-75 59-60-41-57 38-70-04 after the
initial word, which differs from tablet to tablet.[50] Underneath
come items that typically consist of a single word plus the
ideogram |≡| , the double-mina sign ⚖ and a numeral (see
above, p. 73). Later in contrast comes another formula
05-12-45 08-59-60-41-36 77-44-75 followed by words that
are taken to be men's names, and the numeral Ⅰ after every
such word.[51] The two formulae were observed quite early
by Ventris (Work Note 9, pp. 75-76, item E 1), who furthermore pointed out the alternation between 59-60-41-57

and 08-59-60-41-36,

and made it his prime example of a prefix. His ingenuity
somehow missed the inference that the meaning of the 08-
prefix is negative, although he had surmised the value a for
this character on account of its preeminent frequency at the
beginning of words (see above, p. 80). A negative prefix a-
would have constituted the strongest indication accessible
to him in 1951 that the Linear B language was Greek or related to Greek. Since we have verified the value of 08
in a-no-we 'earless' and a-pi-po-re-we 'amphoras,' we can add
that in the Jn tablets 08- corresponds to ἀ- 'un-, without,
-less.' It is furthermore likely to have a counterpart expressing 'with, having' somewhere in the three words of the
other formula. To be sure, the language could conceivably
leave such a meaning unexpressed, but here 38-70-04 offers
itself as the opposite of 08-. Ventris's transcription e-ko-te =
ἔχοντες ("Evidence," p. 98) is questionable in regard to the
last character, as we shall presently see. But the equation
$38 = e$ accords with the employment of the same character
as a dual or plural suffix of a "third declension" adjective re-

87

ferring to two jugs; and $70 = ko$ can be confirmed by other tablets (see below, pp. 104-6). We conclude that a word which in Greek letters would begin ἐχο- is fully in place on the Jn tablets after *59-60-41-57*, where the ensuing ideographic context expresses something weighed out — while the opposite (i.e., the lack of this kind of ideographic context) is correlated with the negative prefix in *08-59-60-41-36*.

However, a difficulty over the last character of *38-70-04* makes the rest of the word somewhat less secure. The same archaeological campaign at Pylos that unearthed Ta641 unearthed many new Jn tablets besides; of these, Jn658 and 706 begin *77-44-75 59-60-41-57 38-70-41* (not *-04*) with no previous word. In Ventris's transcription it becomes *ka-ke-we ta-ra-si-ja e-ko-si* 'smiths have an allocation,' while the more common formula would be 'smiths having an allocation.'[52] But if the difference between *38-70-41* and *38-70-04* is indeed that they are finite verb and participle respectively, we do not then see why the variable initial word should be associated with *38-70-04*. Ventris takes the variable word to be a place name — in no instance identified with a known village of the Pylos area or even with anything Greek.[53] A certain word *08-44-27-54* (followed by *77-44-75*, etc.) opens the tablet- or paragraph-heading of three Jn tablets, but the sequel does not favor the effort to regard them as records of smiths in a town called *a-ke-re-wa*. None of the men's names recur from one tablet to another.[54] The paragraph in question on Jn693 is damaged so that just one name remains, but the other two paragraphs (310.1-12, 725.23-25) have at least twelve and four respectively. It is hard to imagine the smiths of a small, forgotten town either being so numerous or going through such a complete turnover in the interval between records. On archaeological grounds all the Pylos tablets are considered nearly coeval.

Greek syntax does not provide Ventris's interpretation with

any clue to justify the strange consequence, that if the place is expressed before the formula, then at the end of the formula it entails a participle instead of a finite verb. The most we can grant is that syntax would not absolutely forbid such an alternation between the verb ἔχουσι and the participle ἔχοντες; at any rate, both are plural. But until we hear an explanation of the varying Linear B formula, we can fairly doubt whether this syntax of 38-70-41 and 38-70-04 is really as Ventris says. Even in regard to 38-70-, the ideographic proof that it means something opposite to 'without' or 'un-' is not so clear-cut as the drawings of tripods and jugs were. So I accept Ventris's value 38 = e with some hesitation.

Furthermore, to us at this stage the transcription signifies that 38 in the words 37-53-61-75-38 and 38-70-04, 38-70-41 corresponds to the Greek ε. We are not thereby committed to a phonological interpretation, either excluding a consonant before the vowel or identifying which consonant was there. Before the Greek dual and plural suffixes -ε, -ες a sigmatic stem loses the consonant that is preserved in the singular, as in ἀμφῶες. The intervocalic loss of this consonant is one of the touchstones of Greek, serving to distinguish it from other Indo-European languages. Similarly in the Greek verb ἐχ- 'have,' the lack of the sibilant before the vowel (while it is preserved immediately before the consonant χ in the aorist ἔσχον, σχών, etc., and in the Sanskrit cognate sah-) is a touchstone of Greek. But we have so far no proof that the Linear B character 38 stands for e not preceded by a sibilant or some related consonant. We need to see, for example, a case where it demonstrably corresponds to a Greek ε cognate with a (not sa) in Sanskrit, or with e (not se or re) in Latin. A reason given as early as Work Note 8 (p. 22) for regarding 38 as a "pure vowel" with no consonant is its high frequency at the beginning of words.[55] That is an intelligent surmise, provided the Linear B language had a phonological structure not too different from Greek. In Greek a very large proportion of the ἐ- words are accounted for by the prefixes ἐν-, εἰσ-, ἐκ-, ἐπι- and the augment for past tenses. Since these turn out to be rare or lacking in Linear B as transcribed by Ventris, except for *e-pi-*,[56] we are less justified in arguing that the frequency of 38- fits the frequency of ἐ-. The value 38 = *e* is just a normalization; it would be premature to elevate it to a phonological statement about the Linear B language, that 38 = /e/, a front vowel of intermediate aperture, not preceded by a consonant.

07-03 = *di-pa* (*conjectural*). It is tempting, perhaps, but unwarranted to go along with Ventris and connect the first word of the jug entries in Ta641 with the Greek word δέπας 'cup, goblet' (*Il.* 11.632, etc.), which has no Indo-European connexions. The enthusiastic title of his article, "King Nestor's Four-handled Cups: Greek Inventories in the Minoan Script,"[57] of course went too far; but even the sober second thoughts of Chadwick (*Decipherment*, p. 82) labor under a fallacy. One part of the description of Nestor's goblet, οὔατα δ᾽ αὐτοῦ/ τέσσαρ᾽ ἔσαν 'its ears (handles) were four,' signifies merely that a δέπας could be big and heavy indeed: one man would be hard put to budge it from the table (ἄλλος μὲν μογέων ἀποκινήσασκε τραπέζης/ πλεῖον ἐόν, Νέστωρ δ᾽ ὁ γέρων ἀμογητὶ ἄειρεν, 11.636-637); obviously to carry it would take more than one woman attendant using both hands. This does not justify a presumption that *any* vessel heavy enough to need four handles might be called δέπας. The meaning of the word in Greek does not have nearly the range of fluctuation that we noted in φιάλη (see above, p. 85). δέπας in every Greek passage is something to drink from — granted that it may have been clumsy to sip from Nestor's four-handled one when it was full. Nothing in the drawings of the four-handled 07-03 or any other on the tablet suggests a vessel for drinking. Homer's description does not suit these drawings except for the number of handles; notably he mentions two stands or supports (δύω δ' ὑπὸ πυθμένες ἦσαν), whereas the drawings show none.

While δέπας does not fit the context of the Linear B tablet, an obscure Cypriotic word may possibly be made to fit. Conceivably we can detect a Greek word *διπας in the first three characters of a lost Cypriotic text, described as follows:

Inscription on a cylindrical alabastron (or alabaster vase), with downward flaring rim and small solid ears. From Golgoi. The vase went to England and was copied there, but it appears never to have reached America. It is here copied from General di Cesnola's notes in manuscript. The text is in one vertical line below one of the ears, apparently 2½ inches long. The vase was 11¾ inches high. The characters were apparently ⅝ inch high.

ti. pa. se. i. ti (or, *wo*). *to. te.*

A copy in [Moriz] Schmidt's *Sammlung kyprischer Inschriften* (Tafel xix, 4), and there attributed to Dr. Birch, omits the second *ti*, and reads

ti. pa. se? a. to. te.

The character here given as *se?* is a little doubtful, since in one of di Cesnola's manuscript copies it looks much like a mutilated *i*. Yet in his other copy it is a plain *se*. In the circumstances, the reading is a little uncertain.[58]

The text in Cypriotic characters was published only by Schmidt, and with no representation of the vase itself. I have not been able to locate any fuller description of the vase, nor any copy of it, published or unpublished, although the notice reads as if Cesnola's notebook contained one copy of the vase with the inscription and one of the inscription alone.[59] To judge from the description, "cylindrical" and "with downward flaring rim," the lost Cypriotic vase could not have looked much like the jugs of the Linear B tablet Ta641. Yet the vase and the jugs may have been more like each other than any vessel called δέπας in classical Greek. So, if *ti-pa-se* were the Cypriotic word for such a vase, it would tend to prove the correctness of Ventris's decipherment in regard to *07-03*. Deecke (p. 41, no. 102) proposed to interpret *ti-pa-se* as δίπας, but that leaves the rest of the characters of the inscription quite enigmatic. We do not know where any word boundary falls in this text; it remains unintelligible. We could not safely assume, contrary to the rule of vase inscriptions, that this one begins with a word designating what sort of object it is (see p. 101, note 46).

The upshot is that no evidence of Greek, either in the Greek alphabet or in the syllabic characters of Cyprus, confirms Ventris's transcription of *07-03* as *di-pa* and the corollary that *di-pa* means a jug of the shape shown in Ta641. The close graphic similarity of the Linear B character *03* to the Cypriotic *pa* (✝ or ✢) is what led Ventris to this valuation in the first place (see above, p. 23); and it invites us to look for Linear B words which the value *03 = pa* will demonstrably fit. But *07-03* is not such a word; nor do the many other occurrences of *03* afford any proof of the value *pa* in Linear B (see below, p. 125). Whatever led Ventris to the equation *07 = di* escapes me. He put it into the "vowel 1" column and a row all by itself near the bottom of the grid in its second state. That column was marked -*i* ? in the third state; but we still do not see how he figured out the consonantal component of the character. Since the discovery of Ta641, much effort has been spent — I might say, wasted — on the difference in sound between δέπας with *e* and *di-pa* with *i*, as though *07 = di* were a fact.[60]

Conclusions about Ta641. Although Ventris was understandably elated when he first saw a copy of the all-important tablet,[61] it behooves us to feel only moderately cheered by our exhaustive examination of it. Ventris's values for several characters are now established; of these, some would have remained hypothetical if not for the tripod-and-jug tablet. There would be no cause for disappointment, except that he and his supporters claimed too much for the decipherment, and the scholarly world at large granted too much, on the strength of this one text, all the while that a considerable part of the text remained obscure. No one, to be sure, insisted that the whole thing was clear; but it would have been more judicious to recognize that the Ventris transcription yields several Greek words but not a Greek text. Precisely eight words on the tablet are securely identified, the ones transcribed *ti-ri-po-de* 'tripods' in the first item, *ti-ri-po* 'tripod' in the second and third, *qe-to-ro-we* 'four-eared' in the fifth and seventh, *ti-ri-o-we-e* and *ti-ri-jo-we* 'three-eared' in the sixth and eighth respectively, and *a-no-we* 'earless' in the ninth. These were the words that impressed the mature, expert mind of Blegen when he first wrote the good news to Ventris, and these are still the only words whose meaning is secure. That makes one word to each item except the fourth. A decipherment that succeeds to such an extent cannot be overthrown; however defective it may be, part of it is surely right. But by a fallacy all too typical of men, and even of scholars, this verified part has been taken for a guarantee that the rest too is correct, most if not quite all of it. Yet twenty-two fully preserved words out of thirty remain in the dark. No two consecutive words can be read and understood; no two words that are construed together.

The eight separate words are secured by the clarity of the ideograms and give us less, not more information than the ideograms. We can see tripods of two kinds, the first with a deeper pot and needing to be lifted by two persons each using both hands; for the handles are larger and notched

(Beattie, *JHS*, LXXVI, 15). But we cannot read any such information in the verbal text.[62] We may hope that in other tablets the values verified in Ta641 will yield Greek texts at least a few words long, from which we can learn things that are not shown by the ideograms. The hope, however, is not achieved in any tablet I have studied, with a single exception that is not clear-cut (see below, pp. 111-2). On the other hand, Ta641 contains two words that are completely transcribed, but in vain: we do not know what to make of them. *78-05 qe-to* (or *te-to*) is the one-word caption beside the drawing of the amphora or pitcher; it is not identifiable with any Greek word. *11-45 po-de* occurs in the entry that begins *37-53-11 ti-ri-po*. It might have something to do with 'foot' or 'feet'; but nobody has made sense of the entry, apart from the initial word. I have verified all but two characters in Ventris's transcription of the four words

$$37\text{-}53\text{-}11 \quad 38\text{-}13 \quad 11\text{-}45 \quad 61\text{-}42\text{-}75$$
$$ti\text{-}ri\text{-}po \quad e\text{-}me \; po\text{-}de \; o\text{-}wo\text{-}we$$

They are *13 = me* and *42 = wo* (see below, pp. 109-10, 123). If we go along with Ventris's values of these two characters, we cannot extract any meaning from *e-me po-de o-wo-we* — not even by forcing *e-me*, as he does, to correspond to ἐνί. For his rendering 'with a *single* handle *on* one foot' is nonsense as a description of a tripod and is recognized by him to be contrary to the ideogram. On the other hand, if we decline to commit ourselves to any particular value for *13* and *42*, our liberty is not rewarded with other values that will give an adequate context for fitting in *po-de*. We are left with an uneasy feeling that the text may not be Greek, even though the one word *ti-ri-po* passes so well for Greek by itself. Of course we do not expect to read it right off like the Greek that we know from Homer and his successors; but these few Linear B words seem to be in a language so far from Greek that it resists our efforts to penetrate it.

Notes to Chapter IV

1. "A necessary corrective to Beattie's article in *MIO*, VI, 33-104," *Mitteilungen des Instituts für Orientforschung*, VII (1959), 180-83.

2. Beattie did not attempt to corroborate his suspicions by such methods, although he did make inferences discreditable to Ventris's character. Upon further study of the Work Notes, Beattie in *Saeculum*, X (1960), 373, revised his reconstruction: "In the light of this evidence I no longer suggest that a copy of Ta 641 was sent to *Ventris* by an unknown person at Pylos on or after 4th June 1952, and I no longer question 1st June 1952 as the date of Worknote 20. Instead I say that the words and ideograms of Ta 641 were known to *Ventris* at latest by 1st June 1951 and that Ta 641 itself or a similar tablet, still unknown, was found long before that." It seems to me that Beattie has gone off the track and quite misunderstood the workings of Ventris's mind, how he would sometimes linger inordinately on a point and sometimes bounce from one to another. That is the natural exuberance of a man who has nobody else to check the free range of his thoughts.

3. The fact that he wrote Work Note 20 so close to the time when Ta641 was unearthed, is not amazing psychologically. About nine months earlier, in Work Note 15 (p. 144), he had written, "Though it would evidently be better to wait until the 'GRID' can be further corrected by the full Knossos evidence, it is conceivable that some happy accident or intuition might lead to such a solution at any time now." Meanwhile, the Knosos material was published in *SM* II, and Ventris undoubtedly knew of the plan to resume excavations at Pylos in the late spring of 1952. Although a hasty look through *SM* II did not bring to Ventris's mind any compelling decipherment, an intelligent surmise would have told him that now there was need for just one more lucky find, such as the campaign at Pylos was likely to yield. If he wanted to achieve the decipherment himself before anyone else, it was a worthy ambition, and he would naturally put forth the keenest effort of thought under the urgency of winning a race. He was at an advantage in having almost perfectly mastered the Pylos material in *PT* (1951) through tireless sifting. So he could abstract the data necessary for sketching a decipherment in Work Note 20, and thus forestall the chance that some unmistakable key to decipherment might turn up in the current excavations and afford an easy opportunity for someone else to obtain the glory of solving the Linear

B script, without the great labors that Ventris had poured into it.

4. Except that a corner of the tablet which must have had the third tripod drawing is broken off and lost.

5. The curve in the Cypriotic *pe* goes the opposite way S from the Linear B character $\mathsf{2}$. However, Ventris had taken the Linear B character 75 for *pe* in "Languages" (p. [x]xv, item 33).

6. In the published grid of "Evidence" and *Documents*.

7. The value *to* is not — in spite of Chadwick, *Decipherment*, p. 93 — substantiated by Sh736 (Pylos):

$$05\text{-}60\text{-}44 \quad 08\text{-}13\text{-}57\text{-}05 \quad 61\text{-}03 \quad 13\text{-}17\text{-}06 \quad 42\text{-}45 \quad 24\text{-}08 \overset{\bullet}{\underset{\bullet}{}}$$

followed by a damaged ideogram and number. The ideogram is restored by Bennett — see *PT* (1955), pp. 86, 185 — as a CORSLET; but Beattie, *MIOF*, VI, 48-49, has exposed the futility of making the first word *to-ra-ke* (θώρᾱκες). The other tablets assigned to the Sh series have an undamaged ideogram on the left (contrary to the usual layout of a Linear B tablet). To identify even the undamaged ideogram as a CORSLET is only a possibility, not a necessity; moreover it is never accompanied by *05-60-44*. Not one word of Sh736 occurs on any other Sh tablet; I wonder that Bennett saw enough similarity to warrant classifying this tablet as Sh. Ventris, *Documents*, p. 379, could not make sense of it. It must not be cited as evidence for *05 = to*, or for *60 = ra, 44 = ke*.

8. "MT" (1958), pp. 50-51, 78, 106; and *Documents*, p. 179.

9. It is probably just a coincidence that on the Pylos tablet, where the character *78* occurs in a word accompanying four-handled jugs, it consists graphically of a circle with *four* short horizontal lines inside, while on the Mycenae tablet, where it serves as an enclitic suffix 'and' linking two words, it consists of a circle with *two* somewhat longer horizontal lines. The difference in the number of strokes could very well be nothing ideographic but just a peculiarity of the individual scribe. The character with four inside strokes is found in a Mycenae tablet Ue611.3,r1, written by a different scribe; "MT" (1958), pp. 74-75, 91.

10. So do the one-word entries that are followed by the ideogram and the numeral ‖ or ⫼.

11. Lang, *AJA*, LXII, 183.

12. Doubtless for the sake of uniformity a two-letter transcription *qe* was preferred to *que* or *kwe*.

13. I postpone until pp. 220-5 the problem of the final -ς.

14. In Greek this -δε means '-ward' or 'to.'

15. From Jn415 we can safely go on to infer the correctness of the total $\frac{2}{2}$ —II [12 double minae] in Jn845, where it is also introduced by 05-12-45 77-70 ⊫ and the eight items above are each $\frac{2}{2}$ I # II; one $\frac{2}{2}$ must equal four # .

16 The omission of -n at the end of a syllable accords with the Cypriotic rule; but the omission at the end of a word does not, nor does the omission of -s or -i in either circumstance. See below, pp. 218-32.

17. First noted by Kober, AO, XVIIᵃ, 390. In As1517.10 the second character of the word, following 05, has an abnormal shape which precludes any definite identification; the ideogram is a seated human figure, not the typical MAN. In As1516.11,19 the two characters 05-12 are followed by a peculiar kind of ideographic mark X before the MAN ideogram. It occurs on many other tablets, almost always in the vicinity of a large number; hence it is inferred to be a check mark. Documents, p. 171, copies it with a bit of stylization that makes it look like the familiar 'times' sign x; KT (1956 and 1959) still more amusingly makes it x, as though it were an algebraic symbol for an 'unknown.' Since 05-12-45 is one of the most copiously recorded words from Pylos — Bennett, PT (1955), pp. 206-7 — it is strange not to find it at all in Knosos.

In both As1516 and 1517 there is a problem of counting: to get the correct total it is necessary to ignore a numeral I in the top line. In C912 (joined to 5027, Knosos) 05-12 accompanies a number too small to be the correct total for the items on both sides of the tablet, and too big for just the items on the same side as 05-12.

18. The Greek word for this is κεφάλαιον (IG² 1.374.255,259,293, etc.).

19. The "third declension" dual ending -ε has no Indo-European cognates either, but the plural ending -ες has some.

20. In the lines following 05-12-45 in Jn310.7,11, 389.11, Documents (pp. 353-354) fails to transcribe the repeated ideographic numeral I which Ventris apparently mistook for the word-divider. Both marks are simply a vertical line; but the word-divider I is short and nearly on a level with the lower part of the phonetic characters, while the numeral I is long and on a level with their upper and middle parts.

21. Ventris in Documents, p. 319, and KT (1956) indicated damage that left the reading 05-31 doubtful. Browning in KT [1955] had

not indicated damage; nor had Ventris in "Evidence," p. 92. Bennett
kindly looked up for me his photograph and notes, and reported that
the ideogram and the number 149 are not found on the same piece as
05-31. Paradoxically the two characters 05-31 showed up quite legibly
before the pieces were joined, but afterwards less so.

22. The identification of the ideogram ⚦ as MAN and 𝝠
as WOMAN would admit of some doubt, were it not that the latter
often in the Knosos tablets (though not in this one) has two dots
representing breasts. Minoan art has familiarized us with the remarkable costume that left the woman's bosom bare while she was
otherwise fully dressed. The WOMAN ideogram in the Pylos tablets
never has the two dots; perhaps the costume of that place was
different in at least one striking aspect from that of Knosos in the
period of the tablets.

23. 05-31-45 is frequent in Pylos texts (but not in Knosos; cf.
above, note 17) and occurs regularly in the vicinity of a numeral;
but nowhere does it indicate a total, except perhaps in Vn10.

24. The meaning of 05-12 will be further studied below (pp.
143-50).

25. Similarly 28-32, the initial word above it, stands well to the
left of the three equine heads on the first line. See *Documents*, pp.
210-11 and pl. II.

All identifiable heads of animals in Linear B ideograms face right.

26. The *po-ro* head in the first line is broken off in such a way
that we cannot prove whether or not there was any indication of a
mane.

27. "The Knossos Horse and Foal Tablet (Ca895)," *Bulletin of the
Institute of Classical Studies of the University of London*, II (1955),
1-3. He read the word 61-52 (in Ventris's transcription *o-no*) as the
Greek ὄνοι but did not then notice any indication of long ears.

28. Grumach, *OLZ*, LII, 340-341, further objected that — as Chadwick himself had recognized — 61-52 occurs in many other contexts
not connected with asses. But that is no serious embarrassment in
the case of such a short word, consisting of frequent sounds; another
word of quite different meaning — a homophone or homograph of
the word for 'ass' — is likely enough. If we were to find a long word
such as 08-39-11-27-75 (transcribed *a-pi-po-re-we*) not only with an
amphora drawing but also with a horse head, that would indeed show
that the decipherment had gone astray.

29. The damage to the third ideogram does not affect the place

on the neck where a sex symbol would be marked. The numeral, however, is lost. Which of the sex symbols stands for MALE was determined by Kober, *AO*, XVII[a], 398, through the presence of 05-12, the masculine word for 'total,' near the animal ideogram in C912.r2, Dw1213 (Knosos) and of 05-31, the feminine, near the corresponding ideogram in C918 (Knosos).

30. An22 in *PT* (1951), p. 13.

31. See *Documents*, pp. 21-22. The resulting vacancy in the *i* square was filled with 28, apparently for no better reason than to read 03-28-05 as *pa-i-to* (the Cretan city Φαιστός), 03-28-37-36 and 03-28-37-57 as its ethnic derivatives *pa-i-ti-jo* (masculine) and *pa-i-ti-ja* (feminine). In placing 28 there, he ignored the violation of the very criterion which had previously inclined him to equate 61 with *i*. 28 = *i* makes a *Cii* sequence in 61-39-28-57-39, transcribed *o-pi-i-ja-pi*, a word frequent in the Knosos chariot tablets (Sd0401, etc.). Homeric instances like ἐπίστορα 'experienced, acquainted' (*Od.* 21.26), Διί (*Il.* 1.578, etc.) are not really parallel to *o-pi-i-*; for a digamma [-w-], omitted in our written text of Homer, can be posited in these words, while Ventris had a separate row of *w*-characters set up. When ἐπι- is prefixed to a morpheme that begins with ι, the ι of the prefix is regularly elided, as in ἐπιϊών 'coming up, approaching' (*Il.* 18.546; cf. 5.238, 13.836, *Od.* 16.42). Since the ι of περι- is not normally subject to elision, the -ιϊ- sequence would arise, least infrequently in the participle περιϊών 'going around.' But the meter of comedy and the spelling of papyri (and of good codices to a considerable degree) favor the single -ι- rather than the double -ιϊ- (Liddell-Scott-Jones, *Greek-English Lexicon*, s.v. περίειμι) — even though the single -ι- entails homophony with περιών 'surviving, remaining.' περίαχε 'it rang around' (Hesiod, *Th.* 678) exhibits the same tendency.

32. Customarily transcribed *ve*, although we have no ground for supposing a pronunciation [ve] rather than [we] in Cypriotic. Ventris never noted this resemblance of 75 to the Cypriotic *we*; for he had his eye rather on the Cypriotic *pe* (see above, note 5). The consonant- and vowel-affinities of 75 were set by him in the second state of the grid.

33. Beattie's objection (*JHS*, LXXVI, 13) — that the Mycenaean form would have had to exhibit a diphthong *ou* (-*o-u*- in Ventris's transcription) — depends upon an Indo-European prototype *-ōus-es, containing the diphthong. But how such a sequence, if indeed it

existed, would have behaved in its Greek evolution, is unfathomable.

34. A comparison with the Latin *auris* by no means proves that the vowel written ου in οὖς is a "genuine" diphthong. On the contrary it is spelled ΟΣ in Attic inscriptions (*IG*² 1.372.201, 1.319.6), where it means 'ear' in the figurative sense of an architectural ornament.

35. Beattie, *JHS*, LXXVI, 13, expressed surprise that the negative prefix should correspond to ἀν- rather than ἀ-, since late Greek authors give ἄουτος 'deaf' (Hesychius), ἄωτος 'without handles' (Philetas, Plutarch, etc.). But he points out further that Homer has both ἄουτος and ἀνούτατος as synonyms in the sense of 'unwounded.' Besides, the ἀν- ~ ἀ- alternation has Sanskrit parallels. So there is nothing amiss in *an-* before a vowel, at any stage of the Greek language.

36. The Etruscan and Oscan alphabet has no letter O but uses V or V̇ instead. See "Languages," pp. xii-xiii.

37. In that item on the suffix -*13-06* ~ -*13-52* he noted "a similar, unexplained, alternation . . . in the Knossos 'chariot' tablets." This had been discovered by Kober, "Evidence of Inflection in the 'Chariot' Tablets from Knossos," *AJA*, XLIX (1945), 143-151. The usefulness of her presentation was unhappily lessened by a graphic confusion between *06* and *36*. Their typical shapes are 帚 and ㄅ respectively; but the scribe or scribes of the chariot tablets shaped them somewhat differently, 𐃌 and ㄅ , and 𐃌 was several times mistaken by her (and later by Bennett in the Vocabulary of *SM* II) for *36*. Bennett has explained to me in a letter that through his more recent palaeographical study he can discriminate between the *06* and the *36* of any given scribe. Ventris, without any comparable scrutiny of the Knosos tablets, escaped the pitfall: he never supposed that *52* and *36* had the same consonant.

38. Work Note 15, p. 144, and the second state of the grid. It is listed in the table immediately preceding the grid (line 50), but I have not located the words containing it in the Work Notes, nor in the Index to *PT* (1951), which he undoubtedly used.

39. Deecke, pp. 27-30, no. 60.3,20. In the first example Deecke's wrong evaluation of the fifth character 𐙶 as *ji* was corrected to *vi* (i.e., *wi*) by Meister, pp. 132, 155, and Hoffmann, p. 68, no. 135. That the next character Ο really contains a consonant *j* (like *y* in *yarn, yard*, etc.) is corroborated by the bilingual inscription no. 59.1 (Deecke, p. 26; *Corpus inscriptionum Semiticarum* 1.89.1), in which the Phoenician name מלכיתן becomes in Cypriotic Greek *mi-li-ki-ja-*

to-no-se (with the Greek genitive ending -ος); for ϝ can hardly stand for any sound in Phoenician or Hebrew but the semivocalic consonant *j*. See Johannes Friedrich, *Phönizisch-punische Grammatik*, Analecta Orientalia 32 (Rome, 1951), p. 25; Meister, p. 242.

40. Cf. the *o* in *o-ru-xe* (= Attic ὀρύξη) '[if anyone] digs'; Deecke, pp. 27-28, no. 60.1,12.

41. The few alleged exceptions in Cypriotic are accounted for by Hoffmann, pp. 37-38, 191-92.

42. "MT" (1958), pp. 64-65, 79, 108. Words written as just a single character are extremely rare in Linear B. *Documents*, pp. 227-28, inaccurately reports this instance of *36* as part of a word *jo-o-po-ro*.

43. It is indistinct in Og0467, on account of damage to the tablet. Browning's edition of *KT* [1955], p. 82, does not indicate it at all, and *SM* II shows only a blur. I wonder whether the subsequent editors of *KT* were influenced by the desire to obtain a Greek word: since the clearly visible characters of the second word are *07-14-*, transcribed *di-do-*, the addition of *-41* makes διδοῦσι 'they give' (*Od.* 1.313, etc.).

44. Not Indo-European; on the ια ~ ιε variation see Schwyzer, I, 243.

45. Helene Miltner in *RE*, XXIX, 2059-2062; Heinz Luschey in *RE*, Supplementband VII, 1026-1030; E. Pottier in Daremberg-Saglio, *Dictionnaire des antiquités grecques et romaines*, s.v. "Phiala."

46. Recognized in *Documents*, p. 324: "The connexion of classical Greek vessel-names with classical shapes is itself to some extent a matter of guesswork . . ."

47. Ventris's transcription calls for *di-pa-e* and *di-pa*, which he tried in vain to connect with the neuter noun δέπας (see above, p. 90).

48. Albert Cuny, *Le nombre duel en grec* (Paris, 1906), pp. 67-68, 78-82, 88 ff., 487 ff.

49. *07-03* in K740 (Knosos), as Chadwick noted ("New Fragments," p. 149), is followed by a drawing of a vessel and the numeral ☰ ' (i.e., 31). He explains that in this tablet the scribe twice neglected to show a plural ending!

50. Jn310 = 693, 320, 389, 415, 478, 601, 692, 750, 845. Also in the first line of a later paragraph on several tablets, Jn310.14, 431+433.16, 725.18 (erased). In Jn725.1 the formula occurs, but

the whole paragraph has nothing ideographic except the numeral I
following most of the words.

51. Jn310.7, 389.11, 413.6, 415.9, 431+433.9,22, 478.9 (only one
subsequent word), 601.11, 692.4. In Jn750.12, 845.10 the third word
of the formula is omitted; in 693.10 both the first and the third,
leaving the essential one *08-59-60-41-36*. See above, note 20.

52. See *Documents,* pp. 352-55. In classical Greek ταλασία refers
exclusively to women's work — i.e., spinning (Xenophon, *Mem.* 3.9.11,
etc.); and no adjective *ἀταλάσιος occurs. In support of the meaning
'allocation' for *59-60-41-57*, applicable to a smith's work, Ventris
noted the etymology of ταλασία from τάλαντον, and compared *pēnsum*
'weighed out,' the Latin equivalent to ταλασία. The validity of this is
not my present concern, because neither the transcription *ta-ra-si-ja*
nor the rendering 'allocation' can be established by the ideographic
context, as *08-* = *a-* 'without' can be.

53. The only evidence that any of them may be a place name
is that *08-44-27-54* of the Jn tablets (310.1, 693.1, 725.23) has an
alternant *08-44-27-54-45* in Vn20.8. The other items on the latter
tablet, from the third line on, all have the same suffix *-45*. We have
taken it to be *-de* (see above, p. 71), which according to Greek
morphology is freely attached — at least in Homeric usage — to
nouns of place, but to very few other nouns. Still Ventris's interpretation of the whole tablet Vn20 (*Documents,* pp. 348-49) is quite
unconvincing: if it is really about the distribution of wine (*42-52*)
to certain towns (*-45*), why does a numeral come after each *-45*
with no ideogram of liquid measure in between?

54. The interpretation that on the Jn tablets the items under
the heading are (apart from the ideograms) men's names was confirmed by the 1957 excavation, in which An1281 was dug up with
two noteworthy lines (see above, p. 69):

| An1281.3 | *03-77 27-10-41-42-78* | MAN II [i.e., 2] |
| An1281.5 | *61-06-09-10 59-30-70-78* | MAN II [i.e., 2] |

27-10-41-42 was already known from Jn692.6 (and 725.19, erased),
61-06-09-10 from Jn601.6, 658.5, 725.4.

55. The first state of the grid, in Work Note 1, put it into the
fifth row, with no specified consonant. However, the third state made
it *ve* ? *re* ? See Grumach, *Gnomon,* XXXII, 683, note 3.

56. At that, *o-pi* (unknown in Greek) is more common in Linear
B than *e-pi*, either as a separate word or at the beginning of longer
words.

102

57. *Archaeology,* VII (1954), 15-21.

58. Louis P. di Cesnola, *A Descriptive Atlas of the Cesnola Collection of Cypriote Antiquities in the Metropolitan Museum of Art, New York,* Vol. III (Boston: Osgood, 1903), part V, no. 17 in supplement following Plate CXLI. The notice of the lost vase was obviously not written by Cesnola himself; we owe the substance and much of the wording to Isaac H. Hall, who had previously published it in "The Cypriote Inscriptions of the Cesnola Collection in New York," *Journal of the American Oriental Society,* XI (1885), 229.

59. Mr. Dietrich von Bothmer, curator of Greek and Roman art at the Metropolitan Museum, courteously informed me that the Museum does not have Cesnola's notebooks. I am left with no clue to the whereabouts of any sketch of the vase, if any still exists.

60. N. Platon objected in Κρητικά Χρονικά, VIII (1954), 161, that the character in Ta641 is not *07* but *06* (*na*). No subsequent author has agreed with his identification, but the negative side of it deserves more attention. ₸ was the standard shape of *07*, on the basis of the Knosos tablets and those from Pylos published in *PT* (1951). In Ta641 and many other Pylos tablets copied in *PT* (1955) we find a character ₸ with three short horizontal lines instead of three short vertical ones right below the longer horizontal top line. Regardless of the phonetic value *di*, I am curious to see the proof that these are variant shapes of the same character.

61. Chadwick, *Decipherment,* p. 81.

62. Palmer interprets *43-44-10*, which is transcribed *ai-ke-u* and accompanies the larger tripod ideogram, as 'with goat's head handles' and *61-42-75* (*o-wo-we*) in the next item as 'with handles' — i.e., with ordinary handles (*Gnomon,* XXIX, 577). But the whole attempt to read the two items, except for the first word in each, is desperate and contravenes the rules of Greek at every point. See *Documents,* pp. 336-37, for a few of the many objections that ought to be raised.

CHAPTER V

OBJECTIVE DEMONSTRATION
WITH TABLETS OTHER THAN Ta641

BESIDES the phonetic values that we have already, with or without reservations, shown to be established, several more can be established with some degree of reliability. We have not exhausted the ideographic data that can contribute to the decipherment, but what remains is of supplementary rather than primary importance.

70 = *ko*. The identification *38* = *e* depended on the meaning 'have' or the like in *38-70-04* and *38-70-41* (see above, pp. 87-9). But we cannot uphold an equivalence to ἐχο- unless we corroborate *70* = *ko* in one other word at least. A good case is found in S8100 (Knosos): *70-26* followed by what looks like a drawing of a helmet.[1] The drawing is not, like most ideograms, set off toward the right edge of the tablet, nor is it bigger than either phonetic character. Strictly speaking, we should consider it a determinative rather than an ideogram. Jane E. Henle criticized Ventris for overlooking the distinction normally made in ancient Near Eastern texts, except for those written purely in a phonetic alphabet.[2] I know very little about the cuneiform and Egyptian writing systems; so far as I understand, a word written out phonetically can only be supplemented by a small nonphonetic sign, called a determinative and not to be pronounced. If a large nonphonetic sign, called an ideogram, is used, it will be accompanied by no more than one phonetic character, or at any rate not by a complete word. Ideograms thus supplemented are numerous in the Aegean area texts; on the other hand, words supplemented by determinatives are rare — unhappily for us in our desire to decipher the script. A writing system that mixes phonetic and nonphonetic signs confesses itself unable to make either means of writing adequate. It seems to me doubtful, *a priori*, whether or not the Linear texts (A as well as B) should be assumed to follow the Near Eastern practice which was opposed to the writing of words in phonetic characters that only repeat or anticipate what is shown in ideograms. But in S8100, anyhow, we cannot object to the redundancy on the ground that the helmet is an ideogram. As a determinative it is irreproachable, and precious for the purpose of justifying the transcription *ko-ru* (κόρυς, *Il.* 12.184, etc.; a word without a clear Indo-European etymology). The only aspect that we must question is why only this word has a determinative while the others on the tablet are followed by numerals.[3] The rest of the tablet admits of only a conjectural interpretation, which at best leaves unexplained the need for a determinative with one word but not with the others.

Ventris placed *70* on its square in the second state of the grid. The only other character in the row was *44* (*ke*), besides the reduced one *74*, which was removed to another row in "Evidence."[4] He adduced two reasons for detecting a consonant common to *70* and *44:* the alternation between *77-70* and *77-44-75* in the Jn tablets (Work Note 14, p. 121, item P 153; see above, p. 87) and the one between *38-70-41* and *38-44-41* in En74.2,12,21, etc. (Work Note 9, p. 74, item C 6). The former alternation he had registered in the abortive first state of the grid (Work Note 1, p. 6, item 18); at that time he remarked, "Not necessarily the same word."

Small as the connexion was between the two characters, he clung to it, with a mere guess about the identity of the consonant, h- ?? in the first state, $^h/\chi$- ? θ- ? in the third, until he finally tried out k- in Work Note 20.

$54 = wa$, $42 = wo$ (*tentative*). 70-54 and 70-42 are among the most frequent words in the Knosos and Pylos tablets alike. Because both of them occur with numerals so often after the WOMAN ideograms (which also have a numeral) and 70-42 but not 70-54 often after the MAN ideogram, it is natural though not inevitable to go along with Ventris and take 70-54 for 'girls' or 'daughters' and 70-42 for 'boys' or 'sons' (Work Note 11, p. 40; Work Note 14, p. 119, item P 138). Since the tablets with 70-42 after MAN are all from Pylos, Evans did not know of them and guessed the opposite about the sex of 70-54 and 70-42. The prior one (70-54) seemed to him to refer naturally to boys, and the other to girls, all the more because the shape $\bar{A}$ of 42 is reminiscent of the WOMAN ideogram (*PM*, IV[b], 708-9). I can add that the shape $\boxed{T}$ of 54 includes two horizontal lines, which elsewhere add the meaning MALE to several ideograms, no less than one of the nearly vertical strokes in $\bigwedge$ adds the meaning FEMALE (see above, p. 77; *Documents*, pp. 49-52). Furthermore, 70 itself, with its shape $\mathbf{8}$, could be an ideogram for CHILD, because it is always decidedly shorter than the MAN ideogram of the Ad tablets and the tall WOMAN ideogram $\mathring{A}$ of the Ab series from Pylos;[5] the top circle would then represent the relatively large head of a child.[6] But these graphic reminiscences are incomplete and liable to be illusory.[7] They would be irrelevant if we were satisfied that the evidence imposes a phonetic function upon the second character of these two words as well as upon the first character, 70, which we can tolerably well establish to be ko in the words for 'helmet' and 'having.'[8] While 70-54 and 70-42 occur within the ideographic section of the tablets, yet the side-by-side arrangement of the characters 70-54 or 70-42 implies that they serve to spell out a word phonetically; for no two ideographic characters are juxtaposed in this manner.[9]

The word for 'girls' in Attic is κόραι, for 'boys' κόροι; but the Homeric forms κοῦραι, κοῦροι (*Il.* 6.420, 1.470, etc.) point to an original sequence κορϝ-, which is actually recorded in the Arcadian (?) form KOPFAI (*IG* 5.2.554, dative singular feminine). The words have no plausible Indo-European cognates. Ventris's transcription *ko-wa* for 70-54, *ko-wo* for 70-42 is attractive but should still be regarded as tentative. The proof of gender, from occurrence in the neighborhood of the WOMAN and MAN ideograms, leaves some reasonable doubt, simple though it is to group both girls and boys with women but only boys with men. No more direct ideographic evidence for the values *wa* and *wo* can be adduced from any other tablets to corroborate Ventris's theory about these two words. The social and familial organization of that Aegean culture is guesswork for us; and the transcription *ko-wo* does not go far enough toward explaining the *double* use of 70-42 in the Ad tablets from Pylos. These are the ones that typically end with

MAN numeral   70-42 numeral

but 70-42 also occurs before MAN, never with a word-divider ﹐ separating it from what Bennett, followed by Ventris, took to be the previous word.[10] Objectively we should regard -70-42 (occurring before MAN) as the end of a long compound word. The former member of the compound usually recurs in an Aa or Ab tablet as a distinct word right before the WOMAN ideogram. The alternation appears in two different patterns, the more frequent of which is typified by the following example:

Ab578   50-02 72-67-37-76   WOMAN^{t} |||| 70-54 || 70-42 ||

Ad694   72-67-37-76-61-70-42   MAN || 70-42 |||

According to this prevalent pattern, *61* (*o*) is inserted between the feminine form and *70-42*. In a few other cases,
however, the feminine word receives the addition *70-42* with
no *61* in between, e.g.,[11]

Aa804   08-39-32-02 WOMAN^{s} ≡ || 70-54 ≡ ||| 70-42 ⁻ |||

Ad690 50-02-08-39-32-02-70-42 MAN ⁻   70-42 |¦   61 MAN|||

Ventris identified the two classes of nouns, here exemplified
by *72-67-37-76* and *08-39-32-02*, with the "first" and "second
declension" respectively, which in Homeric Greek have the
endings

nominative plural   -αι   -οι
genitive plural   -άων -ων.

The "first declension" genitive plural would thus be one
syllable longer than the nominative plural, and the extra
syllable is accounted for by the character *61 = o* Ventris's
interpretation would fit the structure of Greek excellently if
we had any right to regard *72-67-37-76-61-70-42* (and other
sequences that end in *-61-70-42*) as two words. But a compound word whose first member is genitive plural is utterly
foreign to Greek.[12]

    We ought to allow some leeway, because word bound-
aries are not altogether set in any language, and because the
Linear B language is not presumed to be identical with
Greek — quite apart from the possibility of scribal vagaries
in the tablets. Still, the explanation of *61*, in the Ad tablets,
as a genitive plural suffix is inconclusive because none of
these words with *61* occur in any other series of Linear B
texts, where we might hope to show they are separate words

serving in a genitive plural function. A few of the occurrences in Ad tablets are not followed immediately by 70-42. Thus, while six tablets have 53-24-57-61-70-42 (Ad295, 670, 672, 678, 687, 697), another has 53-24-57-61-08-64-57-61-70-42 (Ad326), and still another has 74-29-60-61-70-42-53-24-57-61 (Ad664). The last one shows that the feminine word from the Aa or Ab tablets, when suffixed with 61, does not absolutely need the further suffix 70-42 right after it. But the converse is not thereby established; 70-42 cannot do without a predecessor taken mainly from the vocabulary of the Aa or Ab texts and usually enlarged with 61. The absence of the word-divider implies, at least, a formulaic relation between 70-42 and what precedes it, making the expression into a sort of surname 'Flaxwomen's-sons,' etc. But this is no more than a hypothesis, until the Aa and Ab words that recur in the Ad tablets are read with greater success than Ventris obtained.[13] Meanwhile we cannot safely decide whether the Ad set refers to men and boys that are the sons of groups of women from the other two sets. Consequently we are not ready to ratify the equations $42 = wo$, $54 = wa$. These crucial tablets are far from being adequately interpreted, and no others enable us to pin down values for 42 or 54 with certainty (see below, p. 144).[14] We cannot even rule out altogether the possibility that the Ad series contains masculine derivatives of which 70-42 is properly no phonetic part but rather an unpronounced determinative.

As late as the third state of the grid, Ventris had not put 42 into the -*o* ? column, but instead put it all by itself with "v[owel] 4," whose sound he did not guess at. Yet he had noted the "genitive" use in several tablets, alternating with non-"genitive" uses of 75 and 10 (Work Note 14, p. 104, items P 47, 49; p. 110, item P 79; p. 117, item P 129; p. 121, item P 152). 54 he settled in the -*a* ? column not only in the third state of the grid, but already in the second. My acceptance of

Ventris's value 75 = *we* (see above, pp. 78-9) does not commit me to 42 = *wo* on the basis of the alternations between the two characters. The argument for *wo* is that 42 occurs at the end of nouns in the genitive function, corresponding to -(ϝ)οϲ in Greek. But by the same argument, 75 occurs at the end of nouns in another oblique-case function, and -*we* will not square with the Greek datives that end in -(ϝ)ι or the accusatives in -(ϝ)α. The evidence does not demonstrate that the Linear B words ending in -42 belong to a declension related to the Greek declension whose genitive singular ends in -(ϝ)οϲ. The alternation does not establish the consonant of 42 any more than the vowel. Even a case like 75-01-24-42 alternating with 75-01-24-75, where there may be no semantic difference (see below, p. 133, note 14), does not argue that 42 and 75 differ in their vowel but share a consonant. That principle was indeed Ventris's working hypothesis as he constructed the grid.[15] But the Linear B material is not obliged to bear him out. Proof is needed, but none has been found, that the relation between the two signs is that they share a consonant but differ vocalically, 42 having -*o* instead of the -*e* of 75.

26 = *ru* (*provisionally acceptable*), 28-32 = *i-qo* (*unsettled*). Ventris gave the value *ru* to 26 in Work Note 20, just to make the word 08-60-26-57 come out *a-ra-ru-ja* (see above, p. 36). His procedure on that occasion does not inspire confidence; but two better cases have come up in tablets not available to him then. One is 70-26 accompanying an apparent but not quite incontestable determinative, HELMET see above, p. 105). The other depends on a more indirect argument of necessary supplementation.

The first line of Ta722 (Pylos; *Documents*, p. 345) contains three successive words that consist mainly of characters we have validated earlier in our study, 08-05-02-32 28-32-78

11-26-11-45-78. Ventris's transcription and interpretation of this and related tablets incur many difficulties apart from these three words and have, indeed, no solid foundation.[16] Nevertheless, -78 at the end of successive words is likely to be the 'and' suffix (see above, p. 69); and 28-32 we have met before as the word for 'horse(s).' To be sure, Ventris's 28 = *i* entails a clash with normal Greek phonology (see above, p. 99, note 31); but in no event could we prudently count upon the Linear B language to share with Greek the odd vowel ι in this word, which no Indo-European cognate throws light upon.[17] The Linear B distinction between 32 and 11 — the latter in *po-ro* 'foals,' etc. — is not maintained in Greek: ἵππος, πῶλος (see above, p. 66). We can adopt Ventris's transcription *qo* for 32 on the understanding that it does not commit us to one particular phonetic interpretation — such as that 32 has to be [kʷo]. So far we have only a hypothesis that the Linear B 28-32 is cognate to the word for 'horse' in Greek, Latin, Sanskrit, etc.; but it becomes more convincing when we look at the preceding word in Ta722. *08-05-02-32* becomes *a-to-ro-qo*; and if the last character had been obliterated by damage, it would still be very tempting to take the two words for 'man and horse.' Even at this point we are short of meeting the conditions for proof by supplementation (see above, pp. 48, 67); we need more to show that the 'and' suffix of 28-32-78 connects it closely with the previous word. But the following two words *11-26-11-45-78* *11-30-44-78* end the same way; so Greek syntax encourages us to regard this as a series of four.

Moreover the third one, *11-26-11-45-78*, calls for a transcription something like Ventris's *po-ru-po-de-qe*. Although I hesitated over the value 45 = *de* (see above, p. 74), the two characters -*11-45* do beyond doubt express the meaning 'foot' or 'feet' in *37-53-11-45* 'tripods.' Now in *11-26-11-45-78*, between *po-* and the part of the word that means 'foot,' we can use a syllable that will make a credible Greek word. One syllable only will fit, producing the Greek word πολυποδ- 'many-footed' — i.e., 'poulp, octopus.' Both parts of this compound word have clear Indo-European cognates; the etymology of ἄνθρωπος, however, is problematical. 'Man and horse and poulp' or 'men and horses and poulps' (not to mention the next word *11-30-44-78*, which remains obscure) make a plausible group only in some fantastic context — presumably as the figures comprising a decoration rather than as the ingredients of a stew. Here we have a case where the value of a Linear B character is confined by a context which will not tolerate any other value — provided only that the words can be safely taken to be either Greek or in a tractable relation to Greek. That the context would have to be fantastic weakens the demonstration somewhat;[18] and outside of the immediate context of these few words, the tablet is obscure — which hinders us from feeling as safe with the equation 26 = *ru* as we are with the values supported by unmistakable drawings. Ventris's rendering of the other words in this line and the rest of the tablet is a tissue of conjectures beyond the range of verification.

The relation between *32* and *78* has not been satisfactorily clarified. They alternate in *43-37-36-32* ~ *43-37-36-78* on Eo247, while the former word also occurs on other Pylos tablets (Eb156.2, 846.1, En74.11,12 Ep301.2). This apparently was Ventris's sole reason, in the second state of the grid, for placing the two characters in the same row. In the third state their columns were designated *-o* ? and *-e* ? respectively.[19] He treated the alternation as parallel to the one between *42* and *75* (see below, note 14): the vowel *-o* ? indicates the genitive case, the vowel *-e* ? a different case, which occurs after the frequent word *03-02*.[20] Ventris had to override a difficulty which he had perceived as early as Work Note 9 (p. 73, item B 5): at the end of the third line

112

of Eo247 the last character in 43-37-36-32 was erased and 78 written over it. He remarked, "The construction probably demands - $\frac{11}{1}$ [-32] (Case 2 [= genitive]) as in line 1. This has apparently been changed to conform visually with the - ☉ [-78] of the adjacent lines, where the name is governed by ‡ ✝ [03-02]."

The audacity of Ventris's presumption leaves me gasping. A person in Pylos long ago, accustomed to the Linear B script and language, took the trouble to erase a character and write another over it. Someone else three thousand years later, ignorant of the language and hoping to find the material for a decipherment, judges that the mistake consisted in changing what was right in the first place. In *Documents* (p. 248) Ventris made a similar unscholarly comment on the erasure: "The scribe's original *Ai-ti-jo-qo* (gen.) in line 3 is of course correct; it appears to have been altered to *-qe* under the influence of the *Ai-ti-jo-qe* which occurs (correctly) in all the other entries." His "of course" in 1956 is as unwarranted as his "probably" in 1951. How are we to say when a mistake has been made in the use of a language, either spoken or written?[21] Either we must be masters of the language, knowing the norm of it ourselves; or we must observe what the insiders are not willing to let pass but see fit to correct. Now a few of us have mastered classical Greek, but nobody should pretend to be a master of Linear B, when many Linear B texts are admitted to be still incomprehensible. As for learning from the natives what mistakes are sometimes made, Ventris has done just the opposite: he professes to detect the rare case where a deliberate correction is erroneous. This amounts to vitiating the material that the decipherment needs to take into account, and we must not follow Ventris when he rejects the data.[22] Let us confess, with Socrates, "What I don't know, I don't think I know." When the decipherment does not fit the Linear B data, we are not to say that here is one more case where the data are incorrect.[23] It does us no good to reflect that the Linear B tablets in all probability contain errors like any other extensive body of texts; this just adds to the difficulty of deciphering them. For in general we cannot tell where the errors lie.[24] We are obviously begging the question if we argue that the decipherment is right where it goes along with the text but the text is wrong where it goes against the decipherment. A decipherer's success depends on the luck of hitting upon a sufficient amount of text written with no errors that fundamentally impede decipherment.[25]

The occurrence of 32 in alternation with 78 on the tablet Eo247 is such as to leave the phonetic relation between the two characters quite uncertain. Whereas -78 corresponds to the Greek τε that has labiovelar cognates (-*que* in Latin), we are not entitled to assert that 32 differed from it in having a back vowel (Greek πο with labiovelar cognates). Even in the horse tablet (Ca895), where the very simple context seems to require that 28-32 should be nominative plural, I now doubt whether we can properly posit a back vowel in the ending, as in the Greek -οι. The corresponding nominative plural in pre-classical Latin has the -EI ending; e.g., VIREI 'men' (*CIL*[2] 1.581.19). Our information about Linear B is too meager to settle anything about the vowel in 32. The words 08-05-02-32 28-32-78 in the "footstool" tablet Ta722 leave us just as uncertain, because their construction is obscure. Ventris understands it as instrumental, like the Greek dative, dependent on a preceding word 08-57-13-52, which he transcribes *a-ja-me-no* and infers to mean 'inlaid (with).' Nothing in Greek or any other Indo-European language confirms his interpretation. That does not prove him wrong; but both the transcription and the meaning of *a-ja-me-no* need to be verified before it can be used to prove anything about the case of other words in the tablet.[26]

41 = si (*doubtful*). I have mentioned (see above, p. 91) that the identification of *38-70-41* with ἔχουσι 'they have' leads to an unsolved problem in connexion with the last character. But ideographic confirmation may be claimed for it in the Pylos tablet Cn608 (see Beattie, *MIOF*, VI, 50-53):

numerical transcription	Ventris's transcription (*Documents*, p. 205)		
36-08-09-12-41 41-25-02	*jo-a-se-so-si si-a₂-ro*		
61-39-01-73-36	*o-pi-da-mi-jo*		
39-82	*pi-*82*	PIGS + SI	3
13-59-03	*me-ta-pa*	PIGS + SI	3
etc.	etc.		

Ventris lamely translates, 'How the local inhabitants will *fatten*[27] fat hogs: at *Pi-*82* three hogs, at Metapa three hogs . . .' Each of the remaining seven lines has a different initial word, which Ventris takes for a place name, but the same ideogram of a hog's head with the character *41* intersecting the neck, and at the right a number as low as two and as high as six. That the drawing represents a hog is recognizable mainly from the snout. The second word of the top line is identified with σιάλους. The value *02 = ro* (*lo*) is one of the best verified in the whole Linear B script. *41 = si* accords fairly well with the Cypriotic *si* character (see above, p. 36). Unfortunately, that is the only solid argument in favor of the identification, and the one point is not enough. The cases of Linear B characters whose verified value agrees with that of Cypriotic characters of similar shape are few. The most that the graphic resemblance can serve for in the other characters is to *suggest* phonetic values to try out where the meaning is established, not just guessed at. No occurrence of *41* in the Linear B tablets sufficiently confirms the value *si*.

As early as the second state of the grid, Ventris placed *41* in the square where it was destined to stay and to receive the value θ*i* ? *ri* ? in the third state, *si* in Work Note 20. Three other characters in the same row had already been called *ṣa, ṣe,* and *ṣ*ᵘ in "Languages" (see above, p. 23).

In Cn608 the word *41-25-02* is not close to the hog's head ideograms. Nothing in the layout of the tablet argues that a word with the meaning 'fat hogs' ought to come second in the opening line; it is a mere possibility. The word before it and the word after it, as transcribed by Ventris, do not go with *si-a₂-ro* (σιάλους or any other case form) to make an acceptable Greek sentence. The first word is altogether unidentifiable in Greek; among other things Ventris's transcription makes it begin with *jo-* (see above, p. 83). If the third word is related to ἐπιδήμιοι, it ought not to mean 'local inhabitants' but those who are 'in town' — i.e., visiting or lately arrived after an absence (cf. *Od.* 1.194, Herodotus 2.39.2). The mystery posed by the ideographic part of the text is the small number of hogs in each item, since the Homeric — indeed the well-nigh universal — custom is to keep hogs in sizable herds.[28]

An inconclusive argument, interesting from the standpoint of method, can be drawn from the *41* in ligature with the HOG ideogram. On the first thought we may take *41* for a restriction upon HOG, signifying not hogs in general but some specific class of hogs; the phonetic symbol *41* could very well be the initial syllable of the class word. This reasoning, if there were no obstacle, would favor the value *si,* understood as the abbreviation of σίαλοι 'fat hogs.' But unhappily *41* also occurs in ligature with another character *23,* 𗗚 (Cn418.2,3, Pylos) doubtless representing a different animal; *23* with the sex signs (see above, p. 77) and HOG with the sex signs occur together in the Knosos Co tablets. One of the strokes of *23* could be a horn, but Ventris's identification ox (*Documents,* pp. 195-196, 207) does not merit the certainty he claims for it. He rests his case upon the word *32-61* in Cn3.2, which he transcribes *qo-o*. But this disyllabic word will not square with any case form of βοῦς (βοϝ-) 'ox,' singular or plural, except by the forced assumption of a *scriptio plena*. Besides, if the ideogram stands for horned cattle, the paucity of the entire species in the Linear B tablets — except for 91 bulls (or more) in one Knosos tablet (C5544)! — is startling. As a phonetic character, *23* was given by Ventris the value *mu*. Here, as usual, he did not find any connexion between the ideographic and the phonetic value of a character. The ideographic value was deduced from the meaning of his Greek equivalent to a Linear B word written out phonetically in the vicinity, like *32-61* (transcribed *qo-o* and equated with βοῦς) in the vicinity of the ideographic *23*. The phonetic value of the same character is not contained in the Linear B word expressing, supposedly, the very meaning conveyed also by *23* as an ideogram. Thus Ventris's method, whether or not by original design, does not reason from the ideographic value or meaning of a character to its phonetic value. Now the ideographic value of *41* must be something reconcilable both with HOG and with whatever animal (or other substance) is indicated by the ideographic *23*. From the Homeric expression οὔας σιάλους (*Od.* 14.41; cf. 14.81, *Il.* 9.208, etc.) one might mistakenly infer that σίαλος is an adjective 'fat' or an epithet 'fat animal,' not limited to one species. But that is not the construction; instead the epithet is applied to no other species — just as in συσὶ κάπροισιν (*Il.* 5.783, etc., dat. pl.; cf. 17.21), where the second word means 'boar' exclusively, not the male of any other animal,[29] and in ἴρηξ κίρκος (*Od.* 13.86-87), where the first word means 'hawk' in general while the second is a certain variety of hawk.[30] Therefore the use of *41* in an ideographic ligature adds nothing of weight to Ventris's transcription of the

117

word 41-25-02 as si-a₂-ro (= σιαλο-). The Greek word σίαλος,
to be sure, lacks an Indo-European pedigree; its source in
some unknown language might have been applied to other
kinds of livestock.

We found earlier (see above, pp. 88-9) that the case for reading 38-70-41 as e-ko-si (ἔχουσι 'they have, they hold') was
weak in regard to the last character, because its alternation
with 38-70-04 (equated with ἔχοντες) in the Jn tablets does
not fit the syntactical difference between finite verb and
participle in Greek. In the En and Ep tablets from Pylos
38-70-41 alternates with 38-44; the most precise correspondence is in Ep704.3-4 (*Documents,* pp. 252-53):

38-53-59 28-46-27-57   61-06-05 38-44   44-44-13-06
70-05-06-03-02   01-15   05-12   72-15   ⚏ Ṭ‖

         67-53-04-40-57   61-06-05   38-70-41   44-44-13-06
70-05-06-03-02   01-15   05-12   72-15   ⚏ Ṭ⫶
translated by Ventris:

'§ 3 Eritha the priestess holds the *lease* of a *communal*
    plot from the village; so much seed: 48 1. wheat,
'§ 4 The *k.*-women hold the *lease* of a *communal* plot
    from the village; so much seed: 228 1. wheat . . .'

But nowhere, not even here, is it proved that 38-70-41 is the
plural of 38-44 (transcribed e-ke). Supposing that both
words are verbs, we cannot show that one has a singular subject and the other a plural. By Ventris's rules
67-53-04-40-57 cannot be expected to show a plural suffix;
he transcribes it ki-ri-te-wi-ja and leaves it untranslated,
'the *k.*-women,' with a cross-reference to another tablet
(An607.1; *Documents,* pp. 166-67) where he takes it for an
adjective tentatively derived from κριθαί 'barley.' His whole
interpretation is obviously insecure. Nor can a plurality of
persons be safely inferred from the fact that a larger quantity
follows the ideogram ⚏ in the 38-70-41 item than in the

38-44.[31] The first item of the tablet has a still larger quantity, but its "verb" is *38-44*.

The alleged likeness to the Greek alternation between ἔχει and ἔχουσι is drastically undermined by a further alternation, revealed in the second item of the same tablet:

10-54-73-57 04-61-36 14-38-60 61-06-05 38-44-78 28-46-27-57 44-60 05-12 72-15 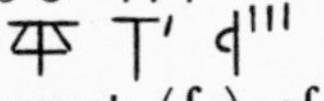

which Ventris translates 'Huamia, servant (f.) of the god, *and* she holds as a *lease* a *geras* [γέρας] of the priestess; so much seed: 18 l. wheat.' His italics in '*and* she holds' treat that part of the interpretation of *38-44-78* or *e-ke-qe* as doubtful. But it is more than doubtful; it is altogether irreconcilable with the syntax of τε in Greek and its cognates in other languages. Even if we were to retranslate 'Huamia [is] a servant of the god, and she holds . . . ,' nevertheless *38-44-78* often occurs as the second word of a tablet or entry, where a conjunction 'and' is quite out of place; e.g., Eb846 (Pylos):

43-37-36-32 38-44-78 61-06-05 44-44-13-06 70-05-06
03-02 01-15 70-05-52-61-70 05-12-45-72-15 (smaller characters) 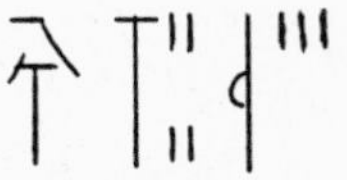

Cf. Ea806 (Pylos):

44-27-04-10 38-44 (large characters) *61-06-05 44-44-13-06 70-05-06* 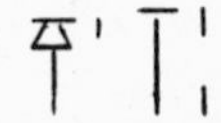

To render Eb846 'Aithioq^{u}s, *and* he holds the lease of a *communal* plot . . .' (*Documents*, p. 252) is absurd – all the more because the other one is rendered simply 'Kretheus holds a *lease* . . .'[32] In the En and Eo tablets the alternation between *38-44* and *38-44-78* is correlated with a change in word order:

En74.22

43-54-57 04-61-36 14-38-60 61-06-05 38-44 05-12-45 72-15 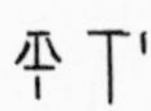

Eo160.2

43-54-57 04-61-36 14-38-60 38-44-78 61-06-05 03-02 39-44-27-75 

Palmer has seen a "prospective" or future meaning in the longer word.[33] Yet for all the ingenuity of his reasoning that

38-44-78 could be a notation for ἕξει, it is just a shot in the dark. The meaning of the words in all of the Ea, Eb, En, Eo, and Ep tablets completely eludes us, so far as it depends on any phonetic values for the characters — even the ones we have verified elsewhere. The great deal of worthwhile interpretation in Bennett's long article is independent of the Ventris transcription; he lapses into unreliable inferences whenever he uses the transcription to get at the meaning of a word.

We come out with nothing in the context to clarify the alternation of *38-44* and *38-44-78*, particularly the way that *61-06-05* as a rule precedes *38-44* but follows *38-44-78*. No clue to the mystery has been adduced from the grammar of any language. The relation of *38-44-78* to *38-44* being unsolved, *38-44* cannot safely be used as the singular *e-ke* to confirm the transcription of *38-70-41* as *e-ko-si*.

06 = na (probable). Ventris's decision to make *52 = no*, which I have accepted, depended upon a prior identification *06 = na*, suggested by the Cypriotic syllabary (see above, p. 80). Besides the alternation that he observed and the similarity in shape to the Cypriotic character — both of which grounds seem to me insufficient in themselves to verify the value *na* — a somewhat stronger argument can be drawn from the Knosos chariot tablets. The drawings show chariots in several degrees of incompleteness or dismantling. Four of the tablets that show a relatively skeletal CHARIOT[c] 𝝘 have also the word *08-06-15-05* (Sf0420, 0421, 0427, Sg0471). The initial *08-* (*a-*) encourages us to presume that the word may be an adjective with a negative prefix; the last character *-to* does not clash with the presumption. Still it can be confirmed only if we find in the Sd series of more complete chariots the word opposed to *08-06-15-05* of the Sf (and Sg) series. Two words *28-21-57* and *08-57-13-06* occur on many Sd and Sf tablets alike; but several other recurrent words on the Sd tablets are still in the running for the role of antonym to *08-06-15-05*. However, five of these Sd words, *40-53-24-36* *61-11-32 44-60-57-39 61-39-28-57-39* (see above, p. 99, note 31) and *11-30-67-57*, appear in Sf0428 along with CHARIOT^d ᴜᴦ, which is even more dismantled than CHARIOT^c. Of the remaining Sd vocabulary, one recurrent word *08-60-02-15-04-13-06* has the advantage of sharing an interior character with *08-06-15-05*. While we may reserve judgement on Ventris's correctness in transcribing that character *15* as *mo*, we still have here a basis for upholding *06* = *na*. From the difference between CHARIOT^c and CHARIOT^b (in Sf and Sd respectively) we have deduced that *08-06-15-05* is a descriptive word negating some feature of CHARIOT^b that is described by *08-60-02-15-04-13-06*. Since the positive word begins with *a-*, the negative counterpart should begin with *an⋮a-*, written syllabically *a-na-*. It comes out shorter than the positive word in spite of adding the negative prefix; but such a difference in length is not unusual in Greek, where ἀ- (ἀν-) is commonly attached to the simple root while in the positive word the root may undergo a considerable extension; e.g., ἄδικον 'unjust,' δίκαιον 'just.' So *15* seems to contain a vital part of the root common to the two words.

Ventris's *15* = *mo* does not meet the test of indispensable supplementation (see above, p. 48): if we had room for one lost character on a damaged tablet between *08-06-*[and]*-05* (*a-na-*[   ]*-to*), we would by no means inevitably be compelled to restore the syllable *-mo-* rather than anything else conceivable, in order to complete a Greek word suitable to the context of CHARIOT^c and opposed to CHARIOT^b. ἀνάρμοστος, as Ventris observed once (*Documents*, p. 387) but elsewhere forgot (p. 362), means 'not fitting' (Xenophon, *Mem.* 3.10.13) rather than 'not put together,' which the ideographic context of the chariot tablets seems to require. The passage in Xenophon refers to breastplates that do not fit on the shoulders; οἱ ἀνάρμοστοι is opposed to οἱ ἁρμόττοντες and could not refer to breastplates that are in pieces, un-assembled, or unfastened.[34] So if we are attempting to read the Linear B chariot tablets as Greek, we should not be content with a transcription of a Linear B word that makes it seem like the Greek word ἀνάρμοστοι 'not fitting.' Unluckily it is questionable whether the tablets record any Greek vocabulary appropriate to chariots. By Ventris's transcription we get only one word that looks tolerably Greek, *08-30-57-39 a-ni-ja-pi* 'with reins.' Even here, the construction with *08-60-26-57 a-ra-ru-ja* ought to mean 'fastened with reins' — which does not make good sense as a description of a chariot (see above, p. 37). Furthermore, Ventris points out (*Documents*, p. 364) that the Sd tablets with the word *08-30-57-39* have no indication of reins in their drawings. The identification of this Linear B word with a Greek word is therefore insecure; no other Greek word pertaining to chariots can be found altogether in this series of tablets.[35]

We are disappointed if we look for the Homeric terms for 'chariot,' 'wheel,' etc., in these texts from the Mycenaean age. Those Homeric terms were presumably not just of local currency, but nearly pan-Achaean; for chariots were a conspicuous part of the common culture and more mobile than most other parts of it. The men of the warrior class not only fought but also traveled in chariots and must have inevitably tended to arrive at a generally understood nomenclature. The nomenclature of the chariot in the Homeric poems ought then to be largely the same as the nomenclature that had been current among the Achaeans of the Mycenaean age. We are puzzled by the lack of this nomenclature in the Linear B chariot tablets — supposing them to be correctly transcribed. Yet the fact that they are from Knosos, not Pylos, may make a great difference. Crete could very well be isolated from the culture of the mainland in regard to the terminology, if not the technique of the chariot. People would not normally have transported their own chariots over the sea when they went visiting, although they would have driven them across the country. After landing, a visitor of consequence would if necessary be lent a chariot and chari- oteer by a gracious host (cf. *Od*. 3.475-84). Accordingly we need not assume that the terms used at Knosos were also in the chariot vocabulary of the mainland, and that the Homeric vocabulary is equally alien to both.

The frequent ending -*13-06* is transcribed -*me-na*, equiva- lent to the Greek middle or passive participle, but in no in- stance has this function or the value of *13* been verified.[36] The ending turns up in two recurrent words of the Sd chariot tablets, *08-60-02-15-04-13-06* and *08-57-13-06*. The relation to another ending -*13-52* is perplexing (see above, p. 114). The forms in -*13-06* occur in fifteen Sd tablets, the longer form showing some internal variation (see p. 137, note 34). All but one tablet have on the left, in big charac- ters, *28-21-57* (*I-QI-JA*), and on the right alongside the CHARIOT drawing a numeral, I or III; in several tablets, how- ever, damage on the left or the right deprives us of part of the text. One of the tablets (pieced together from Sd0415+ 0417+0469) has *08-60-02-15-04-13-06 08-57-13*, with a big word at the left *28-21-36* (*I-QI-JO*) and the numeral II.[37] Still another tablet (Sd0401), not counted among the fifteen, has big *28-21-36* followed by *08-57-13-52* and *08-60-02-15- 04-13-52*; the numeral on the right is unluckily broken off. These facts led Ventris to the hypothesis that *28-21-36* is dual, while *28-21-57* is singular and plural (*Documents*, p. 366). It seemed to follow that the suffix -*13-52* is dual too (-μένω), even though it appears here where no numeral is preserved and contrariwise -*13-06* is recorded in the pres- ence of the numeral II.[38] The idea of a dual characterized by the vowel -*o*, while the singular and plural have -*a*, is nearly desperate. No Greek declension behaves that way; the least unlikely candidate among Greek declensions is the feminine "first." Such nouns have no dual at all in Homeric Greek; so it is not inherently unreasonable that by suppletion the "second declension" dual -ω could be carried over into the other declension.[39] But the Linear B nouns and participles are not suitable for proving that the phenomena here bear any relation to Greek. The interpretation of these Linear B words as Greek is strained and weak; it is therefore gratuitous to insist upon treating their inflexions as Greek or quasi-Greek (see below, p. 180).[40]

Without placing any reliance on the suffix -*13-06*, we still have a fairly strong case for *06* = *na*. It is not so strong, however, as it would be if it occurred in a completely deciphered word. The two converging evidences for it are its occurrence in *08-06-15-05* (*a-na-?-to*) and the shape of the Cypriotic character. Our confidence in the identification should be subdued and circumspect. It does not gain appreciably from the Knosos sword tablet Ra1540,

$$05\text{-}31 \ 03\text{-}77\text{-}06 \ \text{SWORD} \equiv \ ^= [\text{i.e., } 50]$$

The second word consists of smaller characters than the first word and the SWORD ideogram. That the first word *05-31* means or at any rate *can* mean 'total' is shown by L598 (see above, p. 74); that it means 'total' in the sword tablet too is not unlikely, because the other sword tablets, which lack the word, have much smaller numerals, not above 5 in any instance (Kober, *AO*, XVII[a], 395-396). Granted that τόσα (Homeric τόσσα) 'so many' is not precisely the Greek word for 'total,' yet the application of either meaning to the word *05-31* would narrow down the possible meaning of the second word so that it might be 'swords.' In view of the Greek word φάσγανα (*Il.* 15.713, etc.), Ventris's transcription *pa-ka-na* for *03-77-06* has been regarded as a major confirma-

tion of the decipherment (Chadwick, *Decipherment*, p. 93).
However, the proof from context is thin. We are reduced to
guessing why the word is written in smaller characters —
perhaps an abnormal sort of phonetic complement to the
ideogram, which it strangely precedes. The small size of the
characters *03-77-06* is certainly an obstacle to any interpretation of the SWORD drawing as a determinative to accompany the phonetically written word for 'sword.'[41] We are
left in a quandary: we cannot determine whether or not the
word should be taken to mean 'swords'; nor can we decide
whether or not to accept the transcription *pa-ka-na*. The
first character of *03-77-06* looks indeed like the Cypriotic *pa*,
the last one like the Cypriotic *na*. Ventris steadfastly adhered to these among other identifications of Linear B and
Cypriotic characters, but the evidence within Linear B for
03 = pa is nothing to rely on (see above, pp. 23, 92).
If we were sure of *pa-?-na*, we might stretch the principle
of necessary supplementation to identify the middle character as *ka*, on the ground that φάσγανα and no other Greek
word of similar beginning and end would fit the context of
'total' and SWORD.[42] But with only the last character *na* tolerably sure, it is reckless to reconstruct the word and claim
we have something more than a speculation.

Exhaustion of the objective aids to decipherment. I do
not see how to prove the phonetic value of any more Linear
B characters by the same rigorous method. It is a pity, in a
way, that the value *77 = ka* is inadequately established by
the occurrence of *03-77-06* in the sword tablets of Knosos.
It would open up an important chain of probable though not
certain logic, which might end, however, in a worse quandary. Transcribing *77-70* in the Jn tablets as *ka-ko* (see
above, pp. 71, 87), we would almost irresistibly go along with
Ventris in connecting this with χαλκός and agreeing that the

ideogram |Ξ| is BRONZE — which does not in the least conflict with the other ideograms on the same tablets that show it was weighed out in talents and double minae. Next, the word 77-44-75, also in the Jn tablets, could hardly be left in suspense as ka-?-we. The motive of necessary supplementation would lead us to accept Ventris's ka-ke-we, equivalent to χαλκῆ(ϝ)ες 'smiths' (Il. 4.187,216).[43] The acceptance of ke for 44, a very frequent character, would have extensive repercussions, not all of them welcome. It would commit us to e-ke and e-ke-qe for 38-44 and 38-44-78 respectively in the Pylos E tablets, where they are employed altogether unlike the Greek ἔχει and ἔχει τε (see above, p. 119). As long as we remain undecided about the value of 44, we leave the possibility of various solutions in the future, though acknowledging that we have nothing to bank on for the present. But if we make it ke, then the commitment to a vowel -e would argue for taking 44-44-13-06, which is also frequent in the E tablets, as a reduplicated perfect. Given the reduplicated beginning ke-ke-, the rest would almost have to be the participial suffix -me-na, as we have accepted 06 = na. Unhappily, ke-ke-me-na has merely the appearance of a Greek perfect participle, middle or passive. There is no such participle in Greek, nor any verb from which such a derivation is plausible. It does not make the E texts more intelligible; quite the contrary, it gratuitously saddles us with still more problems than are posed by the unclarified data themselves.

Besides, the value me is all the shakier because the Greek suffix -μενος, -μένη, etc., has a singularly incoherent set of Indo-European cognates. To mention just the Indo-Iranian languages, Sanskrit has -mānaḥ, Avestan -mnō (sometimes disyllabic metrically); they clash with each other and with the Greek -μενος as to what comes between m and n. In the Linear B language, which is far from being identical with any known dialect of Greek — even if we choose to label it "Mycenaean Greek" — the value $13 = me$ should be regarded at most as a rough normalization while the real vowel sound in it remains quite obscure.[44]

Recapitulation of ascertained and questionable phonetic values. Each of the following nine characters corresponds unmistakably to the right syllable of a certain Greek word and has its value confirmed independently by another word or by the Cypriotic syllabary or both:

$$02 = ro$$
$$05 = to$$
$$08 = a$$
$$11 = po$$
$$37 = ti$$
$$52 = no$$
$$61 = o$$
$$75 = (w)e$$
$$78 = te^{45}$$

Every one of these occurs in a deciphered word of the tripod-and-jug tablet.

Each of the following eight characters occurs in one unmistakable Greek word but lacks a sure confirmation:

$$26 = ru$$
$$27 = re$$
$$36 = jo \text{ or } o_2$$
$$38 = e$$
$$39 = pi$$
$$45 = de$$
$$53 = ri$$
$$70 = ko$$

127

Eight others of Ventris's values have been demonstrated to be more or less probable in one word at least:

$$06 = na$$
$$12 = so$$
$$28 = i$$
$$31 = sa$$
$$32 = qo$$
$$41 = si$$
$$42 = wo$$
$$54 = wa$$

My examination of $07 = di$ and $03 = pa$ leaves them conjectural. The remainder of Ventris's values — i.e., about forty-five of them — I do not see how to test within the method I have employed hitherto.

A theory for the experimental verification of other characters. I ought to emphasize, to the credit of Ventris, that I have not refuted a single one of his values. Although some serious difficulty has been detected in several of them, in no case did Ventris (at least from the time he embarked upon Work Note 20) overlook a value that is demonstrably correct for a given character and plump instead for a wrong value which some weakness in his method commended to him. He had a truly versatile mind, and as an amateur he was perhaps less liable than a scholar would be to cling to this or that detail which he had previously worked out, in the face of new evidence or insights that suggested a change. When I conclude that the greater part of his work is far from acceptable as it stands, I mean that it is in need not so much of correction as of verification. He and — even more — his adherents were remiss in not sifting his results point by point to affirm only what is really unchallengeable, what will overcome all reasonable doubt. I have verified all that the demonstrative method will allow. I cannot predict whether the supporters of the decipherment will welcome the arguments I have adduced in support of what is, in all, a minor fraction of the transcription. To do so, they might virtually have to admit that the rest of the transcription would be strengthened by a similar corroboration. If such methodical corroboration of all or most of the remaining characters is forthcoming, I dare say nobody on Ventris's side would make a virtue of disdaining it. If it is not forthcoming, the corollary might be that the rest of the transcription is enfeebled; I hope we shall not be told again that the individual parts do not have to be proved. That is the reaction of faith to the sight of wonders, not the response of reason to a scientific statement. For my part I am grateful for any further proof of the value of individual Linear B characters, even if only a little of the decipherment is thereby affected; if more is affected, so much the better.

Having obtained good though limited results by comparing the transcription with the objective, ideographic evidence, I would like if possible to avoid the dead end that confronts us in the exhaustion of this kind of evidence. We have been (to take up again a commercial metaphor) dealing in cash and have found some hard cash in Ventris's decipherment. To determine whether anything in it is sound beyond that, we need to extend a measure of credit. But not what he asked for in "Evidence" (see above, p. 39): that the decipherment "be tested by applying it to the material as a whole." Scholars have done what he wanted, and it amounts to unbridled credit that recognizes no reverse except utter bankruptcy. Most of the Linear B corpus does not come out like Greek at all, or does so only at the price of violent readjustments. Yet such experience does not discredit Ventris's enterprise in the eyes of those who have unwarily consented to the wholesale, undiscriminating test. For any bit of apparent Greek renews their faith, and they lavish their care upon transcribed texts in which — for all they *know* — many of the values are imaginary. I do not want to follow many others into that trap. Instead I propose a deal with Ventris on short-term credit, underwritten for minimum risk. Since my appraisal has determined that a few words, apart from any syntactical construction, are certainly Greek, I will move on to the evaluation of the only Linear B text of several words which, while not amenable to such direct proof, has nevertheless the appearance of being Greek in transcription and needs only some modest assumptions to support an argument that the language is Greek indeed.

Notes to Chapter V

1. First published by Chadwick, "New Fragments," pp. 147-48 and pl. 27. G(S?)5670 (Knosos; formerly X5670) probably contains the same three signs, but only traces remain of 70, the first one.

2. "A Note on the Sword Tablets," in *Minoica: Festschrift zum 80. Geburtstag von Johannes Sundwall* (Berlin: Akademie-Verlag, 1958), pp. 192-96.

3. Except for one word 03-60 in very large characters at the left, which is not accompanied by any nonphonetic sign. Beattie argues there is no drawing of a helmet at all but just the syllabic character 42 obscured by cracks — "Die Entzifferung der mykenischen Schrift: Erwiderung," *Saeculum*, X (1959), 371. Schachermeyr in his rebuttal ("Schlusswort," p. 378) rightly appeals to the photograph against Beattie's identification of 42; but that still leaves room for doubting whether the character really stands for HELMET.

4. The third state of the grid shows both 44 full-sized and 74 reduced in the -e ? square of that row, and two more reduced characters 20 and 45 in other squares of the same row.

5. In the Knosos tablets too, 70-54 and 70-42 are regularly shorter than the WOMAN ideogram.

6. The short WOMAN ideogram 矢 or 仌 of the Aa series is usually no taller than 𝟖 ⷩ or 𝟖 ⴺ. Ventris's concentration upon the decipherment of the phonetic Linear B characters has had the unfortunate effect of drawing attention away from the difference between the two WOMAN ideograms, both numbered 102, which I would transcribe WOMAN[t] and WOMAN[s] in the Ab and Aa texts respectively. The decipherment has not in the least accounted for the correlation between WOMAN[t] and the initial word 50-02 before the main or distinctive word in so many Ab texts, while nearly all Aa's have but a single word in front of WOMAN[s] (the preliminary 50-02 only in Aa61). The rendering *pu-ro* 'Pylos' gives no clue to the difference between WOMAN[t] and WOMAN[s]. Nor does the rest of Ventris's interpretation of the texts as Greek even begin to answer several other questions: Why are the arms shown as distinct lines only in WOMAN[s]? Why, in several Aa tablets (60, 63, 76, 85, 89, 93-95, 98), does the head have an extra horizontal line, possibly a veil? Why is the counting of persons in the Aa's followed almost always by ⊦' ⷩ' (as phonetic characters these are 01 and 59 respectively), while these appear in the Ab's often in reversed order and never

with the numeral, moreover preceded by the 𐂌 and the ✗𐅃 enumerations, which are always identical? (✗𐅃 as a phonetic character is 30.) The difference in the WOMAN ideograms presumably symbolizes a difference in appearance, particularly in dress; and that ought to stand for a difference in status.

The transcription also neglects differences in the MAN ideogram (100). In An857 (transcribed in *Documents*, p. 173) the main section of the reverse side of the tablet shows five times a figure 𐃏 with a horizontal line at the waist and a ripple at the shoulders — altogether lacking in the other MAN drawings on the same tablet, and undoubtedly significant.

7. The MALE sign may be not just the two horizontal lines but rather ‡ (the phonetic character 03) ligatured to the animal ideograms; see below, pp. 186-7.

8. Ventris in Work Note 14, p. 119, remarked, "I am not familiar enough with the Knossos material to explain the forms 𐀪 𐂍 , 𐃀 𐂍 [42-70, 54-70] which are said also to occur." The subsequent publication of *SM* II showed this to have been a misunderstanding. 42-70 and 54-70 do not occur as separate words, nor do they seem, from their ideographic context, to express the meaning 'boys' and 'girls.'

9. Except for the simple line or circle strokes that are manifestly numerals.

10. *PT* (1951), p. 5. The space that Bennett leaves between 70 and the previous character is not justified by his own drawings, made by tracing over photographs, in *PT* (1955). Only in Ad357 — numbered Ad01 in *PT* (1951) — is there an appreciable interval, and it is still too little to count as evidence for a word boundary in a script that habitually uses a vertical line I for that purpose — granted that this stroke is used less regularly in the Ad tablets than in some other series.

11. In Ad690 the first two characters 50-02 are not set off by a word-divider stroke, nor adequately separated by spacing or any other means; but it is evident from many other tablets, including Ab578, Ad671, Ad680, that 50-02 comprises a separate word, either marked off by the stroke I or else placed not on the same line. We have no such evidence that 70-42 is ever thus divisible from the group of characters adjacent to it.

12. See Schwyzer, I, 445-46.

13. His determination to look upon the persons of the Aa and Ab tablets as task groups — flaxworkers, bath attendants, etc. — has driven

him to the strange idea that the quantities of 𝟙 and 𝗫 on each Ab tablet are *equal rations* of WHEAT and FIGS, although his own reference to Cretan inscriptions of the classical period (*Documents*, p. 158) ought to argue that a diet consisting of figs and cereal food in equal amounts would have been abnormal. If 𝟙 truly stands for WHEAT, we must admire the lord for indulgently feeding his menials and their children upon wheat rather than barley. However, we may reflect that a lord would more probably exact the wheat for his own banquet hall.

14. Palmer, *OLZ*, LIII, 110, argues that the value *wo* is proved by a "third declension" genitive singular function in Es644.1: 70-72-27-42 14-12-15, translated 'contribution of Kopreus' (*Documents*, p. 278), as opposed to 70-72-27-10 which is taken to be nominative (Es650.1). Had he cited any more than the first and second lines of these two long tablets, he would have had to remark — as Ventris candidly does — that the word before 14-12-15 is genitive only in that first line.

The thirteen remaining Es tablets are shorter — four lines each, of which the third consists of two words containing an unexplained alternation,

75-01-24-42 14-12-15 (Es645, 648, 651-653, 703, 726-729)
75-01-24-75 14-12-15 (Es646, 647, 649).

Ventris translates both *we-da-ne-wo* and *we-da-ne-we* as a dative, 'contribution to W∼neus' (*Documents*, p. 279; he oddly abbreviates the name of this divinity of his in the manner of a *nomen sacrum*). Furthermore, the usage of the Linear B scribes is inconsistent with the grammar formulated by Ventris: 75-01-24-42 14-38-02 in Es703.1 is translated 'the servant of W∼neus,' but the same word two lines down on the same tablet becomes 'to W∼neus.' Finally *we-da-ne-w°/ₑ* cannot be identified with any god or hero or anything else ever recorded in Greek. In short, neither the base nor the inflexions of this word have anything to do with Greek, as far as we can see.

The decipherment yields particularly bad results in the Es tablets, which were excavated in the same season as the Ta series, famous for the tripod-and-jug tablet. I can point out in the Es a correlation between the verbal and the ideographic parts of not only the third but also the second and fourth lines: where the word is 75-01-24-75, the commodity 𝟙 in each of the three lines is reckoned in two measures 𝖳 and 𝖽 ; where the is 75-01-24-42, it is reckoned only in the smaller measure 𝖽 . I do not see how to fit these facts of the Es tablets into any pattern of the Greek language; but it would be imprudent to brush the correlation aside as a mere coincidence.

15. Even in the first state he inferred that *42* and *54* share a consonant *ś-* ?? because of the words for 'boy' and 'girl' (Work Note 1, p. 10, item 46).

16. The method of the present inquiry does not require a lengthy statement of my objections to what Ventris here asserted without adducing any material proof. In brief let me remark:

(1) The initial word *59-60-55* is unwarrantably translated 'footstool.' By comparing the two-handled ideograms of the tablet with a two-handled footstool which is represented on a signet ring from Tiryns (*Documents*, pp. 332-33), he has proved no more than that the handles do not prohibit the identification of the ideogram as FOOTSTOOL. The identification is not quite impossible, but unproved. It will not serve, therefore, to verify the transcription *ta-ra-nu* (θρῆνυς, θράνυς).

(2) The same word occurs at the beginning of the third line of Ta707 and 708, tablets without ideograms. The two other entries begin *05-52* = *to-no*, which Ventris fills out to *thornos* and translates 'chair' (*Documents*, p. 343); the difference between *θόρνος and θρόνος would be a case of metathesis (Vilborg, p. 54). The idea that *to-no* stands for a piece of furniture was due to the prior supposition that *59-60-55* stands for a different but related piece. But in a writing system that relies so much on ideography, I marvel that a 'chair' should be referred to verbally these four times (plus a fifth in Ta714), with never an ideogram — although a chair is one of the easiest things to make a simple, clear drawing of. See Grumach, *OLZ*, LII, 337-38.

(3) The fourth item in Ta722, and again in 721, repeats the third item identically. Ventris's translations 'one footstool inlaid with ivory *nuts* (twice)' and 'one footstool inlaid with ivory *pomegranates* and *grooves* (twice)' leave us to wonder why the scribe stupidly wrote it out twice instead of just adding a stroke to make the numeral ‖ .

17. The Latin is *equus* (really *ecus* in the spelling of the Golden Age).

18. Ventris was unable to apply to this tablet his own principle: "The simplest, most mundane and least surprising explanation of any inscription is likely to be the correct one. Both the archive tablets

and the Minoan inscriptions written on other objects are likely to have the same general content as similarly-written inscriptions from cultures near in time and space" (Work Note 7, p. 19).

19. An additional miniature 32 was placed in the -a ? column (see above, p. 29).

20. To the latter case he gave the stopgap label "accusative" in the Work Notes (the quotation marks are his own). He noted -32 also in the nominative (Work Note 15, figure 9, accompanying the second state of the grid). This anomaly was smoothed over in "Evidence," p. 91: "ξ, ψ and κʷσ are spelt ka-sa-, ke-se-, pa-sa-, pe-se-, etc., except when final, where they appear to shed the -s and take the vowel of the preceding syllable ([186]wa-na-ka ϝάναξ, [83]ai-ti-jo-qo = Aἰθίοψ."

21. *Mistake*, as I use the term, does not mean a substandard form habitually employed by some but avoided by others; it is a slip which you make through inadvertence or preoccupation, and which you yourself would correct as soon as you become aware of it — provided there is some convenient way to correct it. In speech you would say the word or phrase over, to incorporate the correction (unless the discourse has already passed too far beyond that point); in writing you would cancel and rewrite (unless it would mar the appearance of the writing surface too badly).

22. In Ta641 he marked 13-20-38 after the singular 07-03 as a scribal error for 13-20, while accepting 13-20-38 as correct where it occurs after the dual or plural 07-03-38 in the next item (*Documents*, pp. 336, 400). Here he vitiates the material by forcing a Pylos tablet to yield an example of an alternation between 13-20 and 13-20-38 that is found at Knosos, mainly in the Ak series, following the word 70-54 or 70-42 (see above, pp. 106-7). 13-20 is not recorded at Pylos. At Knosos it is the singular while 13-20-38 comes with the numerals ‖ (i.e., 2) and higher, in all instances where the reading is not jeopardized by any damage to the tablet. However, in one damaged Knosos tablet, Ak7022.2 — *KT* (1959), p. 97 — 13-20-38 probably occurs with the numeral ∣, just as in Ta641 from Pylos. Ventris translates the word 'larger' or 'older.'

Ak tablets also have another alternating word after 70-54 and 70-24; it is 13-40-36 ~ 13-40-36-38 or 13-10-36' ~ 13-10-36-38, which he translates 'younger' (literally 'smaller'). But in no instance do the Knosos tablets show that either 13-40-36 or 13-10-36 is singular.

The numeral in Ak610.3, 5940.2, 5884.2 is II (i.e., 2); in Ak611.2, 612.2 damage leaves us uncertain whether the numeral is I or more. See Beattie, *JHS*, LXXVI, 13 (not quite accurate in regard to *13-20-38* at Knosos).

23. W. C. Brice, "The Decipherment of the Minoan Linear Script B and the Problem of the Linear Script A, "*Man*, LVII (1957), no. 229, p. 183, noted thirty-three instances where the vocabulary of *Documents* assumes a scribal error.

24. Palmer, *OLZ*, LIII, 110, claims a sure method of diagnosing scribal errors. It comes down to calling any deviation from a formula an error, if contrary to the Linear B grammar of Ventris. But his principle is invalid; for unless the language is thoroughly known, such deviations ought to be provisionally received not as erroneous but as significant or at least optional. Besides, his example from the Es tablets is weak, because the formula *po-se-da-o-ne do-so-mo* (*11-09-01-61-24 14-12-15*) is not, as he says, "faithfully adhered to in 10 tablets," but only in three (Es645, 646, 647). In 648, 651, 727, 728, 729 the words come in the opposite order. Furthermore, in the damaged tablet Es652 everything before *11-09-01-61-24* is gone; we have no proof that *14-12-15* was ever there. And in 726 what remains of the formula is *14-12-15 11-09-01-61*[; we do not know whether *24* or *52* or some other character or characters followed or whether the word ended with *61*. Neither the ten tablets nor the first three give us what we would need to reject *11-09-01-61-52 14-12-15* in Es-649 and *11-09-01-61 14-12-15* in Es653 as scribal errors.

I do not understand how a scholar as eminent as Palmer could have contented himself with such a rash procedure. In this one polemical article he was not up to his usual high standard of judgement and objectivity. Chadwick, *Decipherment*, p. 83, affirms a principle like Palmer's: "There are quite a large number of cases where we can say for certain that the scribe has made a mistake; for instance, if a tablet has a constantly repeating formula, and in one case for no reason it is written differently, we need have no fears in putting it down as an error." But he gives no example; the omission does not merit censure, since his book is semipopular; however, scholars must have the proof presented to them.

25. A. E. Housman, "Luciliana," *Classical Quarterly*, I (1907), 53: "The truth is that the difficulties of the text of Lucilius are for the most part inexplicable and its corruptions for the most part irremediable. What more than anything else enables the critic and

commentator of an ancient author to correct mistakes and to elucidate obscurities is their context; and a fragment has no context. An editor of Lucilius or Ennius or Nonius or the reliquiae scaenicae, unless he is grievously self-deluded, must know that the greater number of his corrections, and of his explanations also, are false." The usefulness of a context depends, of course, on its being clearly understood. In a Linear B passage the context is very seldom clear enough to assist in the interpretation — let alone the emendation — of any word; and in the Es tablets the whole text is at nearly the extreme of obscurity.

26. The values *08* = *a* and *52* = *no* have already been established (see above, pp. 63, 80) without bringing in this word, which defies identification, either phonetic or semantic.

27. Italics in the translations offered in *Documents* (see p. 154) indicate a rendering regarded by Ventris and Chadwick as doubtful or controversial.

28. Palmer, *Gnomon*, XXIX, 570, suggests "animals intended for some special purpose" — most likely religious.

29. To be sure, *caper* (the Latin cognate of κάπρος) means 'billy goat.'

30. Not definitively identified by modern ornithologists in spite of the ancient descriptions.

31. On the doubtful significance of this ideogram, see above, note 13.

32. *Documents*, p. 240, cites not this tablet Ea806 but a related one, Ea800, which begins with the same three words. Cf. also Ep301.2 (*Documents*, p. 251).

33. *Gnomon*, XXIX, 571; "Mycenaean Greek Texts from Pylos," *Transactions of the Philological Society*, 1954, pp. 53-53b. See also Bennett, "The Landholders of Pylos," *AJA*, LX (1956), 120-22.

34. The attempt to find a Greek word more or less equivalent to the long word *08-60-02-15-04-13-06* is complicated by the existence of variant forms *08-60-02-15-05-13-06* (Sd0416) and *08-02-15-04-13-06* (Sd0422).

35. *Documents*, pp. 363-64: "Our difficulties begin when we try to interpret the detailed terminology of the Knossos tablets in the light of this picture. Their syntax and the meaning of the *adjectives* describing colour and material are clear enough; but not only do the *nouns* which describe the parts of a chariot fail to agree with the

nomenclature found in Homer, but their identification is equally open to controversy." Adjectives of color and material cannot of course be confirmed by the drawings and do not belong especially to the vocabulary of chariots. See Beattie, *MIOF*, VI, 51.

36. See above, note 22, and Grumach, *OLZ*, LII, 331.

37. *KT* (1955 and 1959) overscrupulously questions the character -06 (-na), doubtless in consequence of the poor photograph in *SM* II, pl. xviii. On Bennett's own photograph, which he generously lent me, it is unmistakable.

38. Ta715.3 (Pylos) does have 08-57-13-52 near the numeral II. As a participle of obscure sense (see above, p. 114) it is taken to be in agreement with the first word of the item, 05-72-20, transcribed *to-pe-zo* and supposed to mean 'tables' (*Documents*, p. 342) — although a simple drawing of a table is strangely absent (see above, note 16). The previous line begins 05-72-17, transcribed *to-pe-za*, and ends with the numeral I; neither 08-57-13-52 nor 08-57-13-06 is present. But on another Pylos tablet, Ta642.1, 05-72-17 and 08-57-13-06 occur in the same line, unfortunately without a numeral. In the next line are 05-72-17 and 08-57-13-[ ]; damage has obliterated a character important to our argument —*PT* (1955), p. 66, inaccurately copied on p. 186.

The alternation, as far as it goes, may be summarized thus:

05-72-20 and 08-57-13-52, both dual, if not plural; definitely not singular (Ta715.3);

05-72-17, definitely singular (Ta715.2);

05-72-17 and 08-57-13-06, presumably not dual but singular (Ta642.1).

39. καλυψαμένω 'covering' (Hesiod, *Op.* 198), cited in *Documents*, p. 84, may be a valid illustration, although it is not uniformly attested — there is some authority for καλυψαμένα, a "first declension" feminine dual of Attic type. A doubt more serious in this case than the matter of attestation lurks in the lengthy construction: "The bad man will injure the better one, addressing him with crooked words, and will swear a false oath. Jealousy [ζῆλος, masculine], malicious, spiteful, hideous, will accompany all of wretched mankind; and then to Olympus from the earth with its highways,

λευκοῖσιν φάρεσσι καλυψαμένω χρόα καλὸν
ἀθανάτων μετὰ φῦλον ἴτον προλιπόντ' ἀνθρώπους
αἰδὼς καὶ νέμεσις

covering their fair skin with their white robes, to the race of the immortals will go [dual], abandoning [masculine or neuter dual] mankind, awe and indignation [both feminine]." The problem is whether already in v. 198 καλυψαμένω is in a feminine context, thanks to the personification, or alternatively there is nothing feminine until we come to the grammatically feminine nouns αἰδὼς καὶ νέμεσις at the very end. χρόα καλόν makes it likely that as soon as the person-ification commences, the poet cannot delay the attribution of female sex. Therefore, if he said καλυψαμένω (and not καλυψαμένᾱ), he know-ingly applied the "second declension" dual because he was con-strained by the lack of a specifically feminine dual. Thus καλυψαμένω should be nearly as certain a case of suppletion here, where it comes two lines before αἰδὼς καὶ νέμεσις, as it would be if immediately preceded by a naturally feminine dual — e.g., *γυναῖκε καλυψαμένω.

40. One of the 28-21-36 tablets (Sd0401) and several of the 28-21-57 tablets (Sd0403, 0405+0410, 0450+0483, 0413 damaged) have the word 08-60-26-57, which Ventris has loosely equated with ἀραρυῖα(ι); see above, p. 36. Even where it is supposed to agree with a dual 28-21-36, it turns up with no modification. But in Sd0408+ 0411, along with]-21-57, it comes out 08-60-26-42-57, which Ventris is obliged to transcribe a-ra-ru-wo-ja but censures as "incorrect fem., contaminated by the neuter plur." (Documents, p. 389). The alleged neuter plural is 08-60-26-42-08 of the Knosos sword tablets. The transcription a-ra-ru-wo-a is interpreted as ararwoa, contrary to his own orthographic rule (pp. 46, 389). In form it does not match the Greek ἀρηρότα (Od. 7.45); nor does the meaning 'fastened' or 'fitted' suit the context. As Henle points out, in several tablets "the swords are still fitted, but fitted with nothing" — (above, note 2), p. 193. In Ra1551 the word 08-60-26-42-08 is added above the main line of writing; so the lack of a construction to tell how the thing is fitted makes the rendering 'fitted' all the more feeble. Besides, the word may have to do for the singular as well as the plural: Ra1542 has]-42-08 followed by the SWORD ideogram and the numeral I; the tablet breaks off, and we cannot tell whether there was any more to the numeral.

Ventris in Work Note 20 (p. 176), while attracted by a-ra-ru-ja, had misgivings over a-ra-ru-wo-a. Probably Chadwick reassured him after they began their collaboration; see "Introductory Essay," p. 7. While the context of the Linear B texts does not bear out a meaning like that of ἀραρυῖα(ι) and ἀρηρότα in Greek, the chances are that 08-60-26-57 and 08-60-26-42-08 are inflected forms of the same word; and we should expect a meaning appropriate both to chariots and to swords.

41. Cf. Henle (see above, p. 104).

42. φάσγανα, like many other words that refer to artifacts, is not convincingly Indo-European.

43. 77-44-75 recurs in many of the mysterious Ma tablets (*Documents*, pp. 289-295), which have been so unsatisfactorily expounded by many scholars.

44. Its shape ⟨Ͳ⟩ is somewhat reminiscent of the Cypriotic *mi*.

45. I cannot verify Ventris's phonological interpretation, contained in the transcription *qe,* that the consonant is not dental but presumably labiovelar.

CHAPTER VI

THE NUGGET OF GREEK TEXT IN THE "OIL" TABLET Gn(OR Fr)1184

Second to Ta641, the most important text for penetrating into the Linear B script was excavated in 1954, after the decipherment had been virtually finished.[1] (See pull-out attached to the front flyleaf.) The words of the first and second lines of Gn1184 can be normalized readily into passable Greek:

Κώκαλος (or Κόκαλος, Κόκκαλος) ἀπέδωκε ἔλαι(ϝ)ον τόσ(σ)ον Εὐμήδεϊ

'K. gave back (paid) so much oil to E.' No other Linear B text can be acceptably normalized in such a way.[2] Even in this one the three words of the last line, transcribed *pa-ro i-pe-se-wa ka-ra-re-we*, do not go into Greek except by violent and arbitrary manipulation. The text has been discussed by many but needs to be re-examined by us now.

The problematical oil *ideogram and the word for 'oil.'* The meaning of the symbol 𝍓 is not obvious on its face. Removing the ligature of 𝟤 (the syllabic character *75;* see above, p. 78), we still do not get an identifiable drawing. It was known from other tablets without the word *38-33-42,* before the discovery of this one, and was already inferred to stand for some measured liquid because it is divisible into fewer parts than the ideograms inferred to stand for dry measure.[3] Which liquid could not be determined, but several were suggested. Evans thought of beer, because the ideogram reminded him of millet (*PM*, IV[b], 625). Arne Furumark, who had not only the Knosos but also the mainland tablets to study, considered wine but was more inclined to oil.[4] Bennett too made "a tentative identification of the meaning of the sign 𐂝 as a particular quantity of olive oil." However, it was all "a suggestion and not a certainty"; he was able to adduce only a slight balance of probability in favor of OIL rather than something else.

Add now the datum *38-33-42* on the line above the ideogram in Gn1184. So far as objective demonstration goes, the case for identifying the ideogram with OIL gains somewhat but not decisively. I reserve for later the question whether it makes any difference — for subjective conviction if not objective demonstration — that the tablet was found after the decipherment had been completed (see below, pp. 164-5). The equation $38 = e$, we have shown, fits *ti-ri-o-we-e* 'three-eared, three-handled' (dual or possibly plural) and *e-ko-*, the beginning of a word that means 'having' (see above, pp. 86-8); we need not hesitate to apply *e* to the present instance. $33 = ra_3$ has nothing solid to recommend it: *39-46-33* next to a two-handled bowl on a stand (Ta709; see above, p. 85) might conceivably correspond to the Greek word φιέλη (pl. φιέλαι); but neither occurrence of *33* is in a word whose meaning is *guaranteed* by the context to be that which is expressed in Greek by a certain word.[5] The third equation $42 = wo$ was made by Ventris in Work Note 20 (p. 175), for the purpose of reading *70-42* as *ko(r)-wo(s)*, *ko(r)-wo(i)*, while *70-54* became *ko(r)-wā*, *ko(r)-wa(i)*. From the context of many tablets, the meaning 'sons' or 'boys' for *70-42* is highly probable, though not quite certain because in the crucial Ad series the function of *-70-42* (and *-61-70-42*) as a suffix remains enigmatic (see above, pp. 106-

110). The phonetic value *wo* entailed the grave assumption by Ventris, in Work Note 20, that the sound *-r-* at the end of the previous syllable was left unwritten (see below, pp. 227-9). However, in a complicated and not unequivocal way that I will set forth, *wo* is confirmed by Gn1184.

The relation between the words 38-33-42 05-12. — ||||⁄|||| is the only thing in the first two lines whose meaning can be directly established without a long and perhaps treacherous chain of reasoning. Since we know it signifies EIGHTEEN, we proceed to inquire what it is a quantity of. All the ideographic evidence together gives a probability that ⊊ stands for some liquid; upon this probability depends the subordinate one that the liquid is oil rather than something else. The many other tablets containing the ideogram contribute nothing verbal toward its identification. We are fortunate that Gn1184 has the word *05-12*, which we have elsewhere found to express something connected with quantity, though otherwise unsettled (see above, pp. 71-5); the quantitative substance is liable to be expressed by a word in the vicinity of *05-12*. We would perhaps expect it to follow *05-12* rather than precede, since in Greek the noun usually follows τόσ(σ)ον 'so much' or any related form.[6] But we are not yet committed to rules of word order for Linear B, whether inferred from Greek or any other source. An internal study of the Linear B corpus, however, brings out no instance — apart from Gn1184 — where the word before *05-12* is likely to be a noun to which an adjective 'so much' or 'so many' is attached.[7] On the other hand, the two words *05-12 72-15* are written more often without the word-divider than with it in Ep212, 301, 539, 617, 704, 705 — which implies a tight syntactical relation between them.[8] We have not been able to verify Ventris's transcription of *72-15* as *pe-mo*, supposed to equal σπέρμα 'seed'; but it is still probable that the word is

143

a noun, modified by the quantitative 05-12. On this analogy, if Gn1184 contains a noun which 05-12 modifies, the noun ought to be 38-10-13-45-28 following 05-12 (although not on the same line), rather than 38-33-42. However, the analogy is not conclusive; 05-12 may follow its noun here for some reason we cannot probe. Even in classical Greek, much as it has been studied, many matters of word order escape us. Common sense may recommend that we figure out the grammar of the Linear B language more from one intelligible text than from a multitude of unintelligible ones, such as those containing 05-12 72-15. The construction 38-33-42 05-12 gives something admissible in Greek if transcribed *e-ra₃-wo to-so* 'so much oil.' ἔλαι(ϝ)ον before τόσον is within the bounds of correct Greek. On the other hand, we get nowhere by trying to make 38-10-13-45-28 go with 05-12, but we can construe it with 08-72-14-44 (see below, p. 151). If we could not find any Greek construction for 38-10-13-45-28, we would be bound to suspect that the construction 38-33-42 05-12 'so much oil' is illusory.

On balance it is probable rather than improbable that if the ideogram stands for some liquid measure, 38-33-42 is the word expressing that liquid. The phonetic value of 42 is then what the last syllable in the Linear B word for 'sons' (or 'boys') has in common with the last syllable of the Linear B word for that liquid. There is only one Greek solution for the value of 42, given these conditions and given also that we already have a strong case for identifying the first character of 70-42 as *ko* and a fairly strong case for the first character of 38-33-42 being *e*. 38-33-42 would have to mean 'oil,' and 42 would have to correspond to (ϝ)ο in the Greek alphabet. The consonant ϝ happens to be attested in the feminine 'girl' but not directly in the masculine 'boy'; it is not attested in the Greek word for 'oil' except for the Latin borrowing *oliuom*.[9] The ϝ can therefore be safely restored as having existed in some dialect forms of both words, *κόρϝοι and *ἔλαιϝον. The value *wo* for 42 should be understood as a normalization of Linear B to the phonology of those dialects, not a commitment to a certain phonological system valid for Linear B itself.

33 =*la*(*i*). The phonetic value of 33 is merely that which will fill a gap of one syllabic character between *e*- and -*wo*. The Greek syllable is -λαι-, but we are in no position to say which phoneme contrasts of Greek may be ignored or neutralized by the Linear B character 33. No character in the Cypriotic syllabary stands for more than a consonant plus a simple vowel, and neither does any Linear B character *which we have verified so far* stand for more. But we see too little of the whole Linear B writing system to set up universal rules for it. We have noted that 02 ignores the Greek distinction between ρ and λ (see above, p. 69); so 33 may ignore it too, but that remains unproved.

Ventris first gave 33 the value *ra*, alongside of 60, casually and without explanation, not in "Evidence" but in another article a little later.[10] He seems to have taken the value for 33 from one word, 39-46-33 next to a drawing of a bowl, while a different-looking vessel on another tablet has the word 39-25-60 (see above, p. 85). To connect either drawing with the Greek word φιάλη/φιέλη (-ᾱ instead of -η outside of Ionic) was a mere guess, but the kind that Ventris loved to make.[11] In *Documents* (p. 23) 33 was labeled *ra₃* (*rai*).[12] The idea of a diphthong instead of a simple vowel arose no doubt because 33 is much rarer than 60 and ought therefore to stand for a less simple and less frequent sound, although the syllabary, in principle, does not admit diphthongs (see below, p. 235-6). Graphically 33 is one of the most complex characters: the bottom half of it looks like *04* ≡|≡ while the top is still fancier. A diphthongal value would be consistent with the Greek words ἔλαι(ϝ)ον and the plural φιέλαι; the drawing next to 39-46-33 is followed by the ideographic numeral III (i.e., 3). But so is the drawing next to 39-25-60; therefore no phonetic difference between 33 and 60 can be established by reference to the Greek nominative plural ending -αι.

The quasi-pronominal function of 05-12. From our examination, so far, of part of Gn1184, we are on the one hand entitled to confidence that the transcription *e-ra₃-wo to-so* has too many contacts with reality to be illusory. On the other hand we are already in serious difficulty. The function of *05-12*, whether or not we accept the value *12 = so*, is unlike that of any word in a Greek text. It is quantitative but does not express any precise quantity; obviously it is not the Linear B word for 'eighteen.' Its function in this tablet and other tablets is (so to speak) pronominal: the precise quantity is given ideographically in another section of the tablet, with empty space intervening unless the scribe is hard up for room. It does not offhand strike us as reasonable that he would have written phonetically 'so much oil' and then ideographically MEASURES OF OIL (with 75 or *we* in ligature) 18. We need a theory to make sense of the apparent wastefulness, especially but not only in regard to *05-12*. Then we may be able to justify the identification of it with the Greek word τόσον and take other steps toward understanding the peculiar character of the Linear B scribal language and its true relation to classical Greek.

It is well known that the Greek numbers above 'four' and under 'two hundred' lack inflexions for case and gender; but nobody has pointed out the full implications of the fact, which has parallels in the other ancient Indo-European languages.[13] The uninflected numbers, in their fundamental use, were not strictly parts of *speech* (μέρη λόγου). The chief

146

occasion for pronouncing them was when there was something to count; to employ such a word in a sentence was only
secondary, when the counted thing was talked about.[14] The
ratio between the non-sentence use and the sentence use of
any particular number tended to determine whether it
would be uninflected or inflected. The lowest numbers must
have been less often needed for actual counting than for
reference within a sentence to something already counted or
else instantly countable by a mere glance of the speaker
without interrupting the flow of words. At the other extreme,
high numbers would mainly occur in sentences, where the
speaker would either know from a previous count or make
an estimate without actual counting. In both of these ranges
the numbers would receive an adjective or noun inflexion
conforming to the pattern of the Greek (or Indo-European)
sentence. But the numbers in between remained basically
alien to that structure. We know them in Greek mostly
through their occurrence in texts consisting of sentences;
but it would be unsafe to judge that in the ordinary spoken
language the same numbers occurred more in sentences than
outside of them. Rather the preserved forms, without inflexion, argue that they were frequently used in separate
counting, where the inflexions would have been excess bag-
gage — so frequently as to resist the analogical tendency to
dress the entire nominal (non-verbal) part of the vocabulary
in case and gender suffixes. A few case forms are attested:
πέμπων, δέκων (Aeolic), ΕΞΑΣΙΝ (Schwyzer, I, 590); but
they never gained currency in Greek.[15] The continued adherence of the Greeks to Indo-European tradition should not
be taken for something obvious and natural, as comparative
grammarians have tacitly assumed. The grammatical difference between the lowest numbers and the next higher ones
was retained not as a mere fossil but because it served in
the economy of the Greek language.[16]

Returning to the Linear B tablets, we observe that the evident purpose of most of them is to record or keep track of quantities of persons or things. They are not like texts whose structure is a series of sentences, which may occasionally convey some numerical information. Quite the contrary, any sentence structure that may be found in a typical Linear B tablet is subsidiary, leading up to the numeral. So much is apparent to us, no matter what language was written in the Linear B characters. As for the numbers written ideographically, such as $-\substack{||||\\||||}$, we know only that the number system was decimal; we have no indication that the writer or the reader of a tablet would normally have pronounced the numbers in Greek, or some other language, or not pronounced them at all. What we are warranted in theorizing is that the numbers, large and small alike, were isolated from the verbal text of the tablets, in some of which we can make out a few Greek words. Our theory need not go so far as to assert that in the Greek spoken before (say) 1000 B.C. numbers could not, as a rule, be incorporated into a sentence. We have no data about the possible range of expression in Greek or any other language of the Aegean in the Second Millennium B.C., beyond what may be mirrored in the tablets from Crete and the Greek mainland. In the language of the Linear B tablets, to judge particularly from Gn1184, the numbers were of paramount importance and were not integrated with the verbal text. *05-12* serves in the verbal text as a prop or surrogate for the numerical designation of quantity, which the style of the scribes — if not also the language of the country — was averse to expressing inside the same verbal unit.

A common observation in modern times is that persons who acquire a second language continue to do their counting in the language that they first learned to count in. It seems so fundamental in the psychology of learning that we may look for indications of the same habit at any time in the past. The usage of the Linear B scribes, who spelled out the word for 'so much' and wrote the actual number ideographically, may be explicable on the hypothesis that they made the count in their own language but wrote the word for 'so much' in another language, along with the adjacent words. I do not jump to the conclusion that the whole verbal text of a tablet is Greek if it includes the word 05-12. The problem is liable to be more complicated (see below, p. 193).

The equations 45 = *de*, 12 = *so*, 31 = *sa*. Within the vocabulary of the known Greek language, the word whose meaning would be most adaptable to such a function is τόσο-, or its compounds with the -δε suffix, such as τοσόνδε. If Linear B is like Greek, the neuter plural and the feminine would replace the second ο with the more open vowel α (η instead of long α in Ionic). Linear B has indeed four words to fit the pattern: 05-12, 05-12-45, 05-31, 05-31-45. The value 05 = *to* is verified without recourse to these words of quantity (see above, p. 69). In the former discussion of 45 = *de*, I hesitated to use 05-12-45 as corroboration for the phonetic value of the last character in 37-53-11-45 *ti-ri-po-de*, because the meaning of 05-12-45 was not proved by the context to

have more than a loose similarity to τοσό$\left\{ \begin{matrix} v \\ o \\ \iota \end{matrix} \right\}$δε. Now, thanks

to our theory, we can attach more credit to the semantic connexion between τόσον and 05-12 in the "oil" tablet. In other tablets, which yield nothing like a Greek construction — much less a sentence — nevertheless 05-12 does at least behave like an antecedent to a number written ideographically. To that extent the meaning of 05-12 is identical in all tablets, and the same meaning is shared by 05-12-45, 05-31, and 05-31-45. Reading the words as Greek would make -45 stand for the suffix -δε.

Furthermore the theory (though not the inescapable facts) requires that 12 be equated with so, because the difference in sound between 12 and 31, which stand next to MAN and WOMAN ideograms respectively in many tablets, should correspond to the difference between τόσοι and τόσαι. Except for the words under discussion now, we cannot bring forward anything that would confirm the values so and sa. The known gender of ἔλαιον in Greek, being neuter, is at least no obstacle to the transcription to-so; however, the graphic identity of masculine plural (and singular) and neuter singular will have to be separately treated in Chapter VIII. In the absence of any Linear B symbol to serve like the Greek letter -ν, we are deprived of proof that the Linear B language has full agreement of adjective with noun — i.e., ἔλαι(ϝ)ον τόσον rather than ἐλαί(ϝ)ου τόσον or some other construction. Neither have we any sign of the accusative case.

From the statement that 05-31(-45) is the feminine of 05-12(-45), it does not follow that if 12 is so, 31 must be sa, except as a normalization of Linear B to Greek — in this case a normalization with no other evidence to confirm it. As a theory — a working hypothesis — we are entitled to assume that Linear B is like Greek on all points where we lack evidence to the contrary. But we beg the question if we confuse the theory with fact, and we pervert it from its proper purpose of helping us to arrive at incontrovertible proofs.

The dative construction. The five apparently Greek words in Gn1184 include three that end in -Co according to Ventris's transcription. They are assigned to the Greek "second declension"; but the failure to show -ς, -ν, or -ι, after the vowel of the final syllable, deprives us of anything morphological to prove that the syntax is like Greek. If we normalize to Κώκαλος and ἔλαι(ϝ)ον τόσον, we are adding a Greek distinction that is not attested by the Linear B script and may not have been in the Linear B language. The lack of a case ending debars us from citing these three words as evidence that the sentence is Greek. Even though there is no objection to *e-ra₃-wo* and *to-so* as Greek words — or rather Greek stems — the missing -*n* is needed to support the theory that the sentence is Greek: *e-ra₃-wo to-so* is taken for the object and *ko-ka-ro* for the subject because such a construction will make sense and it is somewhat favored by the word order of many languages, subject + verb + object; but the indispensable Greek device of nominative and accusative endings has to be imagined — it is not here. However, the other two words *a-pe-do-ke* and *e-u-me-de-i*, though not adjacent, fall admirably into a Greek construction. Palmer rightly insisted upon this as one of the very strongest proofs of Greek revealed in the Linear B corpus by Ventris's transcription (*Gnomon*, XXIX, 580).

$08 = a$ has been demonstrated apart from the "oil" tablet. $38 = e$ and $45 = de$ have been shown to be probable, though not guaranteed. $28 = i$ is weaker: the only ideographic evidence for it is in the word 28-32 'horses' in one Knosos tablet, while in others the same value entails a word of un-Greek structure *o-pi-i-ja-pi*.[17] The other syllables of the words

$$08\text{-}72\text{-}14\text{-}44 \text{ and } 38\text{-}10\text{-}13\text{-}45\text{-}28,$$

which Ventris transcribed   -*pe-do-ke* and   -*u-me*-
respectively, would be merely conjectural apart from their occurrence on this tablet. But the nexus in 'gave back to E.' is too good to let by as a coincidence. It hinges on one character in each word, -*14*- = -*do*- 'give' and the dative ending -*28* = -*i* 'to.' Many possibilities would remain for -*10-13*-, within the bounds of the theory that the five words constitute a Greek sentence. The name need not be Εὐμήδεϊ but

only something in the "third declension" with no consonant at the end of the stem preceding -ι. The values e- and -de- narrow down the possibilities but still leave a considerable leeway for names after the Greek pattern: compounds beginning with Ἐχε-, Ἑκα-, etc., and having a second member -κηδε(ο)-, -κῦδε(ο)-, -ωδε(ο)-, etc. For that matter, the theory does not require that the name must have the structure of a Greek compound and an aristocratic connotation. If the initial name 70-77-02 ko-ka-ro is Greek at all, it must be plebeian, taken from the homely part of the vocabulary; κώκαλον is given by Hesychius as παλαιόν, καὶ εἶδος ἀλεκτρυόνος, and κόκκαλος is a kernel of a pine cone — both of them without an etymology.

If the tablet were damaged and all that remained of the first and second lines were

    ?-?-?]   08-[?]-14-[?]   38-[?]-42   05-12

    38-[?-?]-45-28   𐀰 —꜀꜀꜀꜀

we would have as much evidence of Greek as we have now. Given 38 = e and 42 = wo, we would restore a middle syllable to yield the Greek word for 'oil'; but the meaning of the sentence would leave any other restoration doubtful. That amounts to saying that in 08-72-14-44 the values 72 = pe and 44 = ke are doubtful; so are 10 = u and 13 = me in the last word.[18] But 14 = do is indispensable as one half of the 'give to' construction.

History of the value 14 = do. There is no other evidence for the value *do*. In Work Note 11 (pp. 37-40) Ventris figured that 14-38-02 means 'male servant,' with a feminine counterpart 14-38-60, and asked whether it could be "the original of the Greek word *doulos* 'slave', through an earlier form *do^welo-s*?? I gather that the Indo-European etymologies of this word have not yet been sorted out to everyone's satisfaction."[19] His thinking was bold though brilliant: he found a fair correlation between the last character in words accompanying 14-38-02 in the Eb, Ec, En, Eo, and Ep tablets and accompanying the MAN ideogram in other Pylos tablets, while words accompanying either 14-38-60 or the WOMAN ideogram showed a different correlation. The evidence did not entitle him to say that certain words go with 14-38-02 and with MAN, and that certain other words go with 14-38-60 and with WOMAN. The correlation was only in the endings of the words; and to this day it remains undemonstrated that 14-38-02 and 14-38-60 refer to persons.

Ventris had previously accepted the Cypriotic value *lo* as applicable to Linear B (see above, p. 23). Although in *Documents* (p. 18) he looked back on *do-we-lo* as a "wild guess," it seems to have been his only basis for setting 14 (reduced in size) right above 05 and below 11 in the second state of the grid, and setting 38 in the square where it would get the value *ve* ? *re* ? in the third state.[20] He already had 05 = *to* and 11 = *po* from the the Cypriotic syllabary (see above, p. 27). All in all, his reasoning in regard to 14 leaves the impression of a fluke. I cannot fathom why he derived δοῦλος from a trisyllabic *do^welos*, unless he took the Attic "spurious" diphthong ου (ΔΟΛΟΝ, accusative, in the Golden Age spelling, *IG²* 1.328.3) to be equivalent to *owe* in Cypriotic:

Attic   δοῦναι (ΔΟΝΑΙ)[21] 'to give'   hence δοῦλος
Cypriotic *to-we-na-i*[21]   Linear B *do-we-lo(s)*

In both the second and the third state of the grid he must have perceived that *do* involved a departure from the Cypriotic rule of no distinction between voiced and unvoiced consonants; in the third state he labeled two rows *t-* ? Yet he held to 14 = *do* on the strength of only one slight support in the Pylos material published by Bennett in *PT* (1951): The word 40-14-42-28-36 (Ad17, An24.2) is paralleled by 40-51-42-28-36 (Jn08.3),[22] and 51 is interchanged with 01 in several other words.[23] Neither then nor later was there any particular reason for assuming that in these words *51* has some phonetic relation to *14* on the one hand and to *01* on the other; the meaning of the words is altogether obscure, and the connexion between them merely hypothetical. But the assumption had an advantage, because Ventris was inclined to the Cypriotic value *ta* (including τα, δα, θα) for *01* but could not find in Linear B any interchange between *01* and *05* (Cypriotic *to*) or between *01* and *37* (Cypriotic *ti*). The "wild guess" *14* = *do* was a prop to the idea of another dental series, embracing *14, 01,* and *51* but separate from *05* and *37*, and destined eventually to be restricted to one dental consonant *d-*. In Work Note 20 (p. 174) he seized upon a much better indication that *14* and *01* are related. *SM* II made available the Knosos tablets with the word *70-53-57-14-52* (Ga415, 417, 421-423, 674, 676, 685), which he compared to *70-53-25-01-06* (Un267.5, Pylos) because the two words are accompanied by a similar ideogram.[24] His transcriptions *kori^{j}at^{o}no* and *kori^{j}at^{a}na* (ignoring the special difficulty of *25*, which he later made *a₂*) fascinated him because one resembles the Greek singular, the other the Greek plural. But his main point was that *ko-^{l}/$_r$i-ja-t^o-no* "is strikingly similar to the Greek word *koríannon* 'coriander' . . . , whose by-forms *koríandron, kolíandron, koríamblon* suggest that *-nn-* is a reduction of some more difficult group of consonants."

It is easy but insufficient to object that from first to last the value *14* = *do* was guesswork. The guess turned out to be portentously lucky. Not only does it occur in the acceptably Greek portion of Gn1184; but the intelligibility of the sentence hinges upon this one character. Unless the second word *08-72-14-44* expresses some notion that falls under the heading of 'give,' the sentence is gone. Conceivably something could be salvaged if the second word had to be taken for an epithet, surname, or other qualifier of the first; but with a verb then needing to be "understood" and the subject and direct object both devoid of case endings, the structure would be too flimsy to warrant identification with Greek. In case the character *14* were accidentally obliterated along with its neighbor on either side, we would be tempted but not obliged to restore something including *do;* for that is the root common to all forms of the usual Greek verb for 'give.' However, we would be assuming that none of the less frequently used verbs of related meaning was used in this instance — also (in accord with our present theory) that the Linear B language is like Greek in distinguishing between 'put' and 'give.' Many other ancient languages indifferently express 'put' or 'give' by the same morpheme; e.g., the Latin compound verbs *abde* 'put away,' *redde* 'give back.' In our theory we are entitled to hold *14* = *do,* but it has no strict confirmation outside of Gn1184. Ventris's guesses about words with *14* in other tablets remain unsubstantiated. Nor does the fact that the guesses came first, before he knew of Gn1184, elevate them to adequate reasons. The sequence of events obliges us to admire Ventris; but how to put our admiration properly into practice, calls for further pondering (see below, p. 165).

The case for and against 72 = *pe.* For the beginning of the verb we may need something like ἀπο- or ἀπε-. We have prior proof that *08* = *a.* As between ἀπο- and ἀπε-, since we have also ascertained that another character, *11*, occupies the *po* niche in the syllabary, the simple solution — perhaps naively simple — would be to conclude *72* = *pe.* Thus the Greek augment of past time would be shared by Linear B. It does not matter that no other instance of the augment has been discovered by Ventris's transcription of the Linear B corpus; for the alleged verb forms without augment in

Linear B are all conjectural.[25] That leaves the question open in regard to *08-72-14-44*. *72* could be *pe* or *po₂*; there is no decisive evidence. In studying *37-53-61-75-38* and *37-53-36-75* 'three-eared,' we were unable to define the phonological relation between *61* and *36* and left them in the loose formulation *o* and *o₂* (see above, p. 84). Furthermore the word *61-14-44* at the beginning of Un267.1 (Pylos) is likely to be related to *08-72-14-44*; and until the apparent prefix *o-* is satisfactorily explained, the morphological relation of the two words with *-14-44* cannot be settled — neither can the phonetic value of *72* be safely deduced from its context here in Gn1184.

What prompted Ventris to give *72* the value *pe* is a mystery. In "Evidence" he offered no case of alternation between *72* and other *p-* characters. In the second and third states of the grid he had hesitantly put the reduced character *72* into the same row with *73, 15*, and *80*, which later were called *mi, mo*, and *ma* respectively as a result of the experiment in Work Note 20.[26] The only reason for placing *72* in that row was one "orthographic variation" with *80*.[27] The grid method failed to determine the role of *72* in the syllabary. Ventris chose the *-e* ? column for it because of the alternation

    77-06-72-10 (En74.3,23, Eo160.3, 276.2)

    77-06-72-42 (Eo269.2; Work Note 14, p. 121, item P 152) Work Note 16 (especially p. 150) gave arguments for and against identifying the alternation with the -ευς declension of Greek; the third state of the grid, in Work Note 17, shows he decided that any penultimate character before such an alternation has the vowel *-e* ? Right after finishing Work Note 20, he experimentally read these words as *ka-na-pe-u*, *ka-na-pe-wo* 'fuller' (nom. and gen. sing.; Greek κναφεύς or γναφεύς).[28] The meaning was from the outset unlikely in tablets of the E series dealing presumably with agriculture (cf. Beattie, *MIOF*, VI, 41); and Ventris adduced no other words with *72* that add appreciably to the probability of this value *pe*, even by the loose standards which he recognized (see above, pp. 37-8).

The suitability of *pe* to the context of Gn1184 is even more of a fluke than the suitability of *do*. However, the case for *pe*, which is otherwise so weak, is not much strengthened by Gn1184, because it is far less essential to the construction than *do*. The meaning does not have to be 'gave back'; it could be 'gave in exchange, gave in return' — ἀντίδωκε or ἀντέδωκε.²⁹ The semantic sphere of the two prefixes ἀπο- and ἀντι- with this verb is not sharply delimited, although ἀντ ʹ̔ξ δωκε would preferably have not only a direct object in the accusative but also a genitive to express the thing received by the subject. The Linear B text in Gn1184 does not enable us to prove either an accusative or a genitive case ending; but this circumstance neither enhances nor lessens the possibility that an exchange is involved. What the subject received may be referred to in the three obscure words of the bottom line and the ideographic numeral THIRTY-EIGHT. But those three words make the question insoluble; for they exhibit nothing to indicate they are Greek. We end up with *pe* a possible but quite insecure value for *72*.

The case for 44 = ke. To get a Greek sentence, the transcription *ke* for *44* in *08-72-14-44* is no more indispensable than *pe* for *72*. The middle ἀπέδοτο 'sold' would make as good sense as the active ἀπέδωκε 'gave back, paid.' There is a further possibility of the verb being plural like ἀπέδοσαν, ἀπέδοντο, since we are not guaranteed that the previous word *70-77-02*, which would seem to be the subject, is singular. Finally it could be first person, ἀπέδωκα, ἀπεδόμην (-μᾱν), or even ἀπέδομεν; for in Greek a written statement may take the form illustrated in the letter of Themistocles: Θεμιστοκλῆς ἥκω παρὰ σέ 'I, Themistocles, have come to you' (Thucydides 1.137.4).[30] As outsiders approaching the Linear B corpus, we are not warranted in relying on a subjective preference for *a-pe-do-ke* with *-ke* rather than any alternative in the last syllable.

Apart from Gn1184 Ventris had a little more reason for *44 = ke* than for *72 = pe*. He did connect *44* with *70* by the distributional method (see above, p. 126); so by assigning the value *ko* to *70* in Work Note 20 (p. 173) he implied *44 = ke*, and so it remained. We must reckon the grid successful to the extent that *ke* slips neatly into place to make a syllable of a Greek sentence in Gn1184 — not that *ke* is the only value that a syllable at that point in the sentence could have.

The dative ending of Linear B. The pivotal identifications for the Greek sentence in the "oil" tablet are *14 = do* and *28 = i*. The latter agrees with what was found in Ca895: *28-32* next to the horses' heads (see above, p. 111); so Linear B, in two independent instances, uses *28* where Greek has ι. The Linear B nouns of consonantal stem ("third declension") were previously supposed to form a dative singular by adding *-e* to that consonant, unlike the -ι of Greek but perhaps corresponding to the rare and problematical vestiges of an -ει ending, chiefly in the god's name ΔΙΕΙ.[31] The alleged dative singular forms of Linear B, graphically identical with the nominative plural, were recognized by occurring right after *03-02*, which is transcribed *pa-ro* and boldly equated with παρά.[32] However, παρά is liable to be followed by an accusative, a genitive, or a dative in Greek, depending on the sense of the clause. It was never shown that the contexts where *pa-ro* occurs would require a dative by the rules of Greek. We are still in the dark about the relation to Greek, if any, that may be lurking in *03-02* and in the case — as yet unidentifiable — which goes with it. Just as unreliable are the few instances where, it is claimed, a Linear B dative singular ends in -i.[33] Neither the -e nor the -i "datives" found outside of Gn1184 are impressive, even in a superficial, illusory way. We had better restrict our discussion of the dative in Linear B to the one tablet, although we must treat it with some reserve until independent, converging evidence turns up from another source.

The identification of 28 with the Greek vowel ι fits the word for 'horses' in Ca895; it enables us to read three consecutive words in an otherwise obscure text (Ta722) as Greek, 'man and horse and poulp' — a fantastic grouping, to be sure; above all, it makes a Greek sentence out of five words in Gn1184. $28 = i$ is still not as strong as the first nine equations recapitulated in my list near the end of the preceding chapter (see above, p. 127); those nine can be doubted only in defiance of reason. It would not be unreasonably cautious to keep $28 = i$ in suspense; we would then be implying that the Greek sentence which ends 'to E.' may somehow be an illusion. However, we go ahead with the theory that the sentence is real; we have found many points in its favor — not enough, indeed, to establish it conclusively — but none that seriously militate against it. A reasonable doubt ought to be raised and answered in regard to the unGreek sequence -pi-i- in a recurrent word 61-39-28-57-39 of the chariot tablets (see above, p. 99, note 31). $39 = pi$ is justified by one occurrence only, in a-pi-po-re-we beside the drawing of an amphora (see above, p. 84); but in that one occurrence -pi- is demanded by the adjacent syllables a- and -po- and further supported by -we, so that the Greek word is unmistakable. No single point in favor of $28 = i$ stands as firm as $39 = pi$. Neither value is so strong as to rule out the other if the two are incompatible, as they seem to be in 61-39-28-57-39.

We must in any case recognize something alien to Greek in the word transcribed *o-pi-i-ja-pi* (of which only the fourth syllable can be left in limbo as a mere speculation). If we use the word to cast doubt on 28 = *i*, we still shall not obtain in the Greek vocabulary a word to fit the syllabic pattern *o-pi-?-?-pi* and the ideographic context of the chariot tablets. Nor shall we arrive at a Greek word by sacrificing 39 = *pi*. It is better to leave room in our theory for the possibility that an unknown Linear B word may have a sequence *-pi-i-* foreign to Greek phonology, than to posit either that the Linear B word for 'amphoras' has something different from *-pi-* (-φι-) for its second syllable or that the dative case ending in Linear B is not *-i* where Greek would have -ι. To admit that Linear B contains something non-Greek *in structure* is a momentous departure from the theory and even more from the practice of Ventris's adherents, who are inclined to see nothing foreign to Greek in Linear B except some items of vocabulary and many proper names. I will set forth in the next chapter my reasons for theorizing that a great deal of the structure as well as vocabulary of Linear B is alien to Greek.

For the moment, in discussing Gn1184, I need only remark that the Greek ends with the fifth word. The "OIL" ideogram contains a ligature of the character 75, as also in Fn101 from Mycenae. Other Pylos tablets exhibit the "OIL" ideogram with a different ligature — *o8*, *o3*, or *11* — or none; and the Knosos tablets have it with no ligature (Bennett, *OOTP*, p. 16). Bennett and others have attempted — either ingeniously or halfheartedly, but in any event fruitlessly — to make out the characters in ligature to be abbreviations of Greek words. Success was precluded by the meagerness of the data; for 75, although we have the phonetic value *we* for it, no Greek word that describes oil and begins with ϝε- is even on the horizon. The three words in the last line of

Gn1184 are not Greek, if transcribed according to Ventris's decipherment; or if we transcribe only those characters that we have more or less verified, even so I see little prospect of filling out ?-*ro i-pe*-?-*wa* ?-?-*re-we* to make Greek.

60 = *ra* (*lai*) *in Fr1223* (*problematical*). As soon as we grant that 38-33-42 corresponds to the Greek word ἔλαι(ϝ)ον 'oil' in Gn(or Fr)1184, we must of course extend the same identification to other occurrences of the word, provided that the same ideogram accompanies it. Other tablets do not quite meet this condition; for they exhibit the ideogram either with no ligature or with a different ligature instead of 75. The meaning of the ligatures remains apparently insoluble, in spite of Bennett's efforts (see below, p. 187). Yet probably enough the variation in the ligature does not compromise the meaning OIL for the ideogram itself. Now in the first line of Fr1217 we find

$$38\text{-}33\text{-}42 \quad 03\text{-}70\text{-}75 \quad 75\text{-}57\text{-}27\text{-}72$$

followed by the ideogram with the ligature 08 in the third line; and the first line of Fr1223 has the words

$$37\text{-}52\text{-}45 \quad 38\text{-}60\text{-}42 \quad 03\text{-}70\text{-}75 \quad 75\text{-}08\text{-}27\text{-}72$$
$$\uparrow$$

(38 written over 03)

followed immediately by the ideogram again with the ligature 08. Anyone not prejudiced against the decipherment will acknowledge some relation or other between 38-33-42 and 38-60-42, and between the obscure last words of the phrase 75-57-27-72 and 75-08-27-72. We lack the data to show whether the difference in the second character of one pair of words is correlated with the difference in the second character, again, of the other pair. Within Greek no inflexions would adhere to such a pattern; and dialect variation would not be very plausible in one locality — indeed in one room of the palace of Pylos, though the handwriting is different.[34] In an unknown language it could be a significant alternation, but beyond our power to judge. Our identification of 38-33-42 with ἔλαι(ϝ)ον in Gn1184 does not warrant a presumption that Fr1217 and 1223 are in Greek. Every word in both of them is obscure except 38-33-42 (and 38-60-42), and ἔλαιον is naturally not an item of Indo-European vocabulary but belongs to the olive culture of the Mediterranean.

We are checked in our desire to figure out the relation between 33 and 60. That they are not simply interchangeable appears from an erasure in Eb866 (Pylos): the scribe had 80-60-54 but changed the second character to 33. We get no light from the preceding word 37-52-45 in Fr1223; the transcription *ti-no-de* is irreproachable but does not yield anything meaningful in itself — let alone anything that will illuminate the choice of -60- rather than -33- in the ensuing word. Nor can we unhesitatingly apply the sort of argument that gave us a result in the case of

37-53-61-75-38 'three-eared' (dual or plural)

37-53-36-75 'three-eared' (singular; see above,
pp. 81-4)

Given the transcription *ti-ri-o-we-e* for the five-character word, the sound of 36 cannot be in doubt beyond certain limits: it must be reconcilable with a word of the Greek structure *τριῶϝες. Even though the compound adjective itself is not attested in Greek, its elements are, and they meet perfectly the requirements for pure Greek of Indo-European origin. Some other words on the tripod-and-jug tablet may not be Greek; so we cannot utterly rule out the thought that the alternation between 61 and 36 may be non-Greek. But at least the starting point for any theory about the deformation of the word away from Greek must be a Greek form virtually identical with *τριῶϝε(ς). On the other hand, the relation between 38-33-42 and the attested Greek but non-Indo-European word ἔλαιον imposes no limit known to us upon the second character of 38-60-42. The alternation is liable to be altogether non-Indo-European and not reflected anywhere in Greek (see below, pp. 202-3).

Again it is unsafe to argue that the Greek identifications of two Linear B words, *38-60-42* 'oil' and *14-38-60* 'female slave,' converge independently to support *60 = ra*, which Ventris hit upon in Work Note 20 (see above, p. 36). The fact that in Greek ἔλαιον and δούλη (-ᾱ) have [la] in common does not establish, by convergence, a value for the Linear B character *60*, because the identification of *14-38-60* with the Greek word for 'female slave' is only tentative. Moreover, apart from the meaning 'slave' for the root, it is not proved that the suffix is feminine — i.e., that *14-38-60* is the feminine of *14-38-02* (see above, p. 153), whose last character is known to be *ro* (*lo*). Ak824.1 (Knosos) begins

    08-39-32-28-59 14-38-60 WOMAN ≡ıı [i.e., 32]

but the tantalizing An607 (Pylos), in which all items close with WOMAN and a numeral, has the word *14-38-60* in some items, *14-38-02* in another, and both words in still another. The phonetic as well as the semantic relation of

14-38-60   and   *38-60-42*
to *14-38-02*   to *38-33-42*

remains doubtful; and *60 = ra* has insufficient confirmation.

The decipherment enhanced by the reading of Gn1184. The research of the present chapter has not arrived at any point of incontestable certainty like the values of several characters in Ta641. We have tried out a theory that we explicitly founded upon a number of probabilities, and we have obtained a few more values that are probable, though not certain. First, two characters whose value would otherwise by wholly hypothetical:

$$14 = do$$
$$33 = la(i)$$

Next, five values for which there was some demonstrative evidence (see above, pp. 127-8), strengthened now by a probable confirmation in Gn1184:

$$12 = so$$
$$28 = i$$
$$38 = e$$
$$42 = wo$$
$$45 = de$$

Furthermore, four values which have passed the test at least negatively — i.e., they have not been ruled out as impossible:

$$10 = u$$
$$13 = me$$
$$44 = ke$$
$$72 = pe^{35}$$

None of Ventris's values have failed the test of the new tablet, except in the sense that the ones which make up the last three words, *pa-ro i-pe-se-wa ka-ra-re-we*, give nothing intelligible as Greek. Finally, Gn1184 indirectly and tenuously supports the experimental value $60 = ra$.

So much, and no more, I judge to be the contribution of Gn1184 to the decipherment; so much would the tablet have helped Ventris or any other inquirer, had it been on hand when the decipherment was worked out. I hesitate to say whether it has some greater significance on account of being dug up subsequently. We have seen how several of the values that are either necessary for the reading of the sentence or at any rate workable — $14 = do$, $28 = i$, $33 = ra(_3)$, $72 = pe$ — had been fastened upon by Ventris for the slenderest of reasons. Offhand I would call it a fluke that they fit the subsequently discovered tablet so well. Beattie, to detract from Ventris's enormous fame, reconstructs a "rational explanation" of how Ventris obtained a value for 33: "a text containing both *e-ra₃-wo* [i.e., 38-33-42] and 130 [the "OIL" ideogram] (or alternatively a pair of texts which made it possible to associate the word and the ideogram) had become known to Ventris as early as the summer of 1953 or even before then" (*MIOF*, VI, 100). But the "rational explanation" is not backed by any testimony or documentary proof; nor does it touch the values *do, i,* and *pe,* which Ventris announced in 1952 or earlier. The most rational course for us is, paradoxically, to acknowledge that Ventris indulged his hunches in advance of any adequate reasons, and that the future bore out his hunches to an extent beyond the random.

It is therefore extremely difficult to assess Ventris and his decipherment at precisely their true worth; but we must try. The degree of his success, as we have looked into it, entitles him and the decipherment to a further extension of credit, but not unbounded credit. Several of his hunches turned out to be good, none of those expressed from Work Note 20 on have been actually refuted, but many remain in suspense — and most of the Linear B corpus is still unintelligible. It does not become us as scholars either to treat Ventris's transcription as worthless except where we have been able to check it, or to treat it as equally reliable throughout. Scholars ought on the one side to follow every track that offers even the slightest prospect of fuller knowledge. On the other side, they have a right and even a duty to be conservative, to refrain from picturing on the same level what is really on firm ground and what is up in the air. Demonstrated facts must not be confused with theory, nor must the organic parts of a well-coordinated theory be confused with a set of guesses. My analysis of the decipherment has verified a small part of it as unassailable fact, and upheld a good deal more as a tenable theory. But still neither I nor anyone else has worked out a critical method for appraising the greater part of the decipherment. There may be a lot that is worthwhile in it but eludes our grasp.

The minor importance of the grid. The decipherment as a whole, though accepted by many scholars, is warranted neither by an ample array of facts nor by a well-thought-out theory. Instead the scholars have been content with tokens of proof that it works — tokens which give them faith in the author, so that it has not seemed necessary to study his reasons. Their attitude of trustful admiration would have been intellectually disreputable in the world of higher learning, had it not been for the misconception that Ventris deduced his transcription by a rigorous cryptanalytic method, which they could properly respect but not judge competently because it fell within another discipline. The grid inspired in them an esteem it did not deserve. Beattie in his second major criticism, without probing very far into the bulk of the Work Notes, found plenty of proof that the decipherment was not "safeguarded by sound crytographic method or . . . strictly controlled by the grid" (*MIOF*, VI, 47). I, after studying all the Work Notes, can claim further that most of those phonetic values which are demonstrably right, or at any rate in conformity with a tenable theory, were obtained by Ventris not from the grid or his study of alternations, but from the Cypriotic syllabary or from his experimental identifications of certain Linear B words with Greek. The technical cryptanalytic approach certainly helped him to arrive at some of the good values, a minority of them — among them $52 = no$ (see above, p. 80). But some other good values, again a minority of them, including $61 = o$ (see above, p. 77), he got only by overruling the same method when a hunch told him it was impeding his progress. The grid was almost as much a hindrance as a help.

If scholars had understood his procedure to be essentially not scientific but intuitive, they might have been prejudiced and given no serious attention to any of his transcriptions. That would have been more harmful than their uncritical acceptance has been, were it not that the harm could have been rectified sooner, by the publication of the tripod-and-jug tablet. The past cannot be changed, but the present state of available knowledge obliges us to grapple with an unwelcome dilemma where reason does not authorize us to accept nor to reject. The majority of Ventris's values have no scientific standing, as fact or as theory. Of that majority some depend on the grid, others do not. The grid does not deserve to be either accepted or rejected as a whole. Many of Ventris's older hunches he himself discarded; but others that he clung to or conceived later have held up better than the grid, in those cases where they can be tested. What then are we to do with the many hunches, such as $77 = ka$, which he never discarded and we cannot see how to test? It seems to me a matter for individual preference and discretion; but those who set store by such parts of the decipherment should at least do it with their eyes open, being aware that it is an act of faith. They should furthermore not confuse themselves and their readers by placing the truly subjective parts of the decipherment on the same plane as the more objective parts.

Obstacles to the testing of other values. Although I cannot regard Ventris's decipherment as anywhere near a complete success, it does — if seen in its true light — something much greater than any other study of Linear B: it gives us a strong *foothold* which cannot collapse, and it allows a hope of subduing much if not all that remains outside our grasp. As I have shown in the analysis of Ta641, Gn1184, and the few other texts that are relatively manageable, even this foothold is not secure at all points; some of the values in my lists (see above, pp. 127-8, 163-4) may have to be revised. But with all due caution, here is something encouraging — we have more or less trustworthy phonetic values for thirty-two char-

acters out of a total of approximately eighty-eight.[36] Such a
ratio of success at any stage in a problem of modern military
cryptanalysis would almost always be rapidly followed
by a complete solution; the values hitherto undetermined
would pop out when the ones already obtained are applied
to more of the corpus. No such happy result awaits us when
we apply the thirty-two values to the remaining Linear B
material. We do not get more Greek words whose identity
is rendered probable by their suitability to one another
when they are in proximity, or to the ideographic context.
We neither add to the evidence in favor of these values nor
obtain values for the remaining characters by their occurrence in contexts where one Greek word and only one
is possible. We might hope that the few deciphered words,
reappearing in other tablets, would help; but instead they
promptly lead us to a dead end. The ubiquitous *05-12 to-so*
is ill suited to throw light on words in its vicinity; it means
no more than a vague 'so much, so many.' *38-33-42* 'oil' recurs
in several tablets,[37] but the attempts to read them as Greek
are painfully unsuccessful. In one of them, Fr1217, we meet
a long word *27-44-38-05-02-04-53-36*, transcribed *re-ke-e-to-
ro-te-ri-jo*, in which every value but *04 = te* has previously
been found by us to be more or less justified. Yet the whole
word has a structure irreconcilable with Greek morphology.[38]
It does nothing to establish *04 = te* or to strengthen any
other values. The words *70-77-02 ko-ka-ro* and *38-10-13-45
e-u-me-de* (without the dative ending) recur, each along
with *08-27-11-20-61*, which is not recorded except in connexion with one or the other of the these two words (Fg374,
Ea812, 820). No Greek word will fit the pattern *a-re-po-?-o;*
the proposed *ἀλειφοζόος 'ungent-boiler' (see *Documents*,
p. 389), which requires *20 = zo*, is contrary to the vocalic
structure of Greek compounds of the type σακεσφόρος,
βουληφόρος, etc., and to the intransitive meaning of the

verb root in early Greek (e.g., ζέε 'it boiled,' *Il.* 21.365).[39]

There the trail ends, and disciplined scholarship is obliged to halt this particular line of investigation and try another instead. Fantasy, of course, is ready to leap onward, in the unwarranted confidence that the texts must contain a Greek meaning; it abuses every license of farfetched interpretation to create an imaginary language under the guise of recovering an ancient one.

Notes to Chapter VI

1. *Documents,* p. 217; *PT* (1955), pp. 111, 166; *OOTP,* pp. 40-41 and pl. ii.

2. The one which, after Gn1184, comes perhaps the closest to an intelligible Greek phrase, though still not by a long shot close enough, is Ae303 (Pylos), transcribed in "Evidence," p. 93: "*PU-RO: i-je-re-ja do-e-ra e-ne-ka* **ku-ru-so-jo** *i-je-ro-jo:* Women *13* Πύλος · ἱερείας δοέλαι † ἕνεκα χρυσοῖο ἱεροῖο ΓΥΝΑΙΚΕΣ 13." In *Documents,* p. 166, it is translated 'At Pylos: 14+ [the number here agrees with Bennett's copy of the tablet, *PT* (1955), p. 119] female slaves of the priestess on account of sacred gold.' Ventris goes on to remark, "The nature of the transaction is obscure; were the slaves given to the priestess in return for some gold which had been offered? Or are they allocated to look after the gold ritual objects?" The Greek construction is at once arbitrary and incoherent; Beattie, *JHS,* LXXVI, 4, rightly censures it.

I am not going to give credit for the appreciable number of words like *61-06-05 o-na-to* (see above, p. 118) which, although consisting of characters whose values are either ascertained or at any rate quite probable, still do not correspond to anything known or inferable in the Greek vocabulary.

3. Bennett, "Fractional Quantities in Minoan Bookkeeping," *AJA,* LIV (1950), 219; "MT" (1953), pp. 447-48.

4. "Ägäische Texte in griechischer Sprache," *Eranos,* LI (1953), 116-117; LII (1954), 31. He did not settle, in his own mind, which of two ideograms is OIL and which is WINE — these being the two main liquid commodities of ancient Greece. Beattie, *MIOF, VI,* 99-100, seems to have misread Furumark's German sentence: "Es scheint jedenfalls sicher zu sein, dass diese beiden Ideogramme die wohl gewöhnlichsten flüssigen Produkte, Wein und Olivenöl, darstellen müssen." Furumark did not say it is certain that ᵞ is OIL and that the other is WINE. Beattie went on to reason that Furumark could not have been certain of it unless Ventris had been in a position to assure him, and that Ventris therefore must already have seen some unreported tablet with the ideogram ᵞ and the word *38-33-42* as in Gn1184, before Gn1184 itself was dug up! What a fantasy to erect on a mistranslation! Beattie was at pains to deprive Ventris's decipherment of any corroboration from the appearance of *e-ra₃-wo* on the new tablet (see above, pp. 164-5).

5. We do not have a Greek word °τριῶες 'three-eared,' but two Greek morphemes τρι- 'three-' and -ῶες '-eared,' which could combine without any obstacle.

6. In a Homeric passage it does not seem to matter whether τόσ(σ)ον is used retrospectively or prospectively. If the former, it is natural, and in Homeric Greek invariable, to have τόσ(σ)ον close to the previous clause — e.g., πεντήκοντα βοῶν ἀγέλας, τόσα πώεα οἰῶν 'fifty herds of cattle, as many flocks of sheep' (Il. 11.679). Where it is used prospectively, to be explained by a ὅσ(σ)ον clause, it still comes early: τόσσον χρόνον ὅσσον ἄνωγας 'as much time as you bid' (24.670). Only three times does it come after the noun (17.410, 19.202, Od. 8.340); in these it points to something present, conceived quantitatively: κακὸν τόσον 'an evil so great,' μένος οὐ τόσον 'rage not so great,' δεσμοὶ μὲν τρὶς τόσσοι 'bonds three times as many.' But even so the quantitative word more often precedes.

The availability of forms with -σ- and forms with -σσ- virtually obviates any metrical inducement to distort the word order.

7. Only in the unintelligible Un718 has Ventris tried to fit together 14-12-15 05-12 (do-so-mo to-so) into a construction 'so much as a contribution' (Documents, pp. 282-83).

8. The word-divider before 05-12 is regular in these tablets, but sporadically omitted.

9. Plautus, Ps. 301, etc. The more usual Latin word oleum contains no trace of a [w] sound.

10. "A Note on Decipherment Methods," accompanying Chadwick, "Greek Records in the Minoan Script," Antiquity, XXVII (1953), 202.

11. Beattie, MIOF, VI, 100-101, imagined that Ventris would not have ventured upon such a slenderly supported identification but must have secretly known of some tablet like Gn1184 containing the word 38-33-42 and the "OIL" ideogram, before the actual Gn1184 was excavated (see above, note 4). The suspicion on Beattie's part was gratuitous; he allowed too little, at that point, for Ventris's adventurous temperament and had of course no direct information whatever that another such "oil" tablet existed. Beattie's fantasy concerns my subject only as a reaction to the claims of Palmer and others that Ventris "predicted" certain words found later in Linear B tablets (see above, pp. 164-5).

Although 33 is omitted from the grid in "Evidence" and no word containing it is cited in that article, yet Ventris had paid a little attention to it in the Work Notes. The second state of the grid has it in the same row as *o2* and the same column as *o6*, which Ventris always reckoned as equivalent to the Cypriotic *lo* and *na* respectively; so he must then have taken *33* for *la*. The only reason I can see is an unspecified "orthographic variation" between *33* and *6o*, recorded in Figure 9, line 72 (Work Note 15), as "possible." *6o* is in the same row but in a column with *37* (the Cypriotic *ti*); see above, p. 67. In the third state of the grid *33* has been shoved out of the *la*? niche to make room for *26* and is kept on hand in the "vowel uncertain" column though still in the same row. I do not understand the stages of Ventris's reasoning and have not found any word with the character *33* in the Work Notes. *6o* was revalued *ra* and *26 ru* in Work Note 20 (see above, p. 36).

12. *76* was already *ra₂* (*ri-ja*).

13. I am indebted, however, to the contribution of James Gow, *A Short History of Greek Mathematics* (Cambridge University Press, 1884), pp. 2-12. On the cognates of the Greek numbers, see Hermann Hirt, *Indogermanische Grammatik*, III ("Indogermanische Bibliothek"; Heidelberg: C. Winter, 1927), 306-15.

14. Gow, p. 9, called the undeclined numbers "interjections, as it were, thrust into the sentence in brackets, like the dates in a history-book."

15. The Sanskrit cognates of the Greek numbers from 'five' to 'ten' take on case endings outside of the nominative and the accusative. But such cases are relatively rare in the early Sanskrit of the Rigveda, and the undeclined *páṁca, saptá, dáça* also occur. Jacob Wackernagel (and Albert Debrunner), *Altindische Grammatik*, III (Göttingen: Vanderhoeck und Ruprecht, 1930), 351-52; Hermann Grassmann, *Wörterbuch zum Rig-Veda* (Wiesbaden: O. Harrassowitz, 1955; reprint of 1872 ed.), pp. 144-45, 581-82, 715, 759-60, 1436, 1474-75. The break in the Indo-European number system between 'four' and 'five' is illustrated by Wilhelm Schulze, *Zur Geschichte lateinischer Eigennamen* ("Abhandlungen der kön. Gesellschaft der Wissenschaften zu Göttingen [philologisch-historische Klasse]," neue Folge, Band V, No. 5), pp. 49-50.

16. In the development of modern French the isolation of the intermediate cardinal numbers from the sentence structure of the language is manifested by special treatment of both initial and final

sounds. The final consonants of 5-10 are exempt from silencing: *cinq* [sɛ̃k], *six* [sis] *sept* [sɛt], *hu't* [ɥit], *neuf* [nœf], *dix* [dis]; see M. K. Pope, *From Latin to Modern French*, 2d ed. (Manchester University Press, [1952]), p. 220. When they occur before a substantive that begins with a consonant, they have a *sandhi* form dropping their own final consonant; or if the substantive begins with a vowel, then a spirant at the end of the numeral is voiced [siz, nœv, diz]. However, a strong present tendency is to use the counting forms [sɛ̃k, sis], etc., in all contexts. The vocalic beginning of *huit* (< *octō*) and *onze* (< *undecim*) is exempted from *sandhi* processes (elision and *liaison*) which would otherwise unite them syllabically with a consonant from the previous word; thus *je n'en ai que huit* 'I have only eight' [kəɥit], not *[kɥit], *les onze* 'the eleven' [leɔ̃z], not *[lezɔ̃z].

17. See above, p. 99, note 31. Not one of the four values *a, e, de, i* was obtained by Ventris from the grid.

18. Still less does the legibility of the five words as a Greek sentence add to the case for $77 = ka$ in the first word. In a plebeian name, not regulated by the pattern of an Indo-European compound, there is scarcely any limit to the possible range of the middle character — granted that the value of *70* before it and *02* after it is known from other evidence to be *ko* and *ro* respectively. Practically any value for *77* would fit between them.

19. An understatement; those etymologies are really worthless.

20. See Grumach's criticism (*Gnomon*, XXXII, 683-84).

21. IG^2 1.84.25, etc.; Deecke, no. 60.15, pp. 28-29.

22. In *PT* (1955) renumbered Ae344, An5.2, and Jn415.3 respectively. Still another variant will be discussed later (see below, p. 211, note 7).

23. Work Note 9, p. 74, item C 7; Work Note 14, p. 96, item P 1. In Work Note 15, Figure 9, line 25, he reported an "orthographic variation" between *01* and *39*, but he gridded *39* in a different row (as well as a different column) from *01*. *39* became *pi* (see above, p. 85).

24. Later taken to mean CONDIMENT and likened fancifully to a pepper-pot (*Documents*, p. 222).

25. See *Documents*, p. 88; Vilborg, p. 104. *08-50-14-44*, transcribed *a-pu-do-ke*, is the second word of a Knosos text X681.b (the lower line having been written before the upper, according to Chadwick's

inspection); but the tablet is broken, and the seven words that remain cannot be understood as Greek.

26. *13* was already in the *-e*? column but in a row by itself, according to the third state of the grid (cf. Work Note 14, p. 114, item P 104, and Work Note 16, pp. 146-151). By the time of "Evidence," *13* had entered the *me* square; see above, p. 123.

27. Figure 9, line 57. He did not make explicit which words on which tablets contain this variation. He treated a few variations, not involving these two characters, in Work Note 9 (pp. 73-74), adding at the end of the paragraph, "There are probably several other pairs of words which show a suggestive similarity, but I have here only included those so long as to be almost certainly connected, or those whose identity is proved by the context."

Another variation, between *72* and the digraph *44-75* (Work Note 14, p. 127, item K 13), was not used in setting up the grid, in either the second or the third state. From "Evidence," p. 87, line 25, and p. 88, it turns out that the character was not after all 𝕓 (*72*) but the unidentified 𝕓 (*87*; *kwe*? according to *Documents*, p. 23).

28. *Documents*, p. 22; "Evidence," pp. 89, 97.

29. The *-ν-* before a homorganic plosive would be omitted in Linear B, as in Cypriotic and often in early alphabetic inscriptions from Greece; see above, p. 111, (*a-to-ro-qo* = ἄνθρωπο-) and below, p. 219.

30. Cf. the two versions of Pausanias' inscription:
3d person: Ἑλλήνων ἀρχηγὸς ἐπεὶ στρατὸν ὤλεσε Μήδων

Παυσανίας Φοίβῳ μνῆμ' ἀνέθηκε τόδε (Thuc. 1.132.2,
ps.-Demosthenes 59.97, etc.)

1st person: Ἑλλάνων ἀρχαγὸς ἐπεὶ στρατὸν ὤλεσα Μήδων

Παυσανίας Φοίβῳ μνᾶμ' ἀνέθηκα τόδε (*Anth. Pal.* 6.197)

31. *SDGI* 1582.2, Dodona; *CIG* 1869.1, Corcyra. The unclassical orthography of both inscriptions, particularly the latter, leaves some doubt whether the two letters EI really stand for a diphthong. In the compound words διειπέτεος 'fallen from Zeus' (*Od.* 4.477 according to Zenodotus; codd. διιπετέος), the Attic name ΔΙΕΙΤΡΕΦΕΣ (Διειτρέφης *IG*² 1.950.174; genitive ΔΙΕΙΤΡΕΦΟΣ, 1.527.2) 'Zeus's fosterling,' and the Cypriotic name *ti-we-i-te-mi-se* (=Διϝειθεμις, Diecke, no. 60.21, pp. 28-30) 'justice of (from, in) Zeus,' the sense of Διει- is not especially dative.

32. "Evidence," pp. 93-95. Ventris in Work Note 14, pp. 97 ff., had

often used the halfhearted phrase " 'Accusative' after $\neq +$."

33. Not the character 28 but others from the -*i* column of the grid; e.g., *Documents*, p. 86.

34. Bennett, *OOTP*, pp. 14, 48, 53. His tracing of Fr1217 (pl. xi) reveals that 57 in 75-57-27-72 was perhaps written over an incomplete erasure of 08.

35. 77 = *ka* counts as having skipped the test, because no other value could have been ruled out in that context.

36. We cannot give an exact total because, in spite of Bennett's admirable palaeography, a few of the very rare characters are still not *graphically* identified with any certainty. Our chief authority is in doubt whether the individual instances on several tablets are specimens all of the same character (like A a *a* in the Latin alphabet) or specimens of different characters.

37. Fr1217, 1218, 1225, 1240, 1242; Bennett, *OOTP*, pp. 48-49, 55, 63-64.

38. Fr343+1213 has the same word except for the absence of the third character -38-. The shorter word could be Hellenized as *λεχεσ-στρωτήριο(ν)* and compared to *lectisternium*, an occasional ceremony of the Roman religion (Livy 5.13.6, 7.2.2, 22.10.9, etc.); in Greek, however, all festivals are neuter *plural* (Herodotus 1.148.2). The interpretation of *re-ke-to-ro-te-ri-jo* is clouded by the circumstance that *re-ke-e-* (etc.) defies Hellenization. Bennett suggests, "it does not go beyond possibility to suppose the presence of the preposition *ex*, in the form *es*" (*OOTP*, p. 31); but that would clash with the rules of Greek compounding.

39. A word different in only one character, 08-27-03-20-61, occurs in Un267.2 (likewise from Pylos); but the entire text is full of perplexities. I am astonished by Palmer's statement that it "presented a coherent sense 'thus *a-ko-so-ta* gave Thyestes the unguentboiler herbs which he is to boil in the unguent'" (*Gnomon*, XXIX, 563). The syntax of his translation and of Ventris's in *Documents*, p. 224, is altogether arbitrary and contravenes Greek usage.

CHAPTER VII

THE PRESENCE OF ANOTHER LANGUAGE BESIDES GREEK IN THE LINEAR B TEXTS

A PRINCIPLE of correct method, which will determine the reliability of many of our findings, is at stake in the definition of "Greek." The language of the Aegean world in the classical period, written in the Greek alphabet of Phoenician origin, is predominantly Indo-European in structure and in basic vocabulary, but includes many words and even some structural features that do not correspond to anything in the other Indo-European languages. A small part of this apparently non-Indo-European component of Greek has a recognizable Semitic source; but much more is taken from no known language, and its existence in Greek is presumably to be attributed to the contacts of Indo-European speakers with some other language or languages of the Aegean area.[1] Now anything in Linear B which we can recognize to be like Greek is welcome, whether or not of Indo-European origin; for it lessens the profound obscurity of Linear B texts. But a dangerous error of method lurks in the working assumption of most scholars that whatever we cannot recognize as Greek is nevertheless Greek, but Greek of the Mycenaean age. It amounts to begging the question; for properly, if we cannot prove that a certain word or group of words in Linear B corresponds unmistakably to known Greek from later times, any attempt to use Greek as a basis for interpreting it is a purely speculative exercise, leading to imaginary results. To be sure, the theory of comparative Indo-European grammar can guide us somewhat in reconstructing the forerunner of classical Greek in the second millennium B.C., but only to the extent that the language was Indo-European in that millennium and later. The non-Indo-European material is a grave and incalculable limitation upon our capacity to penetrate into the Linear B texts.[2]

It is hazardous to count (as Ventris's supporters have in effect done) upon an essentially constant ratio between the Indo-European and the non-Indo-European components in Greek from the Mycenaean to the classical period. In classical times the European side of the Aegean was solidly Hellenic — the whole Peloponnese and the region beyond it from the Isthmus north to Thessaly. However, barbarian peoples still lived in the region north of the Gulf of Corinth and nearer the Ionian Sea than the Aegean; also, not all of Crete was completely Hellenized: six or seven non-Greek inscriptions in the Greek alphabet have been found at Praisos; one from the Cretan Arcadia has many non-Greek words, ΠΑΡΕΛΑΙΝ, ΣΙΑΚΥΚΑ]ΟΝΙ, ΡΑΧΡΙΝ,]ΕΧΟ and perhaps others — each preceded by the Greek definite article Ο, Α, or ΤΟ and followed by an amount of Roman money, ΔΗΝΑΡΙΩΝ, and a Greek numeral spelled out; finally, one inscription from Dreros has two lines not in Greek followed by three damaged lines in Greek — all five written in the Greek alphabet.[3] But in the major Hellenic area, so far as our data go, nothing remained of other languages except what had been *absorbed* into Greek. That it was already so in the Mycenaean period, is very improbable; and the Linear B evidence makes it appear that more than one language was spoken in the places where the tablets come from, and that the Linear B tablets are by no means restricted to one language identifiable with Greek.

Non-Greek personal names. The great Knosos tablet As1516 includes over five dozen one-word items, each followed by a MAN ideogram and the numeral *1*. These words, with a few exceptions, are fully preserved, and none of them recur within the tablet. However, at the end of the paragraphs comes the recurrent *05-12 to-so,* introducing the total for each paragraph. It is natural to take the one-word items for men's names. Ventris remarks: "There are a number, though not a large proportion, of convincingly Greek names: Philinos, Agoraios, Purwos, [De]xelawos, Khariseus, Opsios, Amphiwastos, Amphilawos. But many others are equally certainly non-Greek: e.g. *pa₂-me-si-jo, mi-ja-ra-ro, si-ja-pu₂?-ro, pi-ja-si-ro, pi-ja-se-me*" (*Documents,* p. 171). I have reservations about both types: Ventris's Greek names, except for the first one, *39-53-52 pi-ri-no* (line 6), contain characters whose values are not adequately verified; so do his non-Greek names. But *11-05 po-to* (line 4), *26-06 ru-na* (line 10), *08-37-36 a-ti-jo* (line 14) consist of verified characters, and the second at least will not square with any man's name known from Greek. Longer names are less likely to consist entirely of verified characters; but on other tablets I have noted the following names that do and are evidently non-Greek:

39-53-05-42 pi-ri-to-wo (with MAN[b], B803.2, Knosos)

70-39 ko-pi (with WOMAN *1*, Ap639.1, Knosos)

28-06-61 i-na-o (with MAN *1*, An209.5, Pylos; cf. Ge603.3, Mycenae)[4]

For the great majority of the names it remains in suspense whether they are Greek or not. According to Ventris's transcription most of them come out unidentifiable with anything known in Greece. The licenses of Ventris's spelling for Linear B will allow the majority to assume a structure compatible with Greek, but only because he postulates unwritten sounds whenever convenient. However, no matter how we might try to correct his work — for instance, changing many of his values — we would doubtless be left with a large number of un-Greek names. The very defective syllabic writing keeps us from knowing whether such names received Greek endings and were otherwise adapted to Greek. It is probable at any rate that no inconsiderable part of the persons named in the tablets were barbarian not only in name but also in speech.[5] While it would not, from this, necessarily follow that the language of the Linear B tablets contains more foreign elements (apart from names) than classical Greek texts do, there are some definite indications of a language other than Greek in both the Knosos and the mainland tablets.[6]

The paucity of Indo-European inflexions. While we have verified several Greek words in the Linear B corpus, including some of Indo-European origin, we have not found unambiguous evidence that any of the endings are Indo-European. The difference between *ti-ri-po* and *ti-ri-po-de* is indeed reminiscent of Greek morphology. But since the latter word refers to *two* tripods, it is likely to correspond to a Greek dual τρίποδε rather than a Greek plural τρίποδες. The ending -ες has Indo-European cognates (-*ah* in Sanskrit, etc.), but -ε does not and is of quite obscure origin. Nearly the same relation comes out again in *ti-ri-jo-we* and *ti-ri-o-we-e*, the latter referring to two jugs. The Greek equivalent of *a-pi-po-re-we* would have to be ἀμφιφορῆ(ϝ)ες, the nominative plural of the "third declension," because the Linear B word refers to three amphoras. Here we have a probable instance of a Linear B ending that matches a Greek ending of Indo-European origin; but it falls short of certainty: (1) the consonantal part -ς of the Greek suffix has no Linear B counterpart and has to be imagined; (2) no singular form of the word is recorded in Linear B — so we have no assurance that in

the Linear B language the vowel in the last syllable of
a-pi-po-re-we is a sign of the plural, lacking in the singular.

One of Ventris's key assumptions, which has never been
proved, is that many words ending in a -*Co* character have
a feminine counterpart ending in -*Ca*. But in all cases, at
least one crucial point remains undemonstrated, either that
the vowel of the feminine form is indeed -*a* (rather than -*i* or
-*u* or something more complex), or that the word in question
is indeed feminine and differs in gender alone from another
word known to be masculine. *05-12* and *05-31* are transcribed *to-so* and *to-sa* respectively; but there is nothing to
confirm either the *o* vowel in the masculine or the *a* vowel
in the feminine (see above, p. 150). On the other hand the
phonetic relation between *52 no* and *06 na* is well enough
established; but in the long words *08-60-02-15-04-13-52* and
08-60-02-15-04-13-06 on the chariot tablets the distinction
is not gender and may rather be number: the -*o* being dual,
the -*a* singular or plural (see above, pp. 123-4). Such an inflexion hardly fits Greek or any other Indo-European language.[7] The suffixes -*13-52* and -*13-06* in other words are
taken to be -μενο- and -μενᾰ̆ in Greek — the former masculine
singular or plural or neuter singular, the latter feminine singular or plural (-αι) or neuter plural; but in every instance
the Linear B noun, which is supposed to determine the gender of the participle with the ending -*13-52* or -*13-06*, is itself
merely hypothetical.[8] The alternation between *14-38-02* and
14-38-60 suggested gender to Ventris in Work Note 11, but
he did not recognize *02* and *60* as one of his *Co* ~ *Ca* pairs
(see above, p. 163). The meaning 'slave,' the indication of
gender in the suffix, and the value *60* = *ra* are all somewhat
clouded still. So we cannot definitely credit Linear B with a
Greek and Indo-European alternation, consisting of a masculine noun with the thematic vowel *o* and its feminine de-
rivative with *a* replacing the *o*.

Structural features alien to Greek. Even more opposed to Greek than the alternation between *-no* dual and *-na* singular and plural is the alternation between *38-44* and *38-44-78*, transcribed *e-ke* and *e-ke-qe* in the Pylos E tablets (see above, p. 119). It is utterly unlike the use of τε in Greek and of its own homograph, the suffix *-78* in the Linear B tablets Au102 and An1281 (see above, p. 69).[9] All attempts to make sense of *38-44-78* betray sheer desperation.

Another obstacle to the identification of the Linear B language as Greek is the peculiar set of words beginning with *36-* (see above, p. 83). It is not enough to reserve judgement on the consonantal part of Ventris's transcription *jo*. *36* can hardly help but bear some resemblace to *61 o*, in view of the alternation in *ti-ri-jo-we* ~ *ti-ri-o-we-e* 'three-eared'; yet nothing meaningful in Greek can be extracted from the occurrences of *36* in initial positions. Moreover, I am at a loss to explain why each word that begins with *36-* ends with *-41* in the Pylos tablets, while the following word ends with *-41* in the Knosos tablets; this does not fit any Greek pattern that comes to my mind.[10] As long as we are in the dark about those words and the tablets they belong to, it would be unsound method to trust sanguinely that it will turn out to be like Greek after all.

The variation in the Es tablets between *75-01-24-75 14-12-15* and *75-01-24-42 14-12-15* (see above, p. 133, note 14) is inexplicable in Greek. Accepting the value *75 = we* — and, a little more hesitantly, *42 = wo* — I must protest that nothing in Greek with an ending at all reminiscent of *-(w)e* can alternate with a related form in *-(w)o* or any other related form, unless there is a semantic motive. A semantic motive may indeed be lurking in the larger measurement written ideographically to accompany *75-01-24-75;* but the rationale can only lie in some unknown language, not Greek.

The word *61-39-28-57-39,* transcribed *o-pi-i-ja-pi,* in the

Knosos chariot tablets seems to violate Greek phonology in the repetition of one *i* sound right after another (see above, p. 99, note 31, and pp. 159-60). There is positive evidence in favor of both values, *39* = *pi* and *28* = *i*. We are ready enough to call the word non-Greek, as it cannot be traced in the Greek vocabulary; furthermore, as it appears in the Linear B tablets, it is not even Hellenized — i.e., it does not conform to Greek phonology. Those tablets actually contain just one affinity to Greek — the alternation between the beginning of a word *a-na-*, describing a dismantled chariot, and the beginning of another word *a-*, describing a nearly complete chariot.[11] For the remainder of the wording of the chariot tablets, if we begin our interpretation by taking the language to be Greek, as Ventris and his supporters have done, we find ourselves obliged to posit so many things in them different from any known Greek dialect that we end up with a language just faintly resembling Greek.

How very faintly the Linear B language resembles Greek in places, is laid bare by Chadwick's struggle with the inflexions of Ge603 and 604 (Mycenae).[12] The two opening words in each of the five lines of the latter have a one-word counterpart in the first five lines of the former (before the ideographic part of the text). (See top page 183.)

The effort to connect the very common word *61-72-02* with ὄφελος (which means 'use, advantage') or some related Greek form, and thus to give it a quasi-Greek meaning 'debt' or 'deficit,' is particularly unfortunate in this Ge tablet, because it is preceded by words with non-Greek inflexions.[14] Confining ourselves to the syllables that we are fairly sure of, we note first that the suffix *-re* in Ge604.3 has no Greek counterpart unless we assume that a final consonant *-r* is left unwritten in Ge603.4 (see below, p. 226); even so, we have no ground for connecting *-e* with the Greek dative singular or any other particular formation (see above, p. 158). More

	Ge603		Ge604
1	*44-11*		*44-38-72 61-72-02*
		cf. Ge604.1	
	ke-po		*ke-e-pe o-pe-ro*
2	*50-44-61*		*28-06-61-04 61-72-02*
		cf. Ge604.5	
	pu-ke-o		*i-na-o-te o-pe-ro*
3	*28-06-61*		*60-44-01-52-27 61-72-02*
		cf. Ge604.2	
	i-na-o		*ra-ke-da-no-re o-pe-ro*
4	*60-44-01-52*		*08-44-27-40-36 61-72-02*
		cf. Ge604.3	
	ra-ke-da-no		*a-ke-re-wi-jo o-pe-ro*
5	*08-44-27-40-36*		*50-44 72-02-02*
		cf. Ge604.4	
	a-ke-re-wi-jo		*pu-ke pe-ro-ro*[13]

---

radically irreconcilable with Greek is the first item. Unless
something can shake the values *11 = po* and *38 = e*, the
relation of *44-11* to *44-38-72* conflicts with everything Greek.
On top of that, whatever grammatical kinship may lurk in
50-44-61 and *28-06-61* by virtue of the same final character,
the former drops its *-o* before *72-02-02*, while the latter
retains it and adds *-04* before *61-72-02*. To suspect the scribe
of "a series of blunders" is idle self-delusion, as though we
had some reason — in spite of the characters he wrote — for
believing that the words of the two tablets are capable of
conforming to a Greek declension.

In the two Ge tablets we may be obliged to recognize still another case of non-Greek morphology: the two syllables common to 61-72-02 and 72-02-02 presumably share a meaning, modified in some way by the prefix *o-* and in another way by the suffix *-ro;* but nothing in Greek fits such a pattern. It would be even more non-Greek if the suffix repeats the previous syllable not just by coincidence but through a morphological process of reduplication. A parallel phenomenon in the Ea tablets of Pylos urges us to recognize a reduplicating suffix in our Mycenae text too. Whereas several Ea's, after the initial word in large characters, show the formula

    38-44 61-06-05 44-44-13-06 70-05-06

(*e-ke o-na-to ke-ke-me-na ko-to-na;* Ea480,806,809), one tablet, Ea305, does not have the very common word 61-06-05 (*o-na-to*) but instead 06-05-05 (*na-to-to*), which does not occur elsewhere.[15] The parallel

Mycenae	Pylos
o-pe-ro	*o-na-to*
pe-ro-ro	*na-to-to*

presents a type of inflexion in which the prefix *o-* is not reminiscent of anything Greek and, still worse, the suffix reduplicates the last syllable of the base — a process alien to Greek and to Indo-European in general, although regular in some other language-groups. In recognizing such inflexions as un-Greek, we do not perversely set aside clear Greek words. On the contrary, the identification of *o-pe-ro* with ὄφελος was always unpromising; and Mycenaean scholars have racked their brains for a Greek interpretation of *o-na-to.*

In the next chapter, dealing with the defects of the Linear B script, I will show that 61-52 *o-no* can hardly stand for the Greek nominative plural ὄνοι. The alleged omission of the second vowel of the diphthong is a fictitious rule set by Ventris to facilitate the manipulation of his decipherment (see below, pp. 230-2).

Characters used both phonetically and ideographically. We can almost always distinguish with certainty the phonetic parts of a Linear B text from the ideographic parts. The characters that have a phonetic value but no meaning individually are grouped into words of two or more characters, and normally one word is separated from another by the word-divider, a short vertical stroke.[16] Each ideographic character has meaning in itself. Of those that stand for numbers, every vertical line (usually longer than the word-divider) signifies ONE, every horizontal line TEN, every circle a HUNDRED. The other ideographic characters are for the most part used singly. Many of them are pictorial; many are not. One of the pictorial ones, the hog's head (85), and a large number of the nonpictorial ones serve as phonetic characters too. We naturally expect some close relation between the phonetic and ideographic uses of a character: as it is phonetically one syllable of many words, it ought to be ideographically an abbreviation of a certain word — i.e., the initial syllable of that word, or possibly some other prominent syllable. Such a relation obtains in other writing systems that employ certain characters both phonetically and ideographically. Whether it really obtains in the Linear B system too, is an open question — the proof that can be adduced is so meager. On the one hand, the phonetic value of 85, the hog's head, was left unspecified by Ventris, apart from a hesitant guess in *Documents* (p. 23) that it might stand for two syllables *si-ja;* his successors have not significantly improved upon that random and improbable fancy.[17] On the other hand, the meaning of the nonpictorial ideographic characters which also have a phonetic value is at best conjectural. It happens, besides, that the phonetic value of only a few of these is established. *70* in its ideographic function (Ge603, Mycenae) is reasonably taken for an abbreviation of what is spelled *70-53-57-01-06* and *70-53-25-01-06* in Ge605.3,4,5. Ventris as early as Work Note 20 (p. 174) proposed to identify the latter with κορίαννον 'coriander,' but that remains nothing more than a possible guess;[18] and the meaning CORIANDER for *70* by itself as an ideogram is correspondingly insecure. Even if the many alleged "spice" terms in the Ge tablets were proved right, it would not argue that the texts are Greek; for such a special vocabulary is likely to be shared by the various languages of a given region.

Other characters that are used ideographically resist interpretation, in spite of a verified phonetic value. *75* (phonetically *we*) before a number ought to mean some kind of animal, as it stands repeatedly in the vicinity of the hog's head and other ideograms marked with either the male or the female sex-symbol (see above, p. 77). If *75* is an abbreviation of a word that begins *we-*, it is still hazardous to say which word, and whether it is Greek; (ϝ)ἔταλον 'yearling' is possible. But even in a fully known language and script, abbreviated words can trick or baffle a reader who has not been given a key to them. In Linear B we are much worse off and cannot even be confident whether the phonetic characters being used ideographically abbreviate Greek or non-Greek words.

Small phonetic characters ligatured or monogrammed with larger ideographic ones. Many ideograms occur sometimes plain, sometimes with a smaller character attached to the top, bottom, or side, or written across a vertical stroke of the ideogram proper. For example, ᛋ is an ideogram often appearing in contexts which suggest it stands for a liquid, quite likely to be OIL (Fr1204, 1238, Pylos; Fpl+31,

5, Knosos; etc.); but it also turns up with the following additional strokes:

with *o8* 𐄷 (Fr1207, etc., Pylos)
with *o3* 𐄸 (Fr1202, etc., Pylos)
with *11* 𐄹 (Fr1203, 1208, Pylos)
with *75* 𐄺 (Fr[or Gn]1184, Pylos; Fo101, Mycenae)[19]

Although we have found a good case for *o8 = a, 11 = po*, and *75 = we*, their meaning in these ideographic combinations is next to unfathomable. Bennett assumes explicitly that *o8* here is an abbreviation of *o8-o2-o3*, which is spelled out next to the ideogram ligatured with *o8* in Fr1225 only;[20] but inasmuch as *o8* is the most frequent initial character in Linear B words, the odds against its serving here as the abbreviation of this word and no other are particularly high. The transcription *a-ro-pa* leads Bennett to equate it with ἀλοιφή (-ᾱ́) 'unguent' or 'grease,' but he is unable to give a meaningful translation of it in the context of Fr1225 (*OOTP*, p. 56). He also assumes that *o3* is an abbreviation of the frequent word *o3-70-75*, which he identified with *σφακό(ϝ)εν 'scented with sage.' The distribution of *o3-70-75* is partly correlated with that of 𐄸 , but not enough to prove identity of meaning.[21] In any event the meaning remains very doubtful. The ligatures with *11* and *75* do not even tempt anyone to guess at their meaning or what Greek words they could possibly be related to — what words suitable as qualifiers of OIL could be abbreviated *po* or *we*.

We are just as much in the dark about the little *78* inside the semipictorial TUNIC ideogram 𐘃 (Sc224, 227, 229, 266, Knosos),[22] or the little *53* inside the same ideogram (Le178+ 281, Knosos). Confident though we may be of *78 = qe* (Greek τε) and *53 = ri*, we are merely guessing if we try to expand the abbreviations into Greek words such as λίνεος 'linen.' It happens somewhat unluckily that the ligatured characters of established phonetic value are found less on

Pylos than on Knosos tablets, where they are never near any verified words which might help to narrow down the possible meaning of the ligatures. If some of the latter are abbreviations of Greek words, we are not in a position to pick out which ones.

The question of a mixture of languages in the Linear B tablets. Ventris remarked in *Documents* (p. 52): "Where the syllabic and ideographic uses of the sign have evidently developed side by side from Linear A and the 'hieroglyphs', the search for a Greek derivation is of course pointless." The counterpart, assumed by him in practice but not stated explicitly, is that the Linear B script expresses no language but Greek, except for holdovers from the other Cretan scripts, somewhat in the manner of £ or *lb.* for POUND(s) in English texts. He misapprehended the problem, and the difficulty applies not just to the ideographic abbreviations but also to words spelled out. Having indeed found *some* Greek in the Linear B tablets, he chose to regard them as virtually pure Greek. The many words, the many whole tablets that he could not make sense of as classical Greek, he accounted for by a general excuse: "To have to interpret them is rather like trying to read Chaucer with only a knowledge of twentieth-century English" (*Documents,* p. 27). The analogy of the earlier and the later period of English implies an essentially self-contained monoglot population, whose language evolves through internal causes; it does not allow, to any significant degree, for the effect of a population changing over from other native languages.[23] I cannot help regretting that *Documents* is much less circumspect in this regard than "Evidence" (see above, p. 40), which acknowledged that a "relatively small portion of the tablets [are] interpreted," and conceived Mycenaean Greek as being "surrounded, possibly closely intermingled, with barbarian languages spoken by peoples of equal or superior culture." We have no method for determining how much of the difference between Linear B and classical Greek we could explain by internal change within a monoglot community (split, of course, into dialects), if only we knew Linear B as fully as classical Greek. With our meager knowledge of Linear B, it is safe to affirm that part of it resembles classical Greek and part of it differs; but most of it we cannot make out one way or the other. "The final classification of a language depends ultimately on its grammar and syntax, and it will be shown in what follows that in this respect Mycenaean displays undeniably Greek features" (*Documents*, p. 70). That is true, but I must add that the undeniably Greek features, particularly those of Indo-European origin, amount to less than the undeniably non-Greek features (see above, pp. 179-84). Therefore we cannot afford to give Greek the benefit of the doubt, as Ventris and his supporters do — to identify as Greek everything in Linear B that by any stretch of reasoning could conceivably be like Greek. Before resting anything upon an identification, we ought to prove that it *must* be so, not merely that it *could* be so.[24]

An inadequate linguistic theory has encouraged the inference that because *ti-ri-po* ~ *ti-ri-po-de* and *a-pi-po-re-we* and a few other Linear B transcriptions are in accord with Greek (granted certain rules of spelling), the Linear B language as a whole is Greek. It overlooks the strong possibility that the language is a jargon. By that I do not mean to apply naïvely a vague aesthetic term. Quite the opposite: unless men who have considerable knowledge of two or more languages are guided by an aesthetic principle or tradition, they tend to mix the languages without concern for structural incompatibility. They tend to do it all the more in writing, particularly in writing not intended for the public, and in a script that is partly ideographic and thus puts more emphasis on content than on verbal grace. Such a written language is to a high degree exempt from the pressure exercised by a speech community for the adoption and maintenance of a style which, if it admits foreign elements, does it judiciously, not promiscuously.

The language situation in Crete according to the Odyssey. The disguised Odysseus, pretending to answer Penelope's question about his origin, begins:

Κρήτη τις γαῖ᾽ ἔστι, μέσῳ ἐνὶ οἴνοπι πόντῳ,
καλὴ καὶ πίειρα, περίρρυτος· ἐν δ᾽ ἄνθρωποι
πολλοί, ἀπειρέσιοι, καὶ ἐννήκοντα πόληες·
ἄλλη δ᾽ ἄλλων γλῶσσα μεμιγμένη· ἐν μὲν ᾽Αχαιοί,
ἐν δ᾽ ᾽Ετεόκρητες μεγαλήτορες, ἐν δὲ Κύδωνες,
Δωριέες τε τριχάϊκες δῖοί τε Πελασγοί·
τῆσι δ᾽ ἐνὶ Κνωσός, μεγάλη πόλις, ἔνθα τε Μίνως
ἐννέωρος βασίλευε Διὸς μεγάλου ὀαριστής,
πατρὸς ἐμοῖο πατήρ, μεγαθύμου Δευκαλίωνος (19.172-180)

'There is a country Crete in the middle of the wine-dark sea, fair and rich, surrounded by water. In it is a large, a countless population and ninety cities. The various peoples have various tongues, intermingled: among them are (first of all) Achaeans, then great-hearted native Cretans, then Cydonians, and Dorians living in three tribes, and noble Pelasgians. Among the cities is Knosos, a great city, where the king was Minos the nine-year gossip of great Zeus and the father of my father, great-spirited Deucalion.'

In my interpretation the salient points are:

(1) The peoples of Crete — Achaeans, native Cretans, etc. — speak different languages (not just differences of dialect such as one would have been bound to encounter in any part of the Aegean area). To be sure, the naming of five peoples does not show that the narrator necessarily supposed no two of them to be speaking related dialects; we

must not press literary expression too strictly. However, at the very least he thought of language as one of the major differences between the peoples of Crete.

(2) The Achaeans are in some way the most prominent in his list (perhaps because Ithaca, where the story is told, is also inhabited by Achaeans); and in most striking contrast to the Achaeans are the indigenous Cretans. It could be that his order is determined by mere convenience of versification, although poetic skill would not have found it necessary to sacrifice a significant order.

(3) To impress Penelope, the shrewd imposter chooses Knosos out of the ninety cities of Crete for his home. By implication, Knosos is famous, or at any rate deserves to be.

(4) μεμιγμένη does not signify that all Crete speaks one jargon, made up of components from Achaean, native Cretan, etc.; for that interpretation would stultify ἄλλη δ' ἄλλων γλῶσσα. Nevertheless, languages in proximity would undoubtedly influence one another, all the more because it is probable that the ninety cities were not each exclusively inhabited by one nationality, even though one nationality predominated in each. A city with a mixed but not merged population is a good setting for large-scale borrowing between languages, as in an inscription from the Cretan Arcadia in Roman times (see above, p. 177).

We do not know whether the poet was thinking more of Crete in his own age, which would have been appreciably after the Linear B period, than of Crete in the heroic age, which would not. Nor do we know whether the language situation there changed fundamentally in all that time. For whatever period he envisaged, his description implies that the contrast of languages was more noticeable in Crete than in most areas within the purview of Achaeans. The Knosos tablets in Linear B script contain a little that agrees demonstrably with Greek — less than the Pylos tablets do. Any

Greek — or perhaps more properly, any Achaean — settlement at Knosos must have been close to speakers of other languages. The environment in which the Knosos Linear B tablets were written was therefore not similar to that in which the great majority of Greek texts, literary and inscriptional, were written in the classical period. It may have been more like that of the inscription found at Sillyia in Pamphylia (*IGA* 505, pp. 141-143). Only snatches of the text, even in its relatively undamaged portions, can be recognized as Greek, though written in the Greek alphabet; and within those snatches some non-Greek structural features turn up several times, such as ΝΙΑΟΙΚΫ, where Greek would presumably have τὸν (ϝ)οῖκον.

Circumstances favoring the formation of a jargon. A language that serves the varied needs of life within a community is in little danger of becoming a jargon, even though another speech community lives close by and actually overlaps the same territory. To be sure, a language in process of being given up does turn into a jargon in the generation or two before the speakers of it complete their shift to another. And people who share more or less knowledge of several languages, all containing usable elements for some special purpose, are inclined to piece together a jargon, unless restrained by pride or the discipline of style. Now one such special purpose is what the Linear B tablets, even before Ventris's decipherment, were considered to have served — the recording of business that concerned the lords of Knosos and Pylos. A very large proportion of the wording of the tablets consists of personal names, including many that no one would take for Greek. To make a practice of Hellenizing them — or alternatively, of reducing them to the structure of some other language — would have been a futile amusement for the palace scribes.[25] As the lord of Knosos almost certainly and the lord of Pylos quite probably had subjects in several speech communities, it was most sensible to keep track of those men and women simply by their real names. Uniformity of language in such records, far from being imperative, would not figure as a great convenience; much more to the point is uniformity of script: it would be a decided nuisance to the scribes if they had to use one writing system for certain names and another system for others.

The balance of probability is, further, that not only the personal names recorded in the Linear B tablets but other matters too were drawn from more than one speech community. There is no reason *a priori* why we should expect the scribes to have systematically rendered everything but the names into one language — Greek or whichever you will. Nor do we find that under examination it all turns out to be in accord with Greek. To put ourselves in the place of those scribes, let us reflect that when you have to write memoranda or notes and the oral raw material comes to you in several languages which you understand well enough and are not hard put to write down, then it is not the simple but rather the ideal procedure to compose the notes in one language. Indeed, to do so under such conditions would take an essentially literary motive, going beyond the purely practical need for keeping records.[26]

Yet it would be an implausible theory to regard the tablets as merely a notation (in a barely passable phonetic script) of oral raw material received by the scribes. They would naturally tend to fasten upon certain favored formulae and repeat them in tablet after tablet, insofar as it was easier to write up the information that way than to sound out each item phonetically. The process would result in a narrow, monotonous regularity of expression, which we ought not to equate with the more subtle pattern of a language that is the general vehicle of a community. A language developed for a special purpose — and at that a purpose achieved in writing rather than speaking — will stabilize rather than integrate the miscellaneous components that it drew in at the early stages. So the Linear B language on the mainland — at Pylos and Mycenae — need not be less of a jargon than the Linear B language at Knosos, even though on the mainland the Greek or Achaean speaking part of the population may have been much larger. The history of the transmission of the Linear B script is not as yet accessible to us; but the resemblances between the Knosos and the Pylos texts are so great as to warrant a presumption that the language used in the tablets was in its essentials transmitted along with the writing system.

Linear scripts as a mark of the Aegean civilization. Before Palmer in 1960 (see above, p. 10), nobody challenged the generally accepted view that the tablets excavated at Knosos are considerably older than the ones from Pylos. I think it is now an open question; but in any case the age of the preserved tablets will not prove where Linear B originated. For the tablets were not baked to insure permanence; so it is just the accident of a conflagration that has preserved some of those which had been inscribed shortly before and allowed to harden.[27] At Knosos the Linear B texts are later than the Linear A, according to Evans's report and reasoning (*PM*, I, 613; IV, 675-676), which go without contradiction so far as I, a non-archaeologist, am able to learn. Linear A was not limited to Knosos but used elsewhere in Crete; Knosos is the one place on the island where Linear B was also used. Linear A has not yielded to efforts of decipherment any more than Linear B did before Ventris; the precise relation between the two scripts, which have many characters in common, remains in doubt. The appearances make it likely that Linear B was a fairly late invention in the Aegean culture, and not a drastically new one but rather a modification of a writing system already well developed.

That the Linear B script emerged in the maturity or even the decline of the Minoan world, has some major theoretical implications. The scripts of other civilizations that afford any sort of parallel authorize us to believe (1) that the language situation shifted in favor of a speech community or communities that had been outside the ken of Minoan writing until the period in which Linear B was developed; (2) that the modified script attempted to embrace the language or languages newly recognized within the civilization, but did not abandon the old. In Asia the cuneiform script began with Sumerian; and when it was adapted to Accadian and then to Hittite, the texts continued to be written partly as Sumerian. A polyglot civilization is naturally loath to give up the unifying elements which cut across the lines between the speech communities; it will tenaciously nurture what it can of the older language which was its first vehicle of written expression and which becomes to some extent familiar to all literate persons regardless of their vernacular. Writing in the older language and writing ideographically go hand in hand; in many particulars they are one and the same thing. Without maintaining that the undiscovered history of the Linear scripts must duplicate the accessible history of the cuneiform, I consider the Linear B script — with its large amount of ideography and its evidence of non-Greek as well as Greek inflexion — to fit a situation in which no one vernacular had so triumphed that the scribes wrote it straight off without drawing upon any other language. Much later, those who wrote classical Greek in a purely phonetic alphabet were altogether emancipated from the earlier languages of civilization. But it is unsafe to assume that the Linear B scribes were in essentially the same state.[28]

The attitude of a scribe toward the language or languages

that he writes may not be obvious to us, but it should not be a mystery beyond our understanding. Learning to write is very different from learning to talk; only under special conditions does it become important to make writing simply the image of speech. In general, a text that needs to be written but is not to reach the ears of the community does not have to be in one language. Some of the symbols in the text may not readily correspond to anything vocal; other symbols may correspond to the spoken words of different languages, provided they belong to the same civilization. Whether writing plays a large or a small role, those who carry it on somewhat as a profession have — during their apprenticeship — learned more than their homoglots about the other languages of the civilization and have acquired the custom of writing not so much whole texts in this or that language as this phrase in one, that phrase in another.

The amount of Greek in Linear B. If the effect of Ventris's work so far has been to spread more illusory that real knowledge, the misstep lay in jumping from *There is Greek in Linear B* to *Linear B is Greek*. It is the logical fallacy of taking the particular for the universal. Men of superior intelligence slipped into it through an unlucky cluster of distracting circumstances. As late as the "Evidence" article, Ventris's transcription of Linear B was wholly experimental; he could not adduce proof that any of his suggested phonetic equations with Greek words were semantically borne out by the context. As none of them were demonstrably right and the whole thing was at the most a controlled speculation, he could fairly point to the large number of words for which a Greek rendering was not impossible, given the latitude of his spelling rules. He had more to display than any predecessor, although none of it was yet certain. Later Blegen announced the excavation of the tripod-and-jug tablet (Ta641), which was followed by Chadwick's finding of the missing piece of the horse tablet (Ca895); these proved that some of Ventris's phonetic values are right and some Linear B words are Greek. At that point entered the paralogism, that because those few words were proved to be Greek, the remainder in the Linear B corpus could be accepted as Greek without proof. All words that could by any means be reconciled with Greek passed then for items of the pre-Homeric Greek language.

In reality the attempt to construe Linear B texts in some relation to Greek was as speculative as before. In the tripod-and-jug tablet no two consecutive words, no more than one word in each entry was explicable as Greek; the rest of the words, far from being securely identified, could not even be guessed at with any plausibility. So the greater part of the text might be in an unknown, even an unheard-of language. However, the discovery of the "oil" tablet (Gn1184) did give an impressive Greek construction, embracing at least two and possibly as many as five of the eight words. In the whole Linear B corpus no other Greek constructions nearly so probable have been found,[29] though many have been read into the ambiguities of the transcription.

From the small amount of Greek that has been authenticated in Linear B writing, we can (if we will) imagine either that a large part of the corpus is Greek or that only a little of it is. We are in no position to judge securely most of what Ventris cited in "Evidence" and *Documents*. We can properly say it is not demonstrably Greek but looks as if it might be Greek, but then again it might be something else, because any other language of the Aegean civilization is lost to us. If a scholar is searching for English in an obscure medieval text that is known to contain some, he can be certain of what is written there in other languages; so the residue, if it has the appearance of English, can be safely taken as such. But in Linear B we have not isolated all that is non-Greek, so as to be confident of the residue. Since we have found some Greek and some non-Greek in Linear B, but not their ratio, there is no sound presumption *a priori* that a given word is Greek; a particular reason needs to be adduced in every case. Where a word consists entirely of characters whose phonetic values are tolerably well established — e.g., *70-05-52-61-70 ko-to-no-o-ko* (Eb369.2, etc., Pylos) — it is of course worth trying to identify the word with something Greek. In such cases the ambiguity of the syllabary is liable to allow several phonetically possible Greek identifications. But whether it allows just one or more than one, no identification is reliable unless the *meaning* can be proved from the rest of the tablet. Otherwise, for all we know, the word in question may be meaningful only in a lost language.

Unverified phonetic values in unverified Greek words. Many of Ventris's experimental Greek words, published in "Evidence," were then and have remained doubly doubtful: Nothing is known about the context to require of the word *60-54-44-59* in An724.7 (Pylos) a meaning close to the Greek λᾱγέτᾱς 'leader, commander of the people,' or of *51-26-05-15* in Vn10.1 (Pylos) a meaning close to δρυτόμος (-οι) 'woodcutter(s),' etc.[30] Neither is Ventris's transcription *ra-wa-ke-ta, du-ru-to-mo* justified by the presence of each of the characters in other words that we have demonstrated to be Greek. For several of the characters we have not found any verification. Yet, by a circular argument — not concisely stated, so that it escapes notice — the Greek words have been taken to prove the decipherment, and the decipherment has in turn been taken to guarantee the words. The caution proper to an experiment is forgotten; and the Greek words thus "deciphered" become not a hypothetical but an illusory context for interpreting other words in the same tablets, words which in Ventris's transcription do not even *look* Greek.

The case of 'Alektruon son of Etewoklewes.' An intelligent argument for the reality of certain Greek words in Linear B was made by Ventris on grounds of mathematical probability: "It is conceivable that any arbitrary system of phonetic values would yield the same limited number of correspondences; but coincidence seems insufficient to account for the exceptionally long name *E-te-wo-ke-re-we-i-jo* Sn01.15, which on values and orthography determined beforehand (and out of 200 billion possible permutations of syllables in an eight-sign word) so exactly yields the patronymic Ἐτεϝοκλεϝήϊος."[31] Ventris's reasoning is not ruined by the circumstance that he set the values *after*, not before, studying this tablet, among many others. The fact is that in Work Note 14 (p. 110, item P 79) he took the first three characters *38-04-42* for a separate word, in accordance with Bennett's index to *PT* (1951).[32] Even the tracing in *PT* (1955) leaves some doubt whether the scribe intended those three characters to be part of the same word as the next five. There is no word-divider between *42* and *44*, as there is before *38* and again after *36*; but starting with *44* the characters are noticeably larger. The question whether there is really an eight-character word *38-04-42-44-27-75-28-36* would remain unsettled, were it not for the subsequent discovery of An654, which contains it split between lines 8 and 9 (*PT* [1955], p. 70). The splitting is abnormal in Linear B and might seem in itself to argue against the eight characters composing a single word; but the unusual length constrained the scribe. He made *38-04-42-44-27-* full-size, then *-75-* much smaller, but still had too little room for *-28-36* and wrote them on the line below. No other Linear B word of such length fits the pattern of a Greek word, unless subjected to some arbitrary distortion. The case for identifying this word with *Ἐτεϝοκλεϝήϊος, an eminently Greek patronymic, is similar in part to the case for the five Greek words in the "oil" tablet (Gn1184): the sequence of characters transcribed as Greek is fairly long and too meaningful to be a mere coincidence. Besides, I recognize that most of the eight characters of the word now at issue have been proved more or less adequately in some other words. *04 = te*, however, would be a great gain to our list of authenticated values, if we could rely on it.[33]

Unfortunately the context is not enough to prove that a patronymic — or, for that matter, any noun — is suitable; so the demonstration of identity is less straightforward than in *38-33-42* = ἔλαι(ϝ)ον 'oil' (see above, p. 142), and proceeds rather by exclusion. No MAN ideogram follows the verbal part of the entry which contains the eight-character word, either in Sn64.15 or in An654.9. The preceding word in the former text is transcribed *ne-qe-u* but not identified with a name or any other word in any language. In the latter text it is preceded by *08-27-81-69-26-42*, which Ventris transcribes *a-re-ku-tu-ru-wo;* so we have fourteen characters susceptible to the Greek reading Ἀλεκτρυὼν Ἐτεϝοκλεϝήϊος. The case for *a-re-* and *-ru-wo* in the first word is clear from the occurrences of the characters elsewhere; but it would be bold to claim that no other values besides *81 = ku* and *69 = tu* could fill in the center of the word.[34] The word will square with Greek only on the assumption that it is nominative (with graphic suppression of the final *-n*); but the context does not show why a nominative should come so late in a sentence here. The three words before it in the sentence, *13-59-78 72-28 38-78-59*, are a frequent formula in the An series, but will hardly pass for Greek when transcribed *me-ta-qe pe-i e-qe-ta.* 'And with them the follower (or attendant) Alectryon son of Eteocles' incurs the objection that while *pe-i* might be reconciled with the Arcadian dative plural ΣΦΕΙΣ (*IG* 5.2.6.10,18), the same dialect has

not μετά but ΠΕ, the truncated form of πεδά (5.2.262.16).[35]
So the supposed Greek phrase μετά τε σφεῖς may be just an illusion.[36]

In the name 'Αλεκτρυών (*Il.* 17.602), which is also applied to the cock (Theognis 864, etc.), -υών is not of clearly Indo-European origin; but the synonym ἀλέκτωρ (Pindar, *Ol.* 12.14, etc.) is irreproachably Indo-European both in its root — cf. ἀλέξω 'ward off, protect' — and in the -τωρ suffix. However, the Linear B word occurs also in the Es tablets with inflexions unlike Greek:

Es650.1-2

67-53-37-36-36 70-72-27-10 / 38-44 05-12-45-72-15 ⟁ ⫶⫶
08-27-81-69-26-42   38-44-05-12-45-72-15 ⟁ ⫶⫶⫶

transcribed

ki-ri-ti-jo-jo ko-pe-re-u / e-ke to-so-de-pe-mo

a-re-ku-tu-ru-wo   e-ke-to-so-de-pe-mo

Es644.1-2

70-72-27-42 14-12-15 75-04-28-75-04-28 ⟁ ⏉ ⫶⫶⫶
08-27-81-69-26-42-52 75-04-28-75-04-28 ⟁ ⏉ ⫶⫶ ⟊⫶⫶⫶

transcribed

ko-pe-re-wo do-so-mo we-te-i-we-te-i
a-re-ku-tu-ru-wo-no we-te-i-we-te-i

Es646.1

70-72-27-10 11-09-01-61-24 14-12-15   ⟁ ' ⏉ ⫶⫶

transcribed

ko-pe-re-u po-se-da-o-ne do-so-mo

Es649.1

08-27-81-69-26-52-24 11-09-01-61-52 14-12-15 ⟁ ⫾⫾ ⏉ ⫶⫶⫶

transcribed

a-re-ku-tu-ru-ṇo-ne po-se-da-o-no do-so-mo[37]

Whatever *14-12-15* may mean and whatever construction it may call for, the inflexions of the words that go with it defy any Greek pattern (see above, p. 133, note 14). So the cogency — not to mention the inevitability — of identifying one of these words as the name Ἀλεκτρυών (genitive Ἀλεκτρυόνος) is diminished. With that slumps the only contextual prop for the patronymic Ἐτεϝοκλεϝήϊος in An654.8-9. The man's name — patronymic and all — is liable to be an illusion.

Phonetic deformation of Greek words in non-Greek contexts. It is a matter of taste rather than reasoning whether to regard the eight characters *38-04-42-44-27-75-28-36* as providing enough context for one another, so that in the absence of anything to prohibit the identification of such a long word with *Ἐτεϝοκλεϝήϊος, the very length would be sufficient guarantee against coincidence.[38] At least for the practical purpose of continuing to look for recognizable, intelligible — i.e., Greek — words and phrases in the Linear B texts, we ought to accept the identification tentatively. In itself it does not lend any strength to the conjectural value *04 = te* or the feebly supported *44 = ke* (see above, pp. 157-8); but there is a chance that further study of the Linear B material will turn up more compelling instances of the two values. As our knowledge stands now, the values *04 = te* and *44 = ke* cannot be reckoned as more than rough normalizations (see above, p. 70) and might be misleading normalizations at that. For even if we recognize in *38-04-42-44-27-75-28-36* the Linear B equivalent to a Greek patronymic, it does not follow that the tablets where it occurs are written in Greek. Take the analogy of a nearly illegible modern text in which we could somehow make out the surname *Macauley* (originally a patronymic). We would not jump to the conclusion that the text is in Gaelic, unless we could read all the neighboring words as Gaelic too. Moreover we would allow quite a bit of room for distortion of the Gaelic sounds by the tendencies of the non-Gaelic language, whatever it might be. In case we could determine that the non-Gaelic language is English, that would at any rate narrow the possible range of distortions from the true Gaelic form, known to us from some other source. We are less well off when we try to deal with a probable Greek name in Linear B, if it happens to be imbedded in a non-Greek text. The non-Greek languages of the Aegean are unknown to us, although we are certain they existed. Some elements from them survived by entering Greek but were distorted in the process of Hellenization. So we are beset with uncontrollable possibilities of change suffered by Greek sounds in non-Greek texts.

Even where we are certain of a Greek word, like 11-02 'foal(s)' or 37-53-11 'tripod' and its dual or plural 37-53-11-45, doubt remains as to how much or how little it may have been barbarized in the pronunciation of the Linear B scribes. Supposing we had some fully and demonstrably Greek texts in Linear B characters (with more than just the three words for 'horses,' 'asses,' and 'foals'), the seriousness of the distortion could be minimized. But at best some distortions of Greek, by no means negligible, seem inherent in the use of the Linear B script. That will be the subject of the next chapter.

The "gods" tablet. Nearly the same reservations that we have placed on the reliability of ('Αλεκτρυὼν) 'Ετεροκλεϝήϊος must also be applied to the apparent names of gods in V52 (Knosos). It consists of two extant fragments:[39]

$$08\text{-}59\text{-}06\text{-}11\text{-}37\text{-}30\text{-}57 \mid [\qquad\qquad x\,(?)$$
$$38\text{-}55\text{-}54\text{-}53\text{-}36 \mid 03\text{-}57\text{-}42[\qquad]11\text{-}09\text{-}01[$$

transcribed   *a-ta-na-po-ti-ni-ja*   1 [$_x$(?)
           e-nu-wa-ri-jo   1   *pa-ja-wo*[   ]*po-se-da*[

The words can be normalized to Homeric Greek: Ἀθήνη πότνια, Ἐνυάλιος, Παιήων, Ποσειδά[ων]. However, the position of *-po-ti-ni-ja* as a suffix is contrary to the order both in Homeric and in later Greek; πότνια or its rare variant πότνα comes before the name or other word in the construction:[40] πότνι' Ἀθηναίη (*Il.* 6.305; *πότνι' Ἀθήνη is lacking), πότνια Ἥρη (8.198, etc.; βοῶπις πότνια Ἥρη, 8.471, etc.), πότνια Ἥβη (4.2), πότνια μῆτερ (6.264; πότνια μήτηρ, 1.357, etc.), πότνια θηρῶν 'mistress of wild beasts' (21.470; epithet of Artemis), πότνια νύμφη (*Od.* 5.149), πότνια Κίρκη (8.448, etc.),[41] πότνα θεά (5.215, etc.). The metrical pattern of πό̄τνῐᾰ and πό̄τνᾰ is insufficient to account for the fact that another word always closes the construction: πότνια would be metrical suitable in the fourth foot of the hexameter, making a "bucolic diaeresis"; πότνα would fit the last foot. In subsequent Greek poetry also πότνια almost always comes ahead; exceptions are rare — μᾶτερ πότνι' (Sophocles, *Phil.* 395), τὰν ἐρώτων πότνιαν (Euripides, fr. 781.16 [*Phaëthon*] Nauck) — and not quite parallel to *'Αθήνη πότνια with the name first and the title second. Evidently the usage of Greek, though otherwise so remarkably free in word order, fixes the position of πότνια, almost as if it did not rank as an independent word. In Homeric Greek, indeed, it is uninflected and limited to vocative and nominative uses.

The transcription *a-ta-na-po-ti-ni-ja* contains several values that are otherwise well established: $o8 = a$, $11 = po$, $37 = ti$, and not so definitely $o6 = na$. But to accept the whole word as the designation of a goddess *a-ta-na-po-ti-ni-ja* we must surmount a high hurdle. Whereas Ἀθήνη is apparently non-Indo-European in origin (like Ἐνυάλιος, Παιήων, and Ποσειδάων), πότνια is Indo-European, corresponding exactly to *pátnī* in Sanskrit. So only *-po-ti-ni-ja* in the transcribed text argues that the text is Greek; for Greek, however, *-po-ti-ni-ja* is wrongly placed with relation to *a-ta-na*. We would have to suppose that the Greek title 'Lady' penetrated into a neighboring language, whose grammar required it to come after the name (somewhat like *-san* in Japanese).[42] 11-37-30-57 occurs also as a separate word in Gg702.2 and M729.2 (Knosos), Cc665 and Tn316.3 (Pylos); at the end of the words

10-11-36-11-37-30-57 (Fn187.8, Pylos)
38-27-40-36-11-37-30-57 (Vn48.3, Pylos)

and with an apparent suffix in

11-37-30-57-75 (Dl 943.A, Knosos)
11-37-30-57-75-36 (Dl 930.A, 946.A, 933
   +968.A, Knosos; Jn431+433.16, Pylos)[43]
11-37-30-57-75-36-36 (Eq213.5, Pylos)
11-37-30-57-40-36 (Qa1299, Pylos)[44]

The first element in *u-po-jo-po-ti-ni-ja* and *e-re-wi-jo-po-ti-ni-ja* is not identifiable as a goddess or anything else. No such suffixes as *-we, -we-jo, -we-jo-jo, -wi-jo* could be added in Greek to πoτνια- under any circumstances (*Documents*, pp. 127, 406). Reciprocal influence of Greek and a non-Indo-European language upon each other would have been likely enough while the populations were mixed; but that brings us back to the same phonetic uncertainty which confronted us earlier (see above, p. 203): we do not know how different Ἀθήνη, etc., may have been in the "Aegean" language of origin, nor what may have happened to πότνια in passing from Greek to an unknown neighboring language.[45] Thus we would have no assurance of the values 59 = *ta*, 30 = *ni*,

57 = *ja* even if we were certain that the word means 'Athene-lady' or the like.

In any case the meaning is not certain. There is at best a small balance of probability in favor of taking the four words to be names of gods. In themselves they admit of such an interpretation; and it is unlikely that a faulty decipherment could by mere coincidence achieve such a degree of cohesion among the four surviving words of a text. To be sure, they are not in any construction with one another, but a Linear B tablet is liable to be just a list. Athene, Enyalios, Paian, and Poseidon are hardly the four that we would expect together, from our knowledge of Greek religion; but the group may have been better rounded out by the other parts of the text which have perished.[46] Yet a serious doubt arises from the number ONE written ideographically after the first word of both lines.[47] We are hard put to imagine why gods should be counted in this fashion. Conceivably the bare number I could stand for ONE offering of some unspecified kind; but the fact that 08-59-06-11-37-30-57 is the very first word argues against interpreting the text as a record of offerings. Offerings ought to be in accord with some ritual and therefore specified ideographically — some animal, fruit, textile, or the like. The place for such an ideogram would be after the word and before the number; but it is lacking altogether.[48] The tablet is therefore to be compared with others that have nothing ideographic except the repeated number I — i.e., the V tablets from Knosos (V60, 77, 147, 151, 466, 488, 492, 503, 653, 831, 832, 1529, 1631) and from Pylos (Vn851, 865, 1191).[49] The decipherment leaves all these tablets in total darkness. So the idea that V52 contains gods' names is unpromising, and we had better abstain from inferences about its meaning and its language.

The inadequacy of the Linear B script for Greek. Ever

since Ventris's first announcement of Greek in Work Note 20, it has been admitted that Linear B can pass for Greek only by the assumption that certain Greek sounds were left unwritten. In the next chapter we shall look for specific proof of unwritten sounds. The evidence that we must acknowledge is much less than Ventris has adduced, but it suffices to show that the Linear B syllabary was an awkward tool for writing Greek — any dialect whatever of it — or any Indo-European language. The advocates of the decipherment have been content to attribute the principles of the script to the phonological structure of some other language of the Aegean area (see *Documents*, p. 69). However, the points distinguishing the Linear B script from Linear A and earlier Minoan scripts argue that Linear B is an adaptation, not just a continuation. The adaptation must have been influenced by the language or languages to be written in Linear B.[50] So it will not do to maintain that the Linear B tablets are solely in Greek, but ill expressed graphically because the script was ill adapted to Greek. The logical tendency of such a view is that Linear B was adapted, not to the first written language of the Aegean, but to some other — and only in the end applied to Greek. But if we have to go so far, we had better question the exclusive presence of Greek in the preserved Linear B texts. It is unlikely that the language for which the script was intended lost out utterly to Greek while the script itself remained in use at Knosos, Pylos, Mycenae, and other places. More probably, Greek and another language (or languages) coexist in the Linear B tablets. Some scholars may object methodologically that to call anything non-Greek is to abandon the effort to interpret it; for we can try and reasonably hope to make sense of whatever is Greek, but the other ancient Aegean languages remain virtually closed to us. I would reply that to insist on interpreting texts as Greek will lead, if in fact they are not Greek, to the creation of an illusory web, in which the genuine Greek is obscured.

The Cypriotic syllabary is acknowledged to have been used both for Greek and an unknown language called Eteocyprian by the moderns (in imitation of the old term Eteocretan).[51] In some inscriptions it is problematical whether the language is Greek or Eteocyprian.[52] Nobody any longer has a stake in calling the Cypriotic inscriptions all Greek. It ought to be like that in Linear B studies: nobody should shrink from recognizing what is not demonstrably Greek and what is demonstrably not Greek, as well as what is demonstrably Greek — let the chips fall where they may.

Texts in other pre-classical scripts. A by-product of Ventris's work upon Linear B has been the stimulus to the study of the other Cretan scripts — Linear A, hieroglyphics, and the Phaistos disk — and of the Enkomi tablets of Cyprus, somewhat as the decipherment of the Old Persian cuneiform in the last century opened the door to the other cuneiform scripts of Asia. Taking his transcription of Linear B as a basis, several scholars and amateurs have attempted to decipher one or more of those other scripts. If any such effort were to succeed, it would reflect great credit on Ventris's decipherment of Linear B — that being the indispensable starting point for all who have subsequently ventured upon unlocking the secrets of the prehistoric Aegean culture. Even if the Linear B texts then remained as obscure as they are now, the success of any secondary decipherment would almost certainly guarantee that the primary one by Ventris must have been a reliable foundation. However, none of the secondary decipherments that have come to my notice are at all cogent. The authors have not made a case that can attract any considerable backing in the scholarly world.[53] It would be gratuitous for me to extend my critique to them;

I had rather grant offhand that they have doubtless brought to light a worthwhile point here and there. That they have accomplished no more, does not count, of course, against Ventris's decipherment of Linear B; for one decipherment is obviously not a skeleton key all ready for other decipherments. In the future there is room for the hope that progress will be made toward the reading of the other Aegean scripts, and that Linear B studies will gain too.

Notes to Chapter VII

1. For simplicity of treatment I am neglecting something that may conceivably have had a degree of importance — the rise within one Indo-European community of novelties and divergences not prompted by any non-Indo-European influence.

2. Practically as baffling as the strictly non-Indo-European is what A. J. van Windekens has for convenience called "Pelasgic"; *Le Pélasgique*, Bibliothèque du *Muséon*, vol. 29 (Louvain, 1952). He means another prehistoric Indo-European language, which is not represented by any texts and whose existence is inferred from vestiges of its influence upon Greek and other recorded languages of the adjacent territory.

3. Guarducci, vol. III, no. VI.1-6,31, pp. 137-142; vol. I, no. V.23, pp. 18-19; Henri van Effenterre, "Une bilingue étéocrétoise?" *Revue de philologie*, XX (1946), 131-138.

4. More can be obtained by a critical scrutiny of Oscar Landau, *Mykenisch-griechische Personennamen*, Studia Graeca et Latina Gothoburgensia 7 (1958).

5. *Documents*, p. 93, presents a contrary view: "Certainly the names cannot be used to support a theory that any language other than Greek was in actual use in the Mycenaean kingdoms." But the Mycenaean kingdom in Crete, unless perhaps it was limited to the vicinity of Knosos, must incontestably have included some non-Greek population (see above, p. 190). On the mainland the extinction of non-Greek languages in various districts is undatable. There are no non-Greek texts written in the Greek or Phoenician alphabet on the mainland; but this cannot prove *ex silentio* that among the illiterate no other language besides Greek lingered on. Much less can we prove that centuries earlier the Pylos or the Mycenae area was wholly Hellenic in speech.

6. Among the scholars who recognize the deciphered Linear B tablets in general to be Greek, Haiim Rosén has called attention to some totally unintelligible ones, such as L588 (Knosos): "In such a state of things it seems to us there is just one interpretation: the second text [L588, as opposed to L587] and the like are not written in the Greek language, and it is evident that the Linear B script could also serve for the notation of a language which preceded Greek in

the same areas, and that it is perhaps the same language that the Linear A texts are written in" — "הכתבים ה''מי'קיניים" ('The "Mycenaean" Documents'), אשכולות (*Eškolot*), IV (1962), 17; English summary reprinted in *Nestor* (1 April 1962), p. 182.

7. In Eo278 (Pylos) *70-05-52 ko-to-no* is taken for a dual of the frequent word *ko-to-na* (which is supposed to equal the Greek dialect word κτοίνᾱ or κτοῖνα, an obscure term of land division). The only thing in the context that might rank as evidence for a dual is $\overset{\shortparallel}{\lambda}\lambda$ in front of *ko-to-no*. Ernst Risch, "Mykenisch *wo-wo ko-to-no*," *Minos*, V (1957), 28-34, meritoriously pointed out that only the former of the two characters is a normal *42* (*wo*); the latter is a mirror image of it, never found except in this digraph — somewhat as *q* in Latin and English is found only in the digraph *qu.* The same Linear B digraph occurs in Eb338.2, this time *after* the damaged word *ko-to-* [   ]. That the digraph amounts phonetically to *duwo* or *dwo* 'two' was suggested to him by three words in other Pylos tablets:

40-14-42-28-36, transcribed   *wi-do-wo-i-jo* (Ae344, An5.2)
40-51-42-28-36, transcribed   *wi-du-wo-i-jo*
                                  or *wi-da₂-wo-i-jo* (Jn415.3)
40-42- ⤂*-28-36* (Ep539.12)

The meager and utterly dissimilar contexts preclude any proof that the three are variant forms of the same word, as was already assumed by Ventris in Work Note 9, p. 74, item C 7, and in "Evidence," p. 88.

The simplest phonetic interpretation of the digraph is that the first part of it stands for the usual sound of *42*, and the second part for a repetition of it with some kind of dissimilation which would not occur in any other environment — perhaps [woʍo], the second consonant being unvoiced. If it were proved to be the Linear B word for 'two,' that would be far indeed from the Greek δύο, δύω and the Indo-European cognates. Risch, while identifying the Linear B digraph with the Greek word, is aware of the difficulty and suggests a virtually ideographic motive for the digraph: "These two signs facing each other compose as it were a pair, and may therefore be a symbol for the number 2."

Subsequent excavations at Pylos have uncovered a tablet containing this word followed by the ideographic " (Sb1315.3; Lang, *AJA*, LXII, pl. xlviii). Lang's transcription on p. 184 is to be corrected in accord with the appendix to her subsequent article, "The Palace of Nestor Excavations of 1958," *AJA*, LXIII (1959), 137. The word and the ensuing numeral are in tiny characters squeezed into a narrow space between two items, *24-54 08-30-57 08-06-50-44* ¦¦¦ [i.e., 5] and *08-50-44* ¦¦¦ [i.e., 9]. If anything can be certain in the interpretation of this tablet, it is that the new item which the scribe inserted did not consist merely of 'two' written once phonetically and once ideographically. Not even the fussy modern practice of redundantly writing, for example, *two* (*2*) *batteries* would prompt a person to waste a very meager space on *two* 2 while not indicating what, whose, or anything else about the two. So the new tablet argues strongly against Risch's interpretation of the extraordinary word Ⱶ'Ⱶ as 'two.' But a possibility remains that the word is somehow connected with the grammatical category of the dual.

The Third International Colloquium for Mycenaean Studies in 1961 resolved to add the digraph to the Linear B syllabary as a single character *90* — wrongly, in my judgement.

8. The broken word]-*70-13-52*, followed by a MAN ideogram in As608.3 and B799.r5 (Knosos), can hardly count as evidence of gender.

9. The writing of the same character -*78* does not insure that the sound was identical; for the script was imperfect.

10. In all there are only six cases; so my predecessors deserve no blame for not remarking on the peculiar distribution of *36*- and -*41*.

11. See above, pp. 120-2; neither word is identified in full. Another possible but quite unproved affinity is Ventris's equation of *08-30-57-39* with *ἁνίᾱφι* 'reins' (instrumental).

12. "MT" (1958), pp. 108-109; Bennett's photographs, tracings, and transcriptions on pp. 66-69, 80-81. Bennett assigns both tablets to one scribe (p. 91).

13. Daringly emended to *pu-ke-<o o>-pe-ro{ro}* in *Documents*, p. 231. But unless we are cocksure that the whole text is simple, straightforward Greek, we ought to be impressed by two peculiarities of the last item: whereas *50-44-61* is second in Ge603, the corresponding word in Ge604 drops to the bottom of the list; and only in that bottom item is the additional word *72-02-02* rather than *61-72-02*. As far as I dare to judge (being unable to identify *72-02-02* and *61-72-02*, and therefore not knowing what they mean), it appears to me that *72-02-02* puts *50-44* into a different category from the

words above it. To emend the data into insignificance is absurdly premature.

14. *Documents,* p. 401, expresses an odd notion that *o-pe-ro* is an "abbrev. for participles act. *ophêlōn* [ὀφείλων], etc. and pass. *ophêlomenon, -mena* [ὀφειλόμενον, -μενα] etc." Those words of more than three syllables do not occur in Linear B; but *61* as an abbreviation for *61-72-02* occurs often.

15. Professor Carlo Gallavotti of Rome very helpfully pointed out *06-05-05* to me at the Third International Colloquium for Mycenaean Studies, held at Racine, Wisconsin, in September, 1961. The last character *-05* is written over an erasure of *44.* I do not understand the inclination of, editors to reject *na-to-to* as a scribal error for *o-na-to,* when the scribe has in fact taken the trouble to correct a quite different mistake that he became aware of — the writing of the first character of the next word while omitting by haplography the last character of this one.

16. Almost never does it set off a one-character word; see above, p. 101, note 42.

17. Bibliography in Vilborg, p. 30.

18. See above, p. 154. The transcription *-da-na* for the last two characters would not accord with the neuter singular noun of Greek, but the plural is frequent (Aristophanes, *Equ.* 676, 682, etc.)

19. *OOTP,* p. 16; "MT" (1958), pp. 48-49; see above, p. 141.

20. The ideographic part of Fr1242 is broken off and has not been recovered; so there is no telling whether *08-02-03* in the preserved part supports a semantic identification with the ideographic ligature *08.*

21. 5 tablets contain *03-70-75* and ideogram with *03*
  (Fr1202, 1224, 1226, 1232, 1235; *03-70* instead of *03-70-75* in Fr1216);

  6 tablets contain ideogram with *03* but not *03-70-75*
  (Fr1205, 1206+1260+1210, 1227, 1228, 1233, 1236);

  3 tablets contain *03-70-75* and ideogram with *08*
  (Fr1217, 1223.1, 1240);

  7 tablets contain ideogram with *08* but not *03-70-75*
  (Fr1207, 1218, 1219, 1221, 1223.2, 1225, 1230).

See *OOTP,* pp. 16-17. I have left out some tablets that are doubtful because of damage.

22. That it is a tunic gains in likelihood from the variant ⌐⫶⌐ (with 67 inside), where the two dots may well represent something designed to accommodate a woman's breasts (L593-595, 870, 5961, Knosos); see above, p. 98, note 22.

23. Granted that much of the English-speaking stock in North America is descended from continental European immigrants who never lived in the British Isles, and that in Great Britain and Ireland most of what was Celtic territory in Chaucer's time has gone over to English (not, for the most part, through displacement of the Celtic population), yet in each generation those acquiring English though not of native parentage were few compared to those inheriting it. Moreover, the standard of English was so securely established in a large educated class of native speakers that there was only a slight chance of its being modified by the substrate languages of the new speakers of English (including the royal family from Germany).

24. Pallotino (above, p. 17, note 8), p. 29, called attention to the idea that the Linear B language is "merely related to Greek, partially influenced by Greek."

25. Even when Latin was enthroned in the Middle Ages, the practice of the scribes who kept registers varied in regard to Latinizing the less tractable of the Germanic, Celtic, Slavic, and other names.

26. Entries under "Personalien" in *Gnomon* illustrate the tendency to settle for a jargon rather than recast altogether into one language the information received in another (doubtless by letter):

> "Cornelius V e r m e u l e, London, Sir John Soane's Museum, ist als Instructor in Greek and Roman Art an die University of Michigan nach Ann Arbor gegangen" — XXVI (1954), 64.

> "Der Directeur des Antiquités von Algerien, Lehrbeauftragter der Altertümer Afrikas an der Faculté des Lettres von Algier Prof. Louis L e s c h i ist am 7. Januar 1954 gestorben" (*loc. cit.*).

> "Der Reader in Comparative philology am Univ. College London G. P. S h i p p ist zum Professor of Greek in Sidney ernannt worden" (p. 496).

> "Zum Direktor der Academia Belgica de Rome ist in Nachfolge von Prof. Fernand Vercauteren (Univ. Lüttich) der Professor an der Univ. Brüssel William L a m e e r e ernannt worden" (p. 560).

The editor of *Gnomon* or his assistant — whoever wrote this way

— had no adequate reason to bother with problems like "Wie sagt man auf deutsch, *Instructor in Greek and Roman Art?*"

27. Carl W. Blegen in "Foreword" to *PT* (1955), p. viii.

28. See Wilhelm Eilers, "Kretisch-Kritisches," *Forschungen und Fortschritte*, XXX (1957), 327-328, 331-332; W. Merlingen, *Das "Vorgriechische" und die sprachwissenschaftlich-vorhistorischen Grundlagen* (Vienna: Gerold, 1955), p. 45.

29. In Ca895 the words for 'horse(s),' 'ass(es),' and 'foal(s)' are not in any construction.

30. See "Evidence," p. 96.

31. "Evidence," p. 94; Sn01 was renumbered Sn64 in *PT* (1955).

32. P. 98. Naturally the other five characters *44-27-75-28-36* are listed as another word (p. 103). The identity of the character between *44* and *75* is unsettled; the tracing in *PT* (1955), p. 10, makes it *02* (*ro*), not *27* (*re*).

33. We would then face the odd syntax of *e-ko-te* and *e-ko-si* in the Jn tablets (see above, pp. 88-9). We might have to theorize that Greek forms close to ἔχοντες and ἔχουσι were employed according to the syntax of some unknown language.

34. Since the Greek word is syllabically ἀ-λεκ-τρύ-ων, it is odd that [k] at the end of a syllable should be written *ku* with the vowel of the next syllable. See *Documents*, pp. 45-46.

35. Part of the letter Π is gone, but enough remains to guarantee it is not M; Gustave Fougères, "Inscriptions archaïques de Mantinée," *Bulletin de correspondance hellénique*, XVI (1892), pl. xix. The first scholar to restore Π was Bruno Keil, "Das Gottesurteil von Mantineia," *Nachrichten von der Königl. Gesellschaft der Wissenschaften zu Göttingen, historisch-philologische Klasse*, 1895, pp. 351, 353. The meaning of ΠΕΤΟΙΣΦΟΙΚΙΑΤΑΙ is plainly 'with those of his household.' In another text ΠΕ[τοδι]ΚΑΣΤΗΡΙΟΝ or ΠΕ[δαδι]-ΚΑΣΤΗΡΙΟΝ (5.2.6.98), the preposition with the accusative may mean 'in the midst of.' Our inscriptions from this backward part of Greece are few until the period when the dialect becomes infected with Atticisms and finally succumbs to the κοινή. ΜΕΤΑ begins to appear in the time of transition (citations in *IG* 5.2, p. 186), and ΠΕ then drops out.

36. Besides, *13-59*, without the third character *-78*, is not in Linear B. So we lack proof that *-78* is here an enclitic suffix 'and.'

37. Only meager vestiges remain of the astonishing character *52*

in the first word, according to Bennett's line drawing — *PT* (1955), p. 68; but he evidently saw more on the tablet itself.

38. In answer to the criticism that Ventris's loose orthographic rules allow a multitude of possible Greek interpretations of many if not all Linear B words, Palmer (*OLZ*, LIII, 109) and others have rightly shown that the possibilities of anything actually Greek would be most numerous in a two-character word and decline sharply with each additional character; so nothing else in Greek besides Ἐτε(ϝ)ο-κλε(ϝ)ῆτος could fit the eight characters transcribed *e-te-wo-ke-re-we-i-jo*. While the defenders win this point in the controversy, with regard to the particular eight-character word, still they slight the other side of their own coin: Many, many Linear B words of three or more characters are doomed by the transcription of their last character to be unidentifiable as Greek. If they were shorter by one character, they could by Ventris's rules be equated with a Greek word; e.g., *tu-na-no* (Lc525.B, etc.; Knosos) minus the last character could be θύννα, a kind of fish. It is futile to say that what nobody is able to equate with Greek is correctly deciphered but not yet interpreted (see above, p. 55).

39. An intermediate piece is lost, but beyond doubt these two belong to the same tablet.

40. Beattie, *JHS*, LXXVI, 4. His other objections to Ventris's reading of this tablet will not hold up. Palmer, *Gnomon*, XXIX, 567, cryptically interprets the Linear B word to mean 'the Lady of Athānā' (= 'the Athens lady'?). Ἀθήνη and Ἀθάνā are limited to poetry; the normal form of the goddess's name is Ἀθηναίη in Ionic, Ἀθηναίā, Ἀθηνάā, Ἀθηνᾶ in Attic, Ἀθāναίā in Doric, Ἀθāνάā in Aeolic.

41. Another word intervenes only in *Od.* 1.14, νύμφη πότνι' ἔρυκε Καλυψώ — meter would forbid the juxtaposition *πότνια Καλυψώ.

42. If in a baffling modern text we were to make out *Lady Mary*, we could be sure that at least those two words are English. But if instead we got *Marylady* (or *Marialady*), the most we could conclude is that *-lady* is an element of English origin in some other language.

43. Damaged in Jn310.14, Ep617.14, Un249.1.

44. Lang, *AJA*, LXII, 184.

45. On a bilingual Lydian-Greek inscription from Pergamon, ΑΘΗΝΑΙΗΙ (dative) corresponds to *asvil;* transcription and photograph of a squeeze in *Sardis*, vol. VI, part II by W. H. Buckler (Leyden: Brill, 1924), p. 57 and pl. xiii. The Lydian letter Ƨ ,

transcribed v, is in some loose way related to *n* (Buckler, p. xiii). AΘHN- therefore has quite a bit in common with *asv*-, but not enough to justify us in identifying the value of the Lydian characters with the Greek sounds expressed in writing by Θ and N.

46. If *po-se-da*[is here in company with three other gods' names, we cannot say as much for *po-se-da-o-ne* in the Es tablets, where the other "three entities" are *ai̯?-ke-te-si, we-da-ne-we* (or *we-da-ne-wo*), and *di-wi-je-we* (*Documents*, pp. 276, 279) — unidentifiable in any connexion with the cults or anything else of the Aegean world (see above, p. 133, note 14).

47. Whether the other words were also accompanied by a number, cannot be determined from the remains of the tablet.

48. It is not quite impossible that an ideogram was abnormally written after the number on the first line. The tablet is broken off a little to the right of the number, and there are no visible remains of another character, ideographic or phonetic. The safest inference is that the number is the last character of the item. Certainly that is so in 38-55-54-53-36 Ɩ on the second line.

49. Vn851 has a cross or check mark after each ONE. The "gods" tablet seems to have a similar mark, which is the only writing preserved above the second line of the right-hand fragment.

50. Fritz Schachermeyr develops an interesting hypothesis in "Die Entzifferung der mykenischen Schrift," *Saeculum*, X (1959), 70-71.

51. Most convincingly demonstrated in a bilingual inscription by Ernst Sittig, "'Αμαθοῦντος δίγλωσσος ἐπιγραφή," in 'Αρχαιολογικὴ ἐφημερίς, 1914, pp. 1-2; "Zur neu gefundenen kyprischen Sprache," *Zeitschrift für vergleichende Sprachforschung auf dem Gebiete der indogermanischen Sprachen*, LII (1924), 194-202.

52. Mitford, *Archaeology*, V, 152: "Several inscriptions, of Golgi and the hinterland in particular, which have long been rendered into a Greek so dubious as to bring the syllabic epigraphy of Cyprus into serious disrepute, now call for re-examination. This will without doubt substantially increase the Eteo-Cyprian total; but it remains for epigraphy to establish the status and relationship of these two languages, alike at Paphos and throughout the island." See below, p. 245.

53. I await a forthcoming publication by Cyrus H. Gordon on Linear A (announced to the readers of *Nestor* in his circular of February 15, 1962), in the hope that it will prove the first major step since Ventris in the reading of the Aegean scripts.

CHAPTER VIII

UNWRITTEN SOUNDS

IN MOST OF THE identifications between Linear B and Greek words which I have upheld, I have had to accept the lack of a final consonant or of -ι, the latter half of a diphthong. My acceptance was intended provisionally, in order to reserve for a separate section a study of the peculiarities of syllabic writing which keep the Linear B script from representing the language adequately. Evidence for the omission of a sound at the end of a syllable within a word is less clear and will be treated later.

The difficulty of indicating a post-nuclear sound. Many scholars have brought out the "open syllable" principle of the Linear B syllabary, like that of the Cypriotic: each character stands for a consonant plus a vowel, or for a vowel alone; but not for a vowel plus a consonant. Prior to any decipherment Ventris and two of his correspondents, Georgiev and Ktistopoulos, had already taken up the principle as a working hypothesis (see above, pp. 19-20). In Work Note 20 (p. 175) Ventris posited an important difference of detail between the Linear B and the Cypriotic script: the masculine *70-42* is rendered $ko(r)$-$wo(s)$, singular, or $ko(r)$-$wo(i)$, plural; the feminine *70-54* is rendered $ko(r)$-$wā$, singular, or $ko(r)$-$wa(i)$, plural. In Cypriotic the sounds

of *r*, *s*, or *i* at the end of a syllable would normally be indicated as follows: **ko-ro-wo-se, *ko-ro-wo-i, *ko-ro-wa,
ko-ro-wa-i (Deecke, p. 10). Given a repertory of symbols
for open syllables only, the writing of post-nuclear sounds
could not be more than a makeshift. Writing in any syllabic
script requires that a word be resolved into syllables — which
is already somewhat artificial; on top of that, to treat the
post-nuclear part of a syllable as though it were a syllable
in its own right must be still more artificial.

However, not all post-nuclear sounds are equally resistant
to an "open syllable" notation. Here the Cypriotic syllabary
reveals an instructive gradation:

(1) In a geminated consonant — e.g., -λλ- in Ἀπόλλωνι —
the syllabary absolutely neglects the post-nuclear consonantal sound at the end of the former syllable: *a-po-lo-ni*
(Deecke, no. 120, p. 44).

(2) Likewise a post-nuclear nasal consonant, assimilated
to the labial, dental, or velar plosive of the ensuing syllable, is uniformly neglected — e.g., *to-pe-pa-me-ro-ne* 'the
five-day period' (accusative or genitive singular, πεμπ-;
Deecke, no. 59.2, pp. 26-27), *a-ti-to-mi-si-to-ne* 'instead
(ἀντί) of the pay' (no. 60.5, pp. 27-29).

(3) The final -ς is sometimes but not usually omitted:
ti-ja-i-te-mi (= Διαιθεμις; Deecke, no. 74, pp. 34-35).[1]

(4) The *i* or post-nuclear part of a diphthong is consistently written in Cypriotic: *e-le-i* (= ἕλει 'marsh,' dative; Deecke, no. 60.9, pp. 28-30), *me-ma-na-me-no-i*
(= μεμνᾱμένοι, μεμνημένοι 'remembering'; no. 71, p. 34).[1]

Now the neglect of gemination and of the nasal in Cypriotic is doubtless graphic rather than phonetic: a post-
nuclear sound was pronounced, but it resembled neither a
simple vowel nor a consonant-plus-vowel enough to be
symbolized in writing. For that matter, early alphabetical
inscriptions from Greece seldom recognize gemination (even

where the meter calls for it) and often neglect a nasal consonant when followed by a plosive; e.g., ΑΠΟΛΟΝΙ (*IGA* 70.1, p. 28), ΗΙΠΠΟΔΡΟΜΕΣΤΟΔΕΔΟΡΟΝ (= Ἱπποδρόμης τόδε δῶρον 'this is the gift of Hippodromē,' 519, p. 150), ΑΦΙΤΡΕΤΑΝ (= Ἀμφιτρίτην in Homeric and Attic; 20.3, p. 5). The Greek alphabet being acrophonic, the basic value of each letter was the sound at the beginning of its name: ἄλφα, βῆτα, λάβδα, μῦ, ῦ, etc.; it could be quite difficult to recognize a sound occurring in the opposite syllabic environment as practically identical with that basic sound. So the omission of such post-nuclear sounds in the Linear B script should without any reserve be accepted by us as a shortcoming no more surprising than the lack of accent signs. The lack of *m* in the first syllable of *a-pi-po-re-we* is no obstacle to identifying the Linear B word with the Greek ἀμφιφορῆ(ϝ)ες, which is demanded by the values $o8 = a$, $11 = po$, $75 = we$ — all three verified elsewhere. The transcription of 28-32 'horses' as *i-qo* is less secure; but at any rate it is none the weaker for having only one consonant to correspond graphically to the geminate in ἵπποι. Nevertheless, the lack of other post-nuclear sounds in Linear B as transcribed by Ventris is less acceptable.

The absence of final -s. The contrast in number between *ti-ri-po* (singular) and *ti-ri-po-de* (dual or plural) requires that the former, if normalized to Greek, must be τρίπος, with the -ς ending of the nominative singular. Similarly the contrast between *ti-ri-jo-we* (singular) and *ti-ri-o-we-e* (dual or plural) 'three-eared' would require that the former be normalized to *τριῶ(ϝ)ες, like Theocritus' word ἀμφῶες 'both-eared, eared on both sides.' And the plural *a-pi-po-re-we* 'amphoras' needs -s to become the Greek ἀμφιφορῆ(ϝ)ες. So we observe that the final -s sound which Greek leads us to expect in these words was either lacking in the Linear B language or at any rate unexpressed in the Linear B script. Several explanations of this difference between Greek (written in the Greek alphabet) and Linear B are possible — all of them theoretical. The explanation preferred by Ventris and most of his supporters is that the difference is not in language at all but only in script: the sound was [-s] both in classical and in "Mycenaean" Greek, but the Linear B syllabic script could not indicate a consonant with no accompanying vowel. On the other hand Vladimir Georgiev has championed the idea that the consonants not written were unpronounced.[2]

The Cypriotic syllabary of classical times usually expressed the equivalent of -ς by the expedient of writing ᛗ , the syllabic sign for *se;* e.g., *sa-la-mi-ni-o-se* for Σαλαμίνιος (see above, p. 82). However, before we conclude that the Linear B scribes could just as well have used the same device if their language had had the same consonant sound at the end of a word, we ought to reflect that something in the history of writing after Mycenaean times may have suggested the device to the Cypriotes. They had the advantage of living while the rest of Greece was employing an alphabet; and although they would not discard their cumbersome syllabary for writing their dialect, they could at least learn a lesson or two from alphabetically written Greek and so mitigate the grossest defects of syllabic writing.

The graphic principle of writing -se for final -s in Cypriotic. The choice of *se* rather than *si, sa, so,* or *su* to stand for final -s may conceivably have been due to mere chance, or to some phonological consideration that *e* is more fundamental in the language than any other vowel phoneme.[3] But a more likely reason for fastening upon *se* (also *ne* for -*n, re* for -*r, xe* for -*x*) is one which the Cypriotes could well have learned from other Greeks: that a character whose name,

when you are spelling a word out, is pronounced /Ce/— i.e.,
a certain consonant followed by the vowel /e/ — is usable
to indicate merely the consonant. To state it another way,
the Cypriotes, unlike the Linear B scribes, were in a position
to learn that the /e/ part of the character's *name* could be
a null, irrelevant to the character's *function* of recording and
evoking part of the total sound of the word.

The Aegean open-syllable writing system, for all its short-
comings, had one pedagogical point of superiority over the
alphabet, so that the conservative and not very clever Greeks
of Cyprus clung to the older way.[4] In spelling out a word,
each syllabic character could be called by a name similar
to a vowel sound or to a consonant-plus-vowel sequence
actually present in the complete word; e.g., the word /anti/
'instead' would be spelled out syllabically /a-ti/. But in
the alphabet, on the acrophonic principle, you need to grasp
that only the initial sound in the name of any character has
a function: thus the character called /alpʰa/ stands for
the sound /a/, the character called /bɛta/ for /b/, etc.; the
word /anti/ would be spelled out alphabetically /alpʰa-nu-
tau-iɔta/. In the name of a vowel letter all sounds after the
initial one are a pure luxury; in the name of a consonant
letter a vowel sound is necessary to make the name pronounceable, although for that purpose any vowel would do.[5]
The Greeks for the most part kept the Phoenician letter
names, of course modifying them to make them more readily
pronounceable in Greek. Only a few of the letter names did
they "streamline": /o/ for O, /mu, nu/ for M, N, /rɔ/ for P,
reducing them to the minimum structure that was practi-
cable.[6] But they found they needed more letters after T,
the last one that they got from the Phoenician. They added
Υ for a certain Greek vowel and called the letter simply
/u/;[7] and the additional consonants Φ, X, Ψ they called
/pʰe, kʰe, pse/.[8] For another complex consonant Ξ, earlier

in the alphabet, they discarded the Phoenician name
(/sámɛk̄/ according to Hebrew tradition) and called it
instead /kse/.[8]

The vowel in the names of these consonant letters is /e/
because the first of them to be added to the Greek alphabet
was Φ, by a deliberate differentiation from Π. Π was called
/pe/ like its Phoenician source, which owed its name and
its original shape to the Phoenician word for 'mouth.' But
the Greek language, unlike Phoenician, had two phonemes,
the more frequent /p/ and the less frequent /pʰ/, differing
only in aspiration; the Phoenician unvoiced plosives (apart
from the "emphatics") were normally aspirate, just as in
English. So it was logical for the Greeks to devise an additional letter for the contrasting and less frequent sound /pʰ/,
and its name /pʰe/ contained a minimal contrast to /pe/,
the name for Π.[9] Happily that was as brief a name as practical for a consonant letter, and was imitated in naming
the following two additional consonants X, Ψ, and in re-
naming Ξ.

From the added letters of the Greek alphabet the Latin
alphabet derived its simple principle of /Ce/ for letters
that stand for plosive consonants: /be/ for B, /ke/ for C,
etc.[10] However, in the Greek alphabet the /Ce/ principle
was just a supplement to a nearly complete set of letter
names, most of which were vocabulary items needing to be
learned individually. The Cypriotes would not take over
the Greek art of writing, which not only handled about two
dozen unfamiliar graphic symbols but also necessitated the
learning of that number of technical terms, the names of
the symbols, all alien to the nontechnical vocabulary of
Greek and many of them requiring more effort to pronounce
than the simple names of the Cypriotic characters /a, ta, ra/,
etc., /e, te, re/, etc.[11] Nevertheless, the Cypriotes could supplement their inherited Aegean script with a rule taken

223

from the supplementary letters of the Greek alphabet: just as the character Φ, called /pʰe/, has the phonetic value /pʰ/, so the character ⱶ, called /se/, can have the value /s/. The reasoning process through which the Cypriotes may have caught on to this improvement is illustrated by an unusual inscription with ΚΑΡΥΞΕΜΙ 'I am a herald' in Greek letters and *ka-ru-xe e-mi* in Cypriotic (Deecke, no. 65, p. 31). In both scripts the character called /kse/ constitutes the /ks/ part of the word for 'herald.'

The phonetic problem of the final -s. While the Cypriotic character ⱶ at the end of the word occurs where the Greek counterpart has -ς, the sound in Cypriotic may not have been [-s] as in most other Greek dialects. Evidence from two sources weighs heavily against identifying the Cypriotic sound with the Greek sibilant. (1) An inscription divided into a section in Greek letters and another in Cypriotic — the latter very ill-preserved — contains the Greek name ΤΙΜΟΔΟΡΟ ⱶ (Deecke, no. 67, p. 32; Meister, p. 156).[12] The motive for resorting to a Cypriotic character in the midst of the Greek section must have been to express a Cypriotic sound different from the [-s] of Τῑμόδωρος. (2) In a bilingual inscription a Phoenician name is מנחם in Phoenician letters but *ma-na-se-se* in Cypriotic. The Hebrew vocalization of this name is מְנַחֵם (II Kings 15 : 14 ff.; Μαναημ in the Septuagint). Whatever sort of guttural sound may have been the value of ח in Phoenician, it would have been inconceivable to transcribe it Σ in the Greek alphabet. Hence ⱶ was hardly [-se-] but something closer to [-he-] or [-xe-] (as in the Spanish word *jefe*).[13]

It would not follow that the Cypriotic character ⱶ never has the sound [se], or [s] at the end of a word. We must, however, refrain from misplacing too much credence in the transcription of ⱶ as *se* or in the phonological interpretation of it as /se/. Either the transcription *se* or the phonological interpretation /se/ is in effect a normalization of Cypriotic to other Greek dialects. The real sound in Cypriotic of the consonantal part of this syllabic sign is likely to have been far from [s].

Still less can we say that in instances like *ti-ja-i-te-mi* (see above, p. 219), where the Cypriotic script has nothing at all to correspond to the Greek -ς, the Cypriotes nevertheless pronounced [s]. They may have pronounced nothing after the vowel of the last syllable, or else a consonantal sound which their writing system could not handle by any means. In Linear B, where we consistently miss any counterpart to the Greek -ς, we do not know what, if anything, may have been pronounced after the last vowel of *ti-ri-po, ti-ri-jo-we, a-pi-po-re-we*. Supposing it was [-s], we can understand why it would have been omitted; but the same cause would just as well account for the omission of any final consonant.[14]

Other final consonants. The normalization of the "oil" tablet Gn1184 to the morphology of a Greek sentence would oblige us to fill out *e-ra₃-wo* (or *e-lai-wo*) *to-so* with an accusative singular case ending: ἔλαι(ϝ)ον τόϲον (or τόϲϲον). But the requirements for normalization cannot dictate the real structure of the Linear B language, which remains quite doubtful on this point — whether a sound [-n] was pronounced but not written, or some different sound was pronounced but not written, or no sound at all after the vowel was pronounced. The only safe observation is that nothing in the Linear B script corresponds to the Greek -ν; even this is not so firmly established by *e-ra₃-wo to-so* as the analogous lack of a correspondent to the Greek -ς is established by the sure Greek words *ti-ri-po, ti-ri-jo-we*, and *a-pi-po-re-we*. The Cypriotic syllabary has no certain instance of final -*n* being omitted, as final -*s* sometimes is.[15] No evidence for an accusative case, distinct from the nominative, has been pointed out in Linear B, nor evidence for a class of neuter nouns having -*on* in the nominative and accusative singular, opposed to the masculine with -*os* in the nominative and -*on* in the accusative.

Final -ρ in Greek is far less frequent than -ς or -ν. The alleged occurrences of an unwritten final -*r* in the Linear B language (*Documents*, p. 99) deserve some notice, especially a word which alternates on the same tablet with another containing the additional syllable -*o2* (-*ro*):

> Jn750.9   38-10-75-05 under the heading 77-44-75
> 59-60-41-57 38-70-04
>
> Jn750.13   38-10-75-05-02 14-38-02 under the heading
> 05-12-45 08-59-60-41-36
> (see above, p. 88)

The transcription of the former as *e-u-we-to* and the latter as *e-u-we-to-ro do-e-ro* suggests an immediate, though inconclusive, advantage in taking *e-u-we-to* as a nominative *'Εὐήτωρ and *e-u-we-to-ro* as its genitive: 'the slave of Euetor.' On the other hand, the name 'Good-heart' is not recorded in classical Greek; and the ideographic context does not show these are two men.[16] Two Cn tablets from Pylos exhibit the following first lines:

Cn40   54-52-36 42-42 03-02 24-37-57-52-27 03-60-36 ⳨ O ☰
[i.e., 140 MALE SHEEP?]

03-02
Cn599   54-52-36 42-42 24-37-57-52 08-44-61-36   ⳨ O
[i.e., 100 MALE GOATS?]

When transcribed, the next-to-last words *ne-ti-ja-no-re* and *ne-ti-ja-no* and the texts containing them cannot be read as Greek. Besides, in view of the insertion of *03-02* in the latter tablet, we cannot make any safe inference about the func-

tion of the final syllable -27 (-re) in the former tablet. Words
ending in -re have been considered dative, as the Linear B
counterpart to the Greek "third declension"; but the theory
remains unfounded. No known Greek name fits the pattern
ne-ti-ja-no(r), nor ra-ke-da-no(r).[17] What would have become of the Greek final -ρ in Linear B is unproved.

The consonant clusters written in Greek as an individual
letter -ξ or -ψ are said to be expressed in Linear B with the
omission of the [s] component (*Documents,* p. 46), so that
54-06-77 *wa-na-ka* would stand for (ϝ)ἄναξ 'king' (Na334,
Ta711.1, Pylos; Vc73, Knosos) and 43-37-36-32 *ai-ti-jo-qo*
for Αἰθίοψ (Eb156.2, 846.1, Ep301.2, Pylos). But the identification of the two Linear B words with anything Greek
is just an unpromising experiment. A difficulty discussed
earlier (see above, p. 113) forbids us to rely on *ai-ti-jo-qo*
as a "third declension" noun. The supposed case-forms of
wa-na-ka

> 54-06-77-05 *wa-na-ka-to* (La622.r1, Pylos)
> 54-06-77-04 *wa-na-ka-te* (Un2.1, Pylos; Ga675, Knosos)

are only by conjecture related to ἄνακτος, ἄνακτι.[18] In short
we have no evidence for the treatment of -ξ and -ψ in
Linear B.

-r and -s after the vowel of a non-final syllable. That 70-42
means 'boys, sons' and 70-54 means 'girls, daughters' is tolerably well established; and 70-42 has to be transcribed *ko-wo*
(see above, pp. 104-9, 144). The case for 54 = *wa* is weak,
but matters little for the present problem of the unwritten
-r. The Homeric κοῦροι and the Attic κόροι presuppose
kórwoi, though the word has no clear Indo-European connexions. The cluster -ρϝ- is actually attested in the Arcadian
dative singular feminine KOPϜAI; the Arcadian word for

'boys' ought therefore to be *κόρϝοι. It is tempting to regard the Linear B word *ko-wo* as just a defective spelling of *korwoi* (or *korwo-*, to reserve for later the question of the omitted final *-i*). At any rate we can conclude that where the classical Greek dialects which are in this respect the most conservative have the cluster *-rw-*, the *-r* is not written in Linear B.

We have no evidence whether it was pronounced. In no classical Greek diàlect is the *r* of a group *-rw-* suppressed; the *w* is much more liable to suppression. It might therefore seem strange to imagine *r* suppressed in the phonology of the earliest recorded Greek. On the other hand, if the Linear B language was a jargon, the simplification of *[rw] to [w] would be less implausible. The Greek dialect of Crete in the classical age was essentially Doric, but noteworthy for assimilating consonant clusters to an extent beyond any other dialect.[19] This tendency is more reasonably attributable to the non-Dorian substratum than to the Dorian immigrants. I see no serious objection to supposing that before Doric spread over Crete the assimilating tendency could have caused a pronunciation something like [kowo] or [kowwo], with the *r* suppressed. There are no instances of it from the classical period in a *rw cluster, but there are in *rn* clusters; e.g., ΕΛΕΥΘΕΝΝΑΙΟΣ, ΕΛΕΥΘΕΡΝΑΙ[ο]Σ (Guarducci, IV, nos. 206F, 387, pp. 282, 379). We also find *ko-wo* in the Linear B tablets of Pylos on the mainland — i.e., outside the area where assimilation was extensive in classical times. That, however, is not opposed to my theory that the language recorded in the Linear B script arose as a jargon in the motley kingdom whose center was Knosos, and that it passed from there to the mainland, not as a general means of communication but for a limited administrative purpose.

So it remains open whether the omission of *r* in *ko-wo* is phonetic or merely graphic. Either way, *ko-wo* entitles us to look for the omission of *r* at the end of a syllable in other Linear B words too, if the corresponding Greek words have ρ. Unfortunately no other word adds any support to what we have obtained by the analysis of *ko-wo;* for every other identification of a Linear B word without *r* and a Greek word with -ρ- is a mere conjecture, not borne out by the context. I may add that the omission of *r* in the interior of *ko-wo* does not afford a fair presumption that *r* would be omitted at the end of a word too.

The omission of *s* at the end of a syllable cannot be so well illustrated as the omission of *r*. The one possibly valid example, less cogent than *ko-wo*, is *03-77-06* — transcribed *pa-ka-na* — in the Knosos sword tablets (see above, p. 124). The context makes it possible, but far from certain, that the word means 'swords.' The value *03 = pa* is not assured; *77 = ka* has no standing apart from this word. So the identification with the Greek φάσγανα 'swords' is not much more than a conjecture. If it could be better verified, it would not only add two important values, besides *06 = na* (which is fairly secure anyhow), but also prove that the Greek σ at the end of a syllable can be left out in Linear B. The question would remain whether the omission is due to an exceptional environment, the sibilant being followed by a *voiced* plosive. φάσγανα was almost certainly pronounced [pʰázgana], with the sibilant voiced in the cluster -σγ-. Now if we project this pronunciation back to Mycenaean times, it is not hard to grasp why the scribe would not sound it out [pʰa-za-ga-na]; [za], with a voiced sibilant before a vowel, was presumably as foreign to his speech as it was later to classical Greek. Nor can we expect him to have sounded it out [pʰa-sa-ga-na], with an unvoiced sibilant contrary to his normal pronunciation. To do this, he would have had to interpret [z], occurring exclusively before a voiced plosive, as an allophone of the

/s/ phoneme. But with only a syllabary, not an alphabet, to help him segment the words, he was not likely to analyze the consonants so skillfully, being tied to a quasi-syllabic analysis of sounds.

The non-writing of the sibilant, if proved, would leave open an alternative inference: either the word was [pʰazgana], but the syllabary was too inelastic to provide a graphic symbol for the sound between [pʰa] and [ga]; or else the word in Linear B did not have a cluster of two different consonants between the first vowel and the second. Supposing it was something like *[pʰaggana], the Cypriotic syllabary would not indicate the gemination of a consonant; nor would an early inscription in the Greek alphabet necessarily do so (see above, pp. 219-20). Still less would the Linear B script tell us whether the word for 'swords' had a cluster [zg] or a double [gg].

The unlikely omission of i in diphthongs. Not only in *ko-wo* but in *o-no* for certain and probably also in the more dubious case of *i-qo* 'horses,' the Greek nominative plural ending -οι is represented in Linear B with no indication of the ι. No parallel can be adduced from Cypriotic; on the contrary, even in the *ei* diphthong, where the two components are phonetically not in sharp contrast, Cypriotic never drops the *i* component, phonetically or graphically (see Hoffmann, pp. 175-177). I do not understand how Ventris and most others have interpreted the Linear B writing to signify that the scribes heard or pronounced a diphthong *oi* but systematically omitted to write the *i* part. In fact, as Ventris has pointed out ("Evidence," p. 95; *Documents,* pp. 43, 84-85, etc.), the characters *o, ro,* etc., are often followed by *28,*[20] which we may with some confidence take to be *i* (see above, p. 159); but such instances of final *-i* never appear to be nominative plural, according to all attempts to interpret the transcribed texts as

Greek. The simple inference ought to be that the Linear B language differed from Greek in the nominative plural of thematic masculine nouns ("second declension"). The difference was not just graphic, but either phonological or morphological.

The morphological problem is somewhat easier to approach than the phonological. Cognates of the Greek -οι ending are found in several Indo-European languages; but others have an unrelated ending, -āḥ in Sanskrit — e.g., áçvāh 'horses' (nom. sing. áçvaḥ). We have no indication what sound, if any, may have been pronounced after the nuclear vowel o in the last syllable of ko-wo, o-no. It is liable to have been one that defied syllabic notation, and to that extent was more like the Sanskrit -ḥ than the Greek -ι. For the rationale of the syllabary seems to demand that a syllable [woi] or [noi], in a word sounded out slowly for the purpose of writing, would be resolved into two graphic units wo-i or no-i.[21]

Conceivably, however, the nominative plural ending in Linear B may have been cognate with Greek rather than Sanskrit, but actualized with a diphthong that verged so on a monophthong as to be unsegmentable. Or a peculiarity of the Linear B language may have been to suppress the [i] part of a diphthong completely, so that a pure monophthong remained, as happens in the English of certain areas in the Southern states, where the diphthong in boil and my is reduced to a monophthong [ɔ:, a:].[22] Such a tendency might be due to a non-Greek substratum, but any evidence of it from Crete in the classical period is slight. The Doric of Crete is not characterized by simplification of diphthongs. But the name of the city of Πραισός (accent uncertain) is subject to a curious variation, all the more interesting because the place remained in classical times the chief center of the Ἐτεόκρητες 'true (or native) Cretans,' who still lived near the eastern end of the island (see above, p. 190). An inscription in the native language, which is unintelligible, shows the sequence of letters ΦΡΑΙΣΟΙ and ΦΡΑΙΣΟΝ; and all the earlier Greek sources record the name with the AI diphthong — e.g., the ethnic ΠΡΑΙΣΙΟΙ.[23] But Strabo (10.475, 478) — who, although after the destruction of the city, cited the historian Staphylus — called it Πρᾶσος;[24] and still later, under Venetian rule, the village on the site was called 'ς τοὺς Πρασσούς. Somehow in the polyglot milieu of eastern Crete it was possible for the place name to be pronounced in such a way that the graphic rendering in the Greek alphabet could be either AI or A. Granted that the monophthong is not so well attested as the diphthong, and that at best the eastern town of Praisos in the classical period is not close to the central city of Knosos nearly a thousand years earlier — yet the AI ~ A alternation gives an idea of what may have happened in the Linear B language to the nominative plural ending which Greek preserves as the diphthong -οι.

But whatever may be the merit of our subtle hypothesis to clarify the phenomena, there is no avoiding one plain inference, that 61-52 o-no is not a defective spelling for onoi with a pronounced [-i].

Variation between the presence and the absence of 28 (i). The case of o-no and ko-wo is not on a par with

70-52   ko-no (Ge602.5, 603.2,3,4,6,7, 604.2, Mycenae)[25]
70-28-52 ko-i-no (Ge606.7, Mycenae).

If the Linear B scribes now wrote 28 and now omitted it, we can fairly maintain that they heard a sound which reminded them of [i] — at least in the case where they took the trouble to write the character 28. For us to assume an [i] sound in other words, where it is never written in Linear B, would be an unwarranted normalization to Greek. But we have reason

to regard *70-52* and *70-28-52* as related forms of the same
word, perhaps differing phonetically, perhaps just graphically; for they occur in the same context, following the item
73-59 72 ‖ [i.e., 2] in Ge602 and 606. However, in these
two tablets where the prior context is identical, *ko-no* is followed by another word *08-11-04-28* in small characters, while
ko-i-no has only an ideographic sequel *45* ╵. The identification of *ko-no* and *ko-i-no* with σχοῖνος (*Documents,* pp.
226-227) is a conjecture beyond any present verification;
σχοῖνος in classical Greek means 'rush' and is applied to
several species not closely related. Doubt about the meaning of *70-52* and *70-28-52,* and of the neighboring words,
forbids us to assert anything for certain about the phonological relation, even though they have in common two
characters *ko* and *no*.[26] The little-known Linear B language
may have more tricks up its sleeve than we can anticipate.
But to judge merely from appearances, we can say it was
not alien to the Linear B script to write as *28* — i.e., as *i* — a
certain sound occurring at the end of a syllable (not the final
syllable), while at other times ignoring that sound in the
same environment, perhaps because it was pronounced
indistinctly.

Besides *ko-no* ~ *ko-i-no,* two more pairs of variants have
been adduced:

Sf0419 (Knosos)] *08-06-28-59* CHARIOT[c] 80
Sf0420.b ” *28-21-57 08-06-59 08-06-15-05* CHARIOT[c] 80
and
Uf981.a, 1031.a (Knosos) *70-05-28-06*
Ea71, etc., etc. (Pylos) *70-05-06*

But these involve further problems. A serious obstacle to
equating *08-06-28-59* with *08-06-59* (transcribed *a-na-i-ta*
and *a-na-ta* respectively) is Bennett's observation that in

233

Sf0419 *08-06-59* was previously written and the last character then erased to make room for *-28-59*. If the same meaning could be optionally expressed either way, we wonder
why the scribe should have taken so much trouble to insist
on one.[27] The longer one has no other word following it;
the shorter one does — as we noted in *ko-i-no, ko-no*. If this
is indeed an alternation between terminal forms with an
infixed or epenthetic [i] and nonterminal forms without it,
the language would seem to betray a *sandhi* or an accentual
system very alien to Greek.

The contexts of the Knosos word *70-05-28-06 ko-to-i-na*
and the Pylos word *70-05-06 ko-to-na* give no basis for connecting the two. Ventris's essential identification ("Evidence," p. 91; *Documents,* pp. 232 ff.) was of *ko-to-na* and
the Greek dialect word κτοίνα, a term of land tenure (see
above, p. 211, note 7). The E tablets of Pylos, even without
decipherment, admitted of an interpretation dealing with
plots of ground. Ventris was on the lookout for Greek words;
and though any attempt to read these tablets as Greek
bristles with perplexities, he fastened upon *ko-to-na* =
κτοίνα. But κτοίνα was chosen for a really negative reason:
identifying *ko-to-na* with any other Greek word was still
more far-fetched, if not impossible. The identification was
a mere experiment, with wholly indecisive results. The only
excuse for bringing in *ko-to-i-na* was that the spelling is
reminiscent of κτοίνα. Any semantic connexion of *ko-to-i-na*
with either κτοίνα or *ko-to-na* is imaginary as long as those
Knosos tablets remain unintelligible.

Diphthongal characters. The Cypriotic syllabary confines
itself unfailingly to the principle of open-syllable notation —
each character standing for a simple vowel with or without
a consonant before it, and with nothing after it. But in the
Linear B syllabary Ventris found himself obliged to allow

for a few characters whose vowel is not simple but diphthongal. *43 = ai* was listed in "Evidence" (p. 86) without explaining or calling attention to the phonological anomaly. None of the words illustrating this value of *43* are verified. The alleged alternations between *43* and *08* (*a*)[28] are in words on unrelated tablets and without any reasonable suspicion of being connected in their meaning. *43* is found almost exclusively at the beginning of a word.[29] If taken for a reflexion of a phonetic phenomenon, the limited distribution of *43* is hardly compatible with the phonology of Greek, in which no syllable is so restricted. If it is just a graphic vagary, it throws a distressing complication into the Linear B system. Some fully known scripts do indeed have graphic rules for the distribution of certain characters regardless of phonetic identity, as in English *duty* with final -*y* while *duties* and *dutiful* have medial -*i*-. In an unknown script such extravagances obstruct the effort of decipherment. Though it would be romantic — at any rate unscholarly — to credit an unknown script in advance with a beautifully systematic rationality, nevertheless our success in solving it will depend on the extent of rationality discoverable in it; so we must require the most cogent demonstration of any apparently or allegedly irrational feature. The value *43 = ai* cannot meet so stringent a test.

We found *33* to correspond to the -λαι- part of ἔλαιον; but even if we should take this to mean that the same sounds [lai] were pronounced in the Linear B language, it still would not prove how much of the phoneme content was recognized by the Linear B notation of the character *33*. In the character *02* the Greek opposition between λ and ρ is neutralized (see above, p. 69); it may be so in *33* too, and *33* may also neutralize the opposition between α and αι. The relation between *33* and *60* is dubious (see above, pp. 161-2); but if *33* were simply equivalent to both λα and ρα, its rarity would be astonishing — granted that the Linear B corpus contains a considerable proportion of Greek. If then the vocalic component of 33 is not the extremely frequent [a] but the diphthong [ai], we are confronted with a dismaying unsteadiness: How far was the script from adhering systematically to certain principles of phonetic segmentation? In the period which the preserved tablets happen to represent, the script does not have nearly enough characters for all syllables consisting of consonant-plus-diphthong; but that would not exclude the possibility of some such characters. The presence of a few diphthongal characters (which is not quite established) invites speculation upon their origin; but — more important — it argues a degree of awkwardness or hesitancy in the scribes' perception of diphthongal sounds.[30]

Homophones and incoherence in the Linear B syllabary. We have no clear proof of homophonous characters in Linear B, like the letters *b* and *v* in Spanish — where, to be sure, orthography prescribes they shall not be written interchangeably, and therefore a correctly spelled text would not betray the identity of sound. A certain syllable of a certain Linear B word may be written now with one character, now with another, although no difference in meaning or construction is perceptible:

Cn599.2 (Pylos)

25-24-10-04 03-02 77-12 08-70-12-59-61 ⨂ = = ¦¦¦ [i.e.,45]

Cn40.7 (Pylos)

08-24-10-04 03-02 80-53-37-40-36 08-70-12-59-61 ⨂ ≡ ≡ ¦¦¦
[i.e., 83]

Cn40.13 (Pylos)

08-24-10-04 03-02 77-59-54 08-70-12-59 ⨂ ≡ ≡ [i.e., 70][31]

25 is transcribed a_2 (with an alternative value *ha* suggested in *Documents*, pp. 23, 47; Vilborg, p. 31); but nothing in

its distribution establishes how it is related to *08* (*a*). In a different alternation Bennett pointed out that the two Er tablets from Pylos, written by one scribe, have *72-80* (transcribed *pe-ma*) before the ideogram ⤳ , while all the other E tablets from there, written by other scribes, have *72-15* (transcribed *pe-mo*) before the same ideogram.[32] Besides the possibility of individual pronunciations, there may even be different writing due to no phonetic difference in the word itself but merely to a difficulty of phonetic analysis, as the scribes could vary in their slow sounding out of the word orally just before they wrote it or mentally while they wrote it. At the stage of our actual knowledge it would be rash to treat the *80* ~ *15* opposition as a clear case of different vowels, while setting up *25* and *08* as homophones. To a small degree we have fair proof of lack of economy in the Linear B script: If 'three-eared' (dual or plural) could be written *37-53-61-75-38*, I can hardly imagine it was *necessary* to write the singular *37-53-36-75* with -*36*- rather than -*61*-. But in other words, where *36* and *61* do not interchange, the scribes presumably had good reason for inventing or maintaining both members of the syllabary. Some rarer characters are likely to have been marginal — not consistent with the general scope of the script and serving, at best, to bring out a few fine distinctions of sound while the script as a whole attempted only broad distinctions. If any Linear B character was an absolute homophone of another — as in Latin the *k* in *Karthago* was a superfluous competitor of *c*—we can understand such duplication as an irrational part of an imperfect system.

The dangerous laxity of Ventris's spelling rules. Near the end of Work Note 20 Ventris wrote, "If pursued, I suspect that this line of decipherment would sooner or later come to an impasse, or dissipate itself in absurdities

. . ." But the rules for unwritten sounds were bound to lead to a multiplication of possibilities rather than a dead end. In the days and weeks after he mailed out that note, he read many Greek words in the Linear B tablets by taking for granted the unwritten sounds—so many words indeed that I can understand why he would have been reluctant to go back and try again without the unwritten sounds to help him. The influence of Chadwick, who began corresponding with him about a month later, tended to quiet the doubts which Ventris himself, as an amateur, continued to feel from time to time. When the decipherment began to be criticized, or accepted with specific reservations, the unwritten sounds were always mentioned as a difficulty. Chadwick (*Decipherment*, p. 79) quotes from a letter Bennett sent to Ventris on July 6, 1952, when Bennett was undecided: "On the face of it I don't like your freedom to supply l r m n t q w e r t, etc., but there were some other things that seemed quite reasonable."[33]

For a time Ventris and Chadwick went on calling the decipherment experimental, but they seemed not to grasp how much less scientific the experiment became because of the *imprecision* that entered with the unwritten sounds. The issue to settle by experiment was this: given the materials—i.e., the Linear B characters in their sequence on the tablets—can one apply to them the phonetic values from the Ventris grid and by that process produce Greek texts? The result of any such experiment with a Linear B tablet is absolutely negative. To get an affirmative result, you need a subsequent process of inserting some Greek elements from the outside, at will. The second process calls for critical attention no less than the first; for if the missing sounds are simply to be supplied whenever convenient, it is like playing poker with deuces wild. You get a flush or a full house much oftener when the deuce is not restricted to its face value but is a null which you can give any value you please.[34]

In all prudence, viewing the decipherment as a search for truth, not a game, we have to recognize that even without the loose rules of spelling Ventris's very first step precluded one stringent test: By positing that the characters stand either for a vowel or a consonant-plus-vowel, he insured that no phonetic values which he might choose — no matter how wrong — could be self-refuting through the manifest unpronounceability of the sequences they would yield. He had reason to posit this; for the Linear B script was visibly related to the Cypriotic, which had been proved to consist of *V* and *CV* characters. But when he later took the big jump of assuming the omission of post-nuclear sounds, which he was free to supply, he opened the door wide to self-deception. Even though I have found warrant for certain parts of his assumption — notably the omission of final -*s* and, not so certainly, of final -*n* — I am bound to emphasize the unwelcome corollary: the lack of evidence about these final consonants deprives us of a major criterion for gauging how close or how far any Linear B text is from the morphology and syntax of Greek. Thereby is lessened the prospect of interpreting a text securely, once it has been correctly transcribed.

Notes to Chapter VIII

1. See Hoffmann, pp. 173-81, 204. The Cypriotic omission of *i* from a "long diphthong" — ᾳ, ῃ, ῳ in the Greek alphabet — is a phonetic, not a graphic simplification; Hoffmann, pp. 185-87, and Deecke, pp. 11-12.

2. "La κοινή créto-mycénienne," *ÉM*, especially pp. 175-78.

3. It is not decidedly the most frequent vowel in the Cypriotic texts I have studied.

4. A fairer judgement upon them may be that they held on to a Linear script as an inheritance from the polyglot civilization which persisted in Cyprus. Whereas in the Aegean the un-Hellenized population sank into insignificance, in Cyprus it continued to participate in the culture of the island, till after the time of Alexander (see above, p. 195).

5. In Phoenician many of the letter names were functional from a quite different pedagogical standpoint. They were common nouns in the language, standing for visible objects, and the letters were simplified sketches of those objects. So the shape of the first letter would remind the learner of the word for 'ox,' which begins with the glottal consonant /ʔ/ in Phoenician, and the acrophonic principle would give that letter the value /ʔ/. Likewise the shape of the second letter would remind him of the word for 'house' — hence /b/; etc.

6. Phonetically these are [ôː, mûː, nûː rʰɔ̂ː] according to the best attested tradition of the Ionic alphabet.

7. Phonetically [hûː], at least in Attic.

8. Phonetically [pʰêː, kʰêː, psêː, ksêː]. The long vowel came to be written EI in Attic of the fourth century B.C., when it ceased to be distinguished from the diphthong, and eventually the sound merged with [iː]. Hence Φ is vulgarly called *phi*, X *chi*, etc.

9. The related but contrasting nasal sounds written M and N were called /mem, nun/ in Phoenician. In Greek the dental nasal is more frequent; and from its proximity to the other in the alphabetic sequence, the vowel /u/ in its name got into the name for the labial nasal. The motive for making both names have the same vowel was to focus attention upon the minimal contrast, which lay in /m ~ n/, and thereby to reenforce the acrophonic principle.

10. /eC/ for non-plosive consonants F, L, etc.

11. I give this *exempli gratia*. The pedagogical sequence of the Cypriotic syllabary is not known to us.

12. Several of the Cypriotic characters are liable to face now in one direction, now in the other. � and ⫙ are graphic variants of the same character, transcribed *se*.

13. Hoffmann, p. 204; Meister, no. 14[d], p. 170 (both have typographical errors in the Phoenician). Authoritatively treated by Julius Euting, "Zwei. bilingue Inschriften aus Tamassos," *Sitzungsberichte der K. preussischen Akademie der Wissenschaften zu Berlin*, 1887, pp. 116 ff.; the Cypriotic sections of the article were entrusted to Deecke. The last Cypriotic character -*se*, in spite of the Phoenician -*m*, is to be explained as a Greek nominative case ending — although conceivably the Cypriotic text may have substituted another Phoenician name; cf. מְנַשֶּׁה (II Kings 20:21, etc.; LXX Μανασση, or in some mss. Μανασσης).

In the other bilingual inscription from Tamassos the Phoenician לרשף אלהיתם (probably without word separation) is a rendering of the Cypriotic Greek *to-i-a-po-lo-ni-to-i-a-la-si-o-ta-i;* Meister, pp. 171-72. Thus the Cypriotic character ⫫ , though transcribed *si*, was scarcely [si] as one might expect from the Greek Ἀλασιώτᾳ, but more like [hi].

14. It may be that final -*s* is one of the hallmarks of classical Greek, although scholars have generally taken it for a heritage from Indo-European. The other Indo-European languages exhibit it to a much more limited extent, except for classical Latin and Gothic — the two most influenced by Greek.

15. It is not written at the end of the article when the noun begins with a consonant — e.g., *to-ko-ro-ne* = τὸν χῶρον 'the place' (Deecke, no. 60.8, pp. 27, 29); but the article is phonologically and graphically not a separate word except by a post-classical convention. Hoffmann, p. 213, cites the omission of -*n* at the end of a few nouns and verbs; but all instances are compromised by doubt as to the meaning of the words or the construction of the passages or the rules of Cypriotic morphology (in regard to the "second declension" genitive singular), so that it is not clear whether we could expect the -*n* sound.

16. Indeed, frequent as *14-38-02* is, it does not occur with a MAN ideogram except in Ae26 (Pylos) and B822.1b (Knosos). On the contrary it occurs with animal ideograms, male and female, repeatedly in C911, and in C912.5, 915.B (Knosos).

17. See above, pp. 158, 182. The other names adduced in *Documents*, p. 99, have the alleged "nominative" with unwritten *-r* in an altogether different tablet and context from the "genitive" in *-ro* and the "dative" in *-re*. Thus it is just a guess that *me-ta-no* (Cn719.3, Pylos) is related in meaning to *me-ta-no-re* (Uf1522.3, Knosos), or *a-ta-no* (Vc569, As1520.2, Knosos) to *a-ta-no-ro* (Fn50.3, Pylos) and *a-ta-no-re* (Vn130.7, Pylos).

18. *54-06-77-04-02 wa-na-ka-te-ro* (En74.3, etc., Pylos) has been taken for an adjective 'royal' (*Documents*, pp. 89, 411). But this is contrary to Greek morphology (see Beattie, *JHS*, LXXVI, 7).

19. C. D. Buck, *Introduction to the Study of the Greek Dialects*, rev. ed. (Boston: Ginn, [1928]), pp. 68-69, 76-77, 152.

20. Cf. Bennett, *A Minoan Linear B Index* (New Haven: Yale University Press, 1953), p. 88.

21. The Latin diphthongs written *oe, ae* show it is possible to identify the /i/ component with *e* rather than *i*. But to ignore that second component altogether is very unlikely, when the script has some means of indicating it.

22. Popular writers, to indicate the speech of Southerners, spell the latter word *mah*.

23. Guarducci, vol. III, no. VI.2.2,6, p. 139; no. VI.7.4, p. 142; see also pp. 134-38 and Herodotus 7.170.1.

24. Gustav Kramer's ed., vol. II (Berlin: Libraria F. Nicolai, 1847), p. 396, notes that two codices of Strabo have Πραῖσον (the case is accusative here).

25. In Ge603.5 the same two characters in reverse order, *52-70*.

26. The occurrences of *70-52* at Knosos and Pylos (F953+955.2,3, Eq213.6; see *Documents*, pp. 308-309) are liable to be mere homographs of the Mycenae *70-52*; for the accompanying words and ideograms in the Knosos and Pylos tablets quite disagree with those from Mycenae. In a short word made up of frequently used characters, homography is much more than barely possible (see above, p. 98, note 28).

27. Another word *a-na-to* is found in

Sg0425	]-57 08-06-05	CHARIOT[c] [
Sg0423+0471	28-21-57 08-06-15-05 08-06-05	CHARIOT[c] [
Sg888	] 08-06-05 61	CHARIOT[c] [

Documents, p. 387, treats *a-na-i-ta* and *a-na-ta* as "incorrect" synonyms of *a-na-to*, because of the Greek rule that adjectives with the negative prefix ἀ(ν)- do not have a special "first declension" feminine. It is preposterous to dispose of the Linear B phenomena thus. What really governs the use of the three words remains a problem.

28. Doubtfully cited by Vilborg, pp. 31-32.

29. C. D. Ktistopoulos, "Statistical Data on Minoan Words," *Minos,* III (1954), 103; Michel Lejeune, "Observations sur le signe *43* (*ai*)," in *ÉM,* pp. 42-43.

30. The examples of diphthongs with the second member *u* are unproved; *e-u-me-de-i* (see above, p. 151) could very well be five syllables, since in early Greek εὖ 'well' is preferably scanned ⏑ ⏑ .

31. Certain other lines of both Cn40 and 599 have identical opening words before *03-02*:

Cn40.5,6, Cn599.8   *38-70-13-52*

Cn40.1,2,3,4, Cn599.1   *54-52-36 42-42*

32. *ÉM,* p. 261. However, the Knosos tablets Ga674, 675, 680.1 have *72-80* in a quite different context.

33. Bennett of course could not have seriously maintained that Ventris was supplying *t, q, w,* or *e*.

34. Nearly all supporters of the decipherment have an irreproachably earnest purpose; but one professor, who is surely not typical, wrote that the transcribed Linear B texts make a fascinating puzzle game. His metaphor seems to express a very human preference for what you can play around with because it is not objectively and indisputably established, but instead arbitrary, accepted by convention, and full of ambiguity. A scholar ought not to mix this up with his proper concern for the truth about the past. The confusion seems to me unworthy of a man who has otherwise done excellent work. I withhold his name and his exact words because his high reputation entitles him not to have attention called to what may have been a passing touch of flippancy.

CHAPTER IX

CONCLUSION

My LENGTHY CRITIQUE has upheld Ventris on perhaps the most important question, the correctness of his transcription. But the favorable verdict has to be severely qualified; for the majority of his values have not been verified nor refuted at all. A substantial minority, including several very frequent characters, have been adequately verified. Certain other characters — again a minority — have been verified doubtfully or incompletely; no two of them are on quite the same footing. It would be easier if I could say, "Accept this, reject that"; but the evidence in most cases does not warrant such a forthright choice. The grid procedure complicated Ventris's work without contributing much to the results, insofar as they are reliable.

In a different sense the decipherment has had very little success up to now: it has not made the Linear B texts intelligible. To get the illusion of readable documents, you must first take on faith the values of many characters, and then supply the missing sounds so as to make Greek or nearly Greek words. All the while you must ignore the chance that those tablets you are dealing with may contain little or no Greek anyhow, but an unknown language instead. Those who have taken the decipherment in full have within a few years extracted much of interest concerning the economy, government, social structure, and religion of pre-classical Greece and Crete. But under scrutiny their discoveries shrivel to practically nothing. Judged objectively, the interpretation of the wording of nearly every tablet is pure guesswork; and so is the interpretation of ideograms, to the extent that it depends on the decipherment of adjacent words. The one exception is the OIL ideogram 𝟋 , which has really gained from the equation of the word 38-33-42 with ἔλαι(ϝ)ον in Gn1184.

Mitford's summary of the history of Cypriotic epigraphy (*Archaeology*, V, 153) contains an important lesson for Linear B studies:

The decipherment of the Cypriot Syllabary in 1871 gave an immediate prominence to these inscriptions. All the known texts were included by DEECKE in 1884 in the *Sammlung der griechischen Dialekt-Inschriften* — excluding the coins, 150 in number. In 1889 MEISTER added 96 to this total in his *Griechischen Dialekte,* and HOFFMANN in 1891 a dozen or so more. This enthusiasm was, however, speedily quenched by the uncritical approach of certain scholars who (as I have noted [see above, p. 217, note 52]) gave their profound learning and their high ability to extracting Greek where Greek did not exist. It became correct, therefore, to set aside all this body of documents, with the exception always of the celebrated Dali Tablet [Deecke, no. 60, pp. 27-30], supported perhaps by some brief and unambiguous funerary texts and certain inscriptions of Soli and Tamassus, which could be controlled by their alphabetic and Phoenician versions. This degree of caution was indeed salutary, but is now in some measure outmoded; for a new approach is opened to the inscriptions when, with each ambiguous text, we are permitted to consider the possibility that it may not be Greek.

The extravagant ingenuity of Ventris and his adherents has deservedly evoked more than a little disbelief and suspicion. So it is right to take stock of what Greek there really is in Linear B writing. The indeterminate but not inconsiderable amount of non-Greek constitutes a dark area to be reckoned with; so long as it is ignored, the reliably Greek parts of the Linear B corpus are overshadowed.

To deflate Ventris's decipherment without crushing it has seemed to me necessary and indeed overdue; the substantial part of it that remains should leave us cheered rather than disappointed. Nor is it a disservice to his memory to show by balanced criticism what in truth he acomplished. It was not a masterpiece of deduction, but something different and perhaps greater. Santayana's third sonnet has a quatrain,

> Columbus found a world and had no chart
> Save one that faith deciphered in the skies;
> To trust the soul's invincible surmise
> Was all his science and his only art.

Actually, both Columbus and Ventris had considerable science and art, but their excellence lay rather in a resourceful, indefatigable will to discover. We do not fail in admiration for Ventris when we compare him to Columbus. But we are reminded that after Columbus died it still had to be shown that the Indies he was looking for were far from his landfalls, and that the true geography of the earth was more complicated than his conception of it. And yet, when at last all the shores of all the seas were known, not one of the many explorers who contributed to this conquest of the globe was worthy of being named with Columbus. It would not surprise me if posterity judges similarly of Ventris.

INDICES

Linear B material is listed in numerical order, according to Bennett's numbering, which is presented here (and throughout this book) in *italics*. Accompanying each item is Ventris's transcription, subject to the slight modifications adopted by the Third International Colloquium (see pull-out inside back cover). The transcription has been added as a convenience to readers accustomed to it, although much of it remains unverified.

Numbers not italicized refer to pages of this book, and small, superscript numbers to notes at the end of a chapter; e.g., 43^{n10} means page 43, note 10.

LINEAR B CHARACTERS AND WORDS

01 da 23-5, 43^{n10}, 153-4, 173^{n23}

02 ro 23-5, 28, 36, 56, 67, 68-9, 70, 80, 115, 127, 145, 153, 163, 172^{n11}, 173^{n18}, 184, 226, 230, 235

03 pa 23-5, 28, 36, 56, 61^{n6}, 66, 90-2, 125, 128, 132^{n7}, 160, 187, 213^{n21}, 229

03-02 pa-ro 112-3, 141, 158, 164, 174^{n32}, 226, 236, 243^{n31}

03-28-05 pa-i-to 99^{n31}

03-28-37-36 pa-i-ti-jo 99^{n31}

03-28-37-57 pa-i-ti-ja 99^{n31}

03-57-42[pa-ja-wo[203-4

03-60 pa-ra 131^{n3}

03-70 pa-ko 213^{n21}

03-70-75 pa-ko-we 187, 213^{n21}

03-77-06 pa-ka-na 124-5, 229

04 te 68, 69-70, 73, 145, 168, 183, 200, 202

05 to 23, 25, 28, 43^{n10}, 56, 68-9, 72, 73, 80-1, 96^{n7}, 120, 127, 149, 153-4

05-12 to-so 72, 73-5, 97^{n17}, 98^{n24}, 99^{n29}, 143-4, 146-51, 168, $171^{n7,8}$, 178, 180, 225

05-12-45 to-so-de 71-2, 73-5, $97^{n15, 17, 20}$, 149-50

05-31 to-sa 74-5, $97\text{-}8^{n21}$, 99^{n29}, 124, 149-50, 180

05-31-45 to-sa-de 98^{n23}, 149-50

05-52 to-no 134^{n16}

05-60-44 to-ra-ke 96^{n7}

05-72-17 to-pe-za 138^{n38}

05-72-20 to-pe-zo 138^{n38}

06 na 23, 25, 34-5, 80, 100^{n37}, 103^{n60}, 120-6, 128, 172^{n11}, 180-1, 204, 229

06-05-05 na-to-to 184, 213^{n15}

07 di 56, 61^{n6}, 90-2, 103^{n60}, 128

07-03 di-pa 86, 90-2, $101^{n47, 49}$, 135^{n22}

07-03-38 di-pa-e 86, 101^{n47}, 135^{n22}

07-14-41 di-do-si 101^{n43}

07-40-46-75 di-wi-je-we 217^{n46}

247

GREEK WORDS AND MORPHEMES

CYPRIOTIC SYLLABARY CHARACTERS AND WORDS